BOYS BOOK OF INDIAN WARRIORS

BOYS BOOK OF INDIAN WARRIORS

AND

HEROIC INDIAN WOMEN

EDWIN L. SABIN

GYAN

Published by

Gyan Publishing House
5, Ansari Road
Daryaganj, New Delhi-110002
Phone: 011-47034999, 9811692060
E-mail: books@gyanbooks.com

Distribution Network
gyanbooks.com
India, USA, Canada, UK, Australia, France

ISBN: 978-81-212-8921-4 (PB)
First Published, 1918

2nd Impression 2023

Printed at: Gyan Press, Delhi.

BOYS BOOK OF INDIAN WARRIORS

AUTHOR: EDWIN L. SABIN

BOYS' BOOK OF INDIAN WARRIORS

CHIEF JOSEPH

Courtesy of The American Bureau of Ethnology.

BOYS' BOOK OF INDIAN WARRIORS

AND

HEROIC INDIAN WOMEN

BY

EDWIN L. SABIN

PHILADELPHIA
GEORGE W. JACOBS & COMPANY
PUBLISHERS

Alas! for them, their day is o'er,
Their fires are out on hill and shore;
No more for them the wild deer bounds,
The plough is on their hunting grounds;
The pale man's axe rings through their woods,
The pale man's sail skims o'er their floods,
    Their pleasant springs are dry;

* * * * * * * *

CHARLES SPRAGUE.

FOREWORD

When the white race came into the country of the red race, the red race long had had their own ways of living and their own code of right and wrong. They were red, but they were thinking men and women, not mere animals.

The white people brought their ways, which were different from the Indians' ways. So the two races could not live together.

To the white people, many methods of the Indians were wrong; to the Indians, many of the white people's methods were wrong. The white people won the rulership, because they had upon their side a civilization stronger than the loose civilization of the red people, and were able to carry out their plans.

The white Americans formed one nation, with one language; the red Americans formed many nations, with many languages.

The Indian fought as he had always fought, and ninety-nine times out of one hundred he firmly believed that he was enforcing the right. The white man fought after his own custom and sometimes after the Indian's custom also; and not infrequently he knew that he was enforcing a wrong.

Had the Indians been enabled to act all together, they would have held their land, just as the Americans of today would hold their land against the invader.

FOREWORD

Of course, the Indian was not wholly right, and the white man was not wholly wrong. There is much to be said, by either, and there were brave chiefs and warriors on both sides.

This book is written according to the Indian's view of matters, so that we may be better acquainted with his thoughts. The Indians now living do not apologize for what their fathers and grandfathers did. A man who defends what he believes are his rights is a patriot, whether they really are his rights, or not.

CONTENTS

CONTENTS

LIST OF ILLUSTRATIONS

BOYS' BOOK
OF INDIAN WARRIORS

BOYS' BOOK OF INDIAN WARRIORS

CHAPTER I

PISKARET THE ADIRONDACK CHAMPION (1644)

HOW HE SCOUTED AGAINST THE IROQUOIS

IT was in early spring, about the year 1644, that the warrior Piskaret of the Adirondack tribe of the Algonkins set forth alone from the island Allumette in the Ottawa River, Canada, to seek his enemies the Iroquois.

For there long had been bitter, bitter war between the vengeful Algonkins[1] and the cruel Hurons on the one side, and the proud, even crueler Five Nations of the Iroquois on the other side. At first the Adirondacks had driven the Mohawks out of lower Canada and into northern New York; but of late all the Algonkins, all the Hurons, and the French garrisons their allies, had been unable to stem the tide of the fierce Iroquois, rolling back into Canada again.

"Iri-a-khoiw" was the Algonkin name for them, meaning "adder." The French termed them

[1] The noun Algonkin, meaning an Indian, is also spelled Algonquin. But the adjective from this noun is spelled Algonquian when applied to Indians, and Algonkian when applied to a time or period in geology.

"Mingos," from another Algonkin word meaning "stealthy." The English and Dutch colonists in America knew them as the Five Nations. Their own title was "People of the Long House," as if the five nations were one family housed all together under one roof.

The Mohawks, the Senecas, the Onondagas, the Oneidas and the Cayugas—these composed the Iroquois league of the Five Nations against the world of enemies. The league rapidly spread in power, until the dreaded Iroquois were styled the Romans of the West.

But nearly three hundred years ago they were only beginning to rise. Their home was in central New York, from the Mohawk country at the Hudson River west to the Seneca country almost to Lake Erie. In this wide tract were their five principal towns, fortified by ditches and log palisades. From here they carried war south clear to the Cherokees of Tennessee, west clear into the land of the Illinois, and north to the Algonkins at Quebec of the lower St. Lawrence River.

Twelve or fifteen thousand people they numbered. Mohawks, Senecas, Onondagas, Oneidas and Cayugas still survive, as many as ever and ranking high among the civilized Indians of North America.

The Hurons lived to the northwest, in a smaller country along the shores of Georgian Bay of southeastern Lake Huron, in Canada.

"Hurons" they were called by the French, meaning "bristly" or "savage haired," for they wore their coarse black hair in many fantastic cuts, but the favorite fashion was that of a stiff roach or mane extending from the forehead to the nape of the neck, like the bristles of a wild boar's back or the comb of a rooster. By the Algonkins they were called "serpents," also. Their own name for themselves was "Wendat," or "People of the Peninsula"—a word which the English wrote as "Wyandot."

They were of the Iroquois family, but for seventy-five years and more they had been at war with their cousins of the south. They, too, had their principal fortified towns, and their league, of four independent nations and four protected nations, numbering twenty thousand. Like those of the Iroquois, some of their bark houses were five hundred feet long, for twenty families. Yet of this powerful people there remain today only about four hundred Hurons, near Quebec, and as many Wyandots in Canada and the former Indian Territory of Oklahoma.

The Algonkins lived farther north, along the Ottawa River, and the St. Lawrence to the east. "Place of spearing eel and fish from a canoe," is the best that we may get from the word "Algonkin." The "Raised Hair" people did the French first term them, because they wore their hair pompadoured. But Adirondack was a Mohawk word, "Hatirontaks," "Eaters of Trees," accusing the Adirondacks of being so hungry in winter that they ate bark.

In summer the men went naked; in winter they donned a fur cape. They were noted warriors, hunters and fishers, and skillful in making shell ornaments. As the "Nation of the Island" also were they known to the French explorers, because their headquarters were upon that large island of Allumette in the Ottawa River above present Ottawa of Canada.

The several tribes of Algonkins found by the French in Canada were only a small portion of those American Indians speaking in the Algonquian tongue. The immense Algonquian family covered North America from the Atlantic to the Mississippi, and reached even to the Rocky Mountains. The Indians met by the Pilgrim Fathers were Algonquians; King Philip was an Algonquian; the Shawnees of Tecumseh were Algonquians; the Sacs and Foxes of Chief Black-hawk were Algonquians; the Chippewas of Canada and the Winnebagos from Wisconsin are Algonquians; so are the Arapahos and Cheyennes of the plains and the Blackfeet of Montana.

The bark lodges of the Algonkins were round and peaked like a cone, instead of being long and ridged like those of the Iroquois and Hurons. Of the Algonkins of Canada there are sixteen hundred, today; there are no Adirondacks, under that name.

Now in 1644 the proud Iroquois hated the Algonkins, hated the Hurons, and had hated the French for thirty-five years, since the brave gentleman adventurer, Samuel de Champlain, having founded Quebec in 1608, had marched against them with his armor, his powder and ball, and the triumphantly whooping enemy.

The Iroquois never forgave the French for this. And indeed a truly savage warfare it had become, here in this northern country on either side of the border between New York and Canada: where the winters were long and piercingly cold, where hunger frequently stalked, where travel was by canoe on the noble St. Lawrence, the swift Ottawa, the Richelieu, the lesser streams and lakes, and by snowshoe or moccasin through the heavy forests; where the Indians rarely failed to torture their captives in manner too horrid to relate; and where the only white people were 300 French soldiers, fur-traders, laborers, priests and nuns, mainly at Quebec, and new Montreal, on the St. Lawrence, and the little trading-post of Three Rivers, half way between the two.

Algonkins and Hurons were accepting the French as allies. They listened, sometimes in earnest, sometimes in cunning, to the teachings of those "Black Robes," the few fearless priests who sought them out. The priests, bravest of the brave, journeyed unarmed and far, even among the scornful Iroquois, enduring torture by fire and knife, the torment of mosquitoes, cold and famine, and draughty, crowded bark houses smotheringly thick with damp wood smoke.

In spite of cross and sword, (trying to tame them,) the Iroquois were waxing ever bolder. They were well supplied with match-lock guns obtained by the Mohawks from the Dutch of the Hudson River. From their five towns ruled by a grand council of fifty chiefs they constantly sent out their raiding parties into the north. These, darting half-crouched in single file through the dark timber, creeping silently in their canoes by road of the dark rivers, suddenly fell like starved wolves upon whomsoever they sighted, be that near Quebec itself; killed them, or captured them, to hustle them away, break their bones, burn their bodies, eat of them; and returned for more.

Algonkins and Hurons were cruel, too, and crafty; but they were being beaten by greater craft and better arms.

So now we come again to Piskaret, of the Adirondacks, whose home was upon that large island of Allumette, governed by the haughty Algonkin chief Le Borgne, or The One-Eye.

Simon Piskaret was his full name as recorded in the mission books, for he and others of Allumette Island had been baptised by the priests. But with them this was much a method of getting protection, food and powder from these French; and an old writer of 1647 says that Piskaret was a Christian only by "appearance and policy."

However, the case of the Algonkins and the Hurons was growing very desperate. They risked their lives every time they ventured into the forests, and Piskaret was ashamed of being cooped in. Once the Adirondacks had been mighty. Hot desire to strike another blow flamed high in his heart. Therefore in this early spring of 1644, ere yet the snows were fairly melted, he strode away, alone, with snowshoes, bent upon doing some great deed.

His course was southeast, from the river Ottawa to cross the frozen St. Lawrence, and speed onward 100 miles for the Lake Champlain country of the New York-Canada border line, where he certainly would find the Iroquois.

By day and night he traveled, clad in his moccasins and fur mantle. Then when he reached the range of the Iroquois he reversed his snowshoes, so that they pointed backward. The Iroquois who might see his trail would know that these were the prints of Algonkin snowshoes, but they would think that here had been only an Algonkin hastening home. If they followed, they would be going in one direction and he in another!

His progress was slower, now, for it is hard to make time in snowshoes pointing backward; and presently he took pains to pick a way by keeping to the ridges and the south slopes from which the snow had melted. His eyes and ears needs must be alert; no sharper woodsmen ever lived, than the keen wolfish Iroquois.

At last, in the forest, he came upon Iroquois sign; next, peering and listening and sniffing, he smelled wood smoke; and stealing on, from tree to tree, he discovered the site of an Iroquois winter village, set in a clearing amidst the timber.

For the rest of that day he hid out; that night, after all had quieted, with war-club and knife ready he slipped like a shadow in among the very lodges. Not even a dog sensed him as he stood questing about for another hiding place.

Aha, he had it! Both the Hurons and the Iroquois laid in large stocks of fire wood, by forming piles of logs slanted together on end; and in one pile, here, was an opening through which he might squeeze into the center space, there to squat as under a tent. The ground in the village had been scraped bare of snow; he would leave no tracks.

Having thus experimented and arranged, Piskaret drew a long breath, grasped his war-club, and stealthily pushing aside the loose birch-bark door-flap of the nearest lodge, peeped inside. By the ember light he saw that every Iroquois, man and woman, was fast asleep, under furs, on spruce boughs around the fire.

Now Piskaret swiftly entered, without a sound killed them *all*, scalped them, and fled to his wood-pile.

Early in the grayness of morning he heard a great cry, swelling louder and louder until the forest echoed. It was a cry of grief and of rage. The strangely silent lodge had been investigated and his bloody work was known. Feet thudded past his wood-pile, hasty figures brushed against it, as the best warriors of the village bolted for the timber, to circle until they found the tracks of their enemy. But if they found any snowshoe tracks made by a stranger, these led out, not in.

So that day the Iroquois pursued furiously and vainly, while Piskaret crouched snug in his wood-pile, listened to the clamor, and laughed to himself.

At evening the weary Iroquois returned, foiled and puzzled. Their nimblest trailers had not even sighted the bold raider. This night Piskaret again waited until all was quiet; again he ventured forth, slipped inside a lodge, killed and scalped, and retreated to his wood-pile.

And again, with the morning arose that shrill uproar of grief and vengeance and the warriors scurried into the forest.

By evening the Iroquois were not only mystified but

much alarmed. Who was this thing that struck in the night and left no trail? An evil spirit had come among them—roosted perhaps in the trees!

If a squaw had removed a log or two from the pile Piskaret would have been torn to pieces, but fortune still stayed with him and he was not molested save by cold and hunger.

Tonight, however, the Iroquois chattered affrightedly until late; and when, after the noises had died away, Piskaret, cramped and chilled but eager, for a third time stole through the darkness to a lodge, he knew that his game was up. In this lodge two watchers had been posted—one at either end; and they were awake.

The same in the next lodge, and the next. Wherever he applied his eye to a crack in the bark walls, he saw two sentries, armed and alert—until finally he arrived at a lodge wherein one of the sentries, the one near the door, was squatted drowsy and half asleep.

So Piskaret softly placed his bundle of scalps where he might find it instantly, on a sudden threw aside the birch-bark door-flap, struck terribly with his club, yelled his war-cry that all might hear, grabbed his bundle of scalps and ran hard for the forest. From every lodge the Iroquois poured in pursuit.

All the rest of this night he ran, making northward, with the Iroquois pelting and whooping after; but the records say that he was the swiftest runner in the North—therefore he had little fear of being overtaken.

All the next day he ran, only now and then pausing, to show himself, and yell, and tempt the Iroquois onward; for he had another plan. At night-fall there were but six Iroquois left on his trail, and these were about worn out.

Now in the gathering darkness, noting his enemies falter, Piskaret sprang aside to a hollow tree and hid himself again. The tired Iroquois straggled near, and when they lost the trail they willingly quit, in order to roll in their bear-skins and sleep until the light of morning.

Whereupon, after granting them a little time, Piskaret crept out, killed every one of them, added their six scalps to his package, and having rested until day, sped north, with his dreadful trophies, to report at the island of Allumette.

That this is a true story of the famous Adirondack warrior Piskaret may be proved by the old French chronicles of those very times.

CHAPTER II

PISKARET THE ADIRONDACK CHAMPION (1645–1647)

HOW HE BROUGHT PEACE TO THE FORESTS

PISKARET was a hero. From lip to lip the story of his lone trail was repeated through the bark lodges of the Algonkins, and the long houses of the fierce Hurons, and even among the gentle nuns and gaunt priests of the brave mission settlements upon the lower St. Lawrence River.

But the nuns and priests did not favor such bloody deeds, which led only to more. Their teachings were all of peace rather than war between men. Yet each and every one of them was as bold as Piskaret, and to bring about peace would gladly go as far as he, and farther.

Now he did not lack followers. In the early spring of 1645, scarce a twelve-month after his famous lone scout, he took with him six other "Christian" Algonkin warriors, again to hunt the Iroquois.

Upon the large island in the St. Lawrence River, just below the mouth of the Algonkin's River Ottawa, the fort and mission of Montreal had been built, much to the rage of the roving Iroquois. It was the farthest up-river of the French settlements, and in the midst of the Iroquois favorite scouting grounds.

So bitter were the Iroquois, that all the fall and all the winter Montreal had been in a state of siege.

Tired of such one-sided warfare, Piskaret resolved to strike another blow. The broad St. Lawrence was fast locked by the winter's ice. His small party dragged their three canoes over the level snowy surface, and on eastward across a tongue of timbered land, to the River Richelieu. This connects Lake Champlain of New York and the St. Lawrence in Canada.

The Richelieu, flowing black and deep, had opened. It was the water-trail of the Iroquois, and especially of the Mohawks. By it they made their forays north to the St. Lawrence and the camps of their enemies.

Every thicket along its banks and every curve in its course was likely to be an ambush; but the fearless Piskaret party ascended clear to Lake Champlain itself. Here they landed upon an island, concealed themselves and their canoes in the wintry forest, and waited.

One day they heard a gun-shot. Some Iroquois were about, upon the lake or upon the mainland.

"Come," spoke Piskaret, to his party. "Let us eat. It may be the last time, for we will have to die instead of run."

After they had eaten, they saw two canoes making straight for the island. Each canoe held seven Iroquois. That counted up fourteen, or two to one.

However, the Piskaret party had the advantage of position. They hid in the bushes at the place for which the canoes were heading.

"Let us each choose a man in the first canoe," directed Piskaret, "and take sure aim, and fire together."

The volley by the Algonkins was so deadly that every

one of the six balls killed an Iroquois. The seventh warrior dived overboard, and escaped by swimming to the other canoe. That had been swift work.

But the Iroquois were brave. Of the Mohawk tribe, these. Instead of turning about, to get help, the eight warriors, whooping in rage, paddled furiously along the shore, to land at another spot and give battle.

Piskaret's Algonkins ran hard to head them off, and met the canoe again. At the shore one of the Iroquois sighted them, and stood up to fire. They shot him, so that he tumbled overboard and capsized the canoe.

The seven Mohawks were now in the water; but the water was shallow, and splashing through, they bored right in, like bulldogs.

The Piskaret Algonkins had need to shoot fast and true. The Mohawks feared nothing, and despised Algonkins. Besides, they now knew that Piskaret was before them, and his scalp they considered a great prize.

The Mohawks lost this battle. Before they could gain shelter, of their seven four had been killed, two had been captured, and there was only one who escaped.

No time was to be lost. The sounds of the battle probably had been heard.

"We have done well," said Piskaret. "Now we may run."

So they launched their canoes, and with two prisoners and eleven scalps they plied their paddles at best speed for the Richelieu.

Down the Richelieu, and down the St. Lawrence,

nothing disagreeable happened, save that, when one of the Mohawks (a large, out-spoken warrior) defied the Algonkins to do their worst upon him, and called them weaklings, he was struck across the mouth, to silence him.

"Where are you taking us, then?"

"We are taking you to the French governor at Quebec. He is our father, and you belong to him, not to us."

That indeed was surprising news. Usually the Hurons and the Algonkins refused to deliver any of their prisoners to the missions or the forts, but carried them away to the torture.

The Richelieu empties into the St. Lawrence below Montreal. On down the St. Lawrence, thick with melting ice, hastened the canoes, until Quebec, the capital of the province, was within sight.

Four miles above Quebec there had been founded another mission for Christian Indians. It was named Sillery. Here a number of Algonkins had erected a village of log huts, on a flat beside the river, under the protection of a priests' house, church and hospital.

As they approached Sillery, the Piskaret party raised their eleven scalps on eleven long poles. While they drifted, they chanted a song of triumph, and beat time to it by striking their paddles, all together, upon the gunwales of their canoes.

The two captives, believing that the hour of torture was near, sang their own songs of defiance.

That was a strange sight, to be nearing Sillery. So the good father in charge of Sillery sent a runner to

Quebec. He himself, with his assistants, joined the crowd of Algonkins gathered at the river shore.

The canoes came on. The scalps and the two prisoners were plain to be seen. Piskaret! It was the noted warrior Piskaret! Guns were being fired, whoops were being exchanged, and the mission father waited, hopeful and astonished.

Now the chief of the Sillery Algonkins, who had been baptised to the name of Jean Baptiste, made a speech of welcome, from the shore. Standing upright in his canoe, Piskaret the champion replied. And now a squad of French soldiers, hurrying in from Quebec, added to the excitement with a volley of salute.

Piskaret landed, proud not only that he had again whipped the Iroquois, but that he had acted like a Christian toward his captives. He had not burned them nor gnawed off their finger tips. And instead of giving them over for torture by other Algonkins, he had brought them clear down the river, to the governor.

The scalp trophies were planted, like flags, over the doorways of the Sillery lodges. The two captives were placed under guard until the governor should arrive from Quebec. The happy Father Jesuit bade everybody feast and make merry, to celebrate the double victory of Piskaret.

The governor of this New France hastened up from Quebec, hopeful that at last a way had been opened to peace with the dread Iroquois.

Clad in his brilliant uniform of scarlet and lace, he sat in council at the mission house, to receive Piskaret and the captives. With him sat the Father Jesuit, the head of the mission, and around them were grouped the Christian Algonkins.

The two Mohawks were brought in, and by a long speech Piskaret surrendered them to the governor. Governor Montmagny replied, praising him for his good heart and gallant deed—and of course rewarding him with presents, also.

The two Mohawks thought that their torture was only being postponed a little, until the French were on hand to take part in it. To their minds, the council was held for the purpose of deciding upon the form of torture. They had resolved to die bravely.

But to their great astonishment, the governor told them that their lives were spared and that they were to be well treated.

Rarely before, in all the years of war between the Iroquois and other nations, had such a thing occurred. To be sure, now and then a captive had been held alive, but only after he was so much battered that he was not worth finishing, or else had been well punished and was saved out, as a reward for his bravery.

So the big man, of the two captives, rose to make a speech in reply to the offer by the governor. He addressed him as "Onontio," or, in the Mohawk tongue, "Great Mountain," which was the translation of the name Montmagny.

"Onontio," he said, "I am saved from the fire; my body is delivered from death. Onontio, you have given me my life. I thank you for it. I will never forget it. All my country will be grateful to you. The earth will be bright; the river calm and smooth; there will be peace and friendship between us. The shadow is before my eyes no longer. The spirits of my ancestors slain by the Algonkins have disappeared. Onontio, you are good: we are bad. But our anger is gone; I have no heart except for peace and rejoicing."

He danced, holding up his hands to the ceiling of the council chamber, as if to the sky. He seized a hatchet, and flourished it—but he suddenly flung the hatchet into the wood fire.

"Thus I throw down my anger! Thus I cast away the weapons of blood! Farewell, war! Now I am your friend forever!"

Naturally, Piskaret might feel much satisfied with himself, that he had followed the teachings of the priests and had spared the enemies who had fallen into his hands.

The two captives were permitted to move about freely. After a while they were sent up-river to the trading-post and fort of Three Rivers, where there was another Iroquois. Having suffered cruel torture he had been purchased by the French commander of the post.

This Iroquois, after seeing and talking with the two, was given presents, and started home, to carry peace talk from Onontio to the Five Nations. The great Onontio stood ready to return the two other prisoners, also, unharmed, if the Iroquois would agree to peace.

In about six weeks the Iroquois peace messenger came into Three Rivers with two Mohawk chiefs to represent the Mohawk nation.

Now there was much ceremony, of speeches and

feasts, not only by the French of the post, but also by the Algonkins and the Hurons. The governor came up. In a grand peace council Chief Kiosaton, , head ambassador, made a long address. After each promise of good-will he passed out a broad belt of wampum, until the line upon which the belts were hung was sagging with more than fifteen.

By these beaded belts the promises were sealed.

Piskaret was here. It was necessary for him to give a present that should "wipe out the memory of the Iroquois blood he had shed," and this he did.

With high-sounding words the Mohawks left by sailboat for the mouth of the Richelieu, to continue on south to their own country. Another council had been set, for the fall. Then the more distant tribes of the Algonkins and the Hurons should meet the Iroquois, here at Three Rivers, and seal a general peace.

At that greater council many belts of wampum were passed—to clear the sky of clouds, to smooth the rivers and lakes and trails, to break the hatchets and guns and shields, and the kettles in which prisoners were boiled; to wash faces clean of war-paint and to wipe out the memory of warriors slain.

There were dances and feasts; and in all good humor the throng broke up.

Peace seemed to have come to the forests. The Piskaret party might well consider that they had opened the way. The happy priests gave thanks to Heaven that their prayers had been answered, and that the hearts of the Iroquois, the Algonkins and the Hurons were soft to the teachings of Christianity.

Now, would the peace last?

Yes—for twelve months, with the Mohawks alone. After which, saying that the Black Robe priests had sent them a famine plague in a box, the Mohawks seized new and sharper hatchets, again sped upon the war-trail to the St. Lawrence; and smote so terribly that at last they killed, in the forest, even Piskaret himself, while singing a peace-song he started to greet them.

The Algonkin peoples and the Hurons were driven like straw in the wind. Many fled west and south, into the Great Lakes country, and beyond.

CHAPTER III

OPECHANCANOUGH, SACHEM OF THE PAMUNKEYS (1607-1644)

WHO FOUGHT AT THE AGE OF ONE HUNDRED

THE first English-speaking settlement that held fast in the United States was Jamestown, inland a short distance from the Chesapeake Bay coast of Virginia, in the country of the Great King Powatan.

The Powatans, of at least thirty tribes, in this 1607 owned eight thousand square miles and mustered almost three thousand warriors. They lived in a land rich with good soil, game and fish; the men were well formed, the women were comely, the children many.

But before the new settlers met King Powatan—whose title was sachem (chief) and whose real name was Wa-hun-so-na-cook—they met his brother O-pe-chan-can-ough, sachem of the Pamunkey tribe of the Powatan league.

A large, masterful man was Opechancanough, sachem of the Pamunkeys. The Indians themselves said that he was not a Powatan, nor any relation of their king; but that he came from the princely line of a great Southern nation, distant many leagues. This may be the reason that, although he was allied to Chief Powatan, he never joined him in friendship to the whites, who, he claimed, if not checked would over-run the Indians' hunting-grounds.

SACHEM OF THE PAMUNKEYS

The Indians of Virginia did not wish to have the white men among them. They were living well and comfortably, before the white men came; after the white men came, with terrible weapons and huge appetites which they expected the Indians to fill, and a habit of claiming all creation, clouds veiled the sky of the Powatans, their corn-fields and their streams were no longer their own.

Powatan, the head sachem, collected guns and hatchets and planned to stem the tide while it was small. But these English enticed his daughter Pocahontas aboard a vessel, and there held her for the good behavior of her father.

Pocahontas married John Rolfe, an English gentleman of the colony. Now for the first time Powatan was won, for he loved his daughter and the honest treatment of her at English hands pleased him.

Opechancanough but bided his time, until 1622. He was a thorough hater; his weapons were treachery as well as open war; he had resolved never to give up his country to the stranger.

Meanwhile, Pocahontas had died, in 1617, aged about twenty-two, just when leaving England for a visit home.

Full of years and honors (for he had been a shrewd, noble-minded king) the sachem Powatan himself died in 1618, aged over three score and ten. His elder brother O-pi-tchi-pan became head sachem of the Powatan league. He was not of high character like the great chief's. Now Opechancanough soon sprang to the front, as champion of the nation.

Pocahontas was no longer a hostage, the English settlements and plantations had increased, the English in England were in numbers of the stars, and the leaves, and the sands; and something must be done at once.

Seventy-eight years of age he was, when he struck his blow. With the fierce Chick-a-hom-i-nies backing him, he had enlisted tribe after tribe among the Powatans. Yet never a word of the plan reached the colonists.

For several years peace had reigned in fair Virginia. The Indians were looked upon as only "a naked, timid people, who durst not stand the presenting of a staff in the manner of a firelock, in the hands of a woman"! "Firelocks" and modern arms they did lack, themselves, but Opechancanough, the old hater, had laid his plans to cover that.

March 22, 1622, was the date for the attack, which should "utterly extinguish the English settlements forever." Yet "forever" could not have been the hope of Opechancanough. Here in Virginia the white man's settlements had spread through five hundred miles, and on the north the Pilgrim Fathers had started another batch in the country of the Pokanokets.

The plan of Opechancanough succeeded perfectly. Keeping the date secret, tribe after tribe sent their warriors, to arrive at the borders of the Virginia settlements in the night of March 21.

"Although some of the detachments had to march from great distances, and through a continued forest, guided only by the stars and moon, no single instance of disorder or mistake is known to have happened. One by one they followed each other in profound silence, treading as nearly as possible in each other's steps, and adjusting the long grass and branches which they displaced. They halted at short distances from the settlements, and waited in death-like stillness for the signal of attack."

A number of Indians with whom the settlers were well acquainted had been doing spy work. It was quite the custom for Indians to eat breakfast in settlers' homes, and to sleep before the settlers' fire-places. In this manner the habits of every family upon the scattered plantations were known. There were Indians in the fields and in the houses and yards, pretending to be friendly, but preparing to strike.

The moment agreed upon arrived. Instantly the peaceful scene changed. Acting all together, the Indians in the open seized hatchet, ax, club and gun, whatever would answer the purpose, and killed. Some of the settlers had been decoyed into the timber; many fell on their own thresholds; and the majority died by their own weapons.

The bands in ambush rushed to take a hand. In one hour three hundred and forty-seven white men, women and children had been massacred. It was a black, black deed, but so Opechancanough had planned. Treachery was his only strength.

This spring a guerilla warfare was waged by both sides. Blood-hounds were trained to trail the Indians. Mastiffs were trained to pull them down. But the colonists needed crops; without planted fields they would starve. The governor proposed a peace, that both parties might plant their corn. When the corn in the Indians' fields had ripened, and was being gathered, the settlers made their treacherous attack, in turn. They killed without mercy, destroyed the Indians' supplies, and believed that they had slain Opechancanough.

There was much rejoicing, but Opechancanough still lived, in good health. He had been too clever for the trap.

Rarely seen, himself, by the settlers, he continued to direct the movements of his warriors. He refused to enter the settlements. Never yet had he visited Jamestown. Governors came and went, but Opechancanough remained, unyielding.

He was eighty-seven when, in 1630, a truce was patched up, that both sides might rest a little. So far the Indians had had somewhat the best of the fighting; the colonists had not driven them to a safe distance.

The white men were growing stronger, the red men were improving not at all, and Opechancanough knew that the truce would surely be broken. He stayed aloof nine years, waiting, while the colonists grew careless. At last they quarreled among themselves.

This was his chance. From the Chickahominies and the Pamunkeys the word was spread to the other tribes. The second of his plans ripened. Opechancanough had so aged that he was unable to walk. He set the day of April 18, 1644, as the time for the general attack. He ordered his warriors to bear him upon the field in a litter, at the head of five united tribes.

Again the vengeful league of the Powatans burst upon the settlers in Virginia. From the mouth of the James River back inland over a space of six hundred square miles, war ravaged for two days; three hundred and more settlers were killed, two hundred were made captives, homes and supplies were burned to ashes.

It looked as though nothing would stand before Opechancanough—indeed, as though the end of Virginia had come. But in the midst of the pillage the work suddenly was stopped, the victorious Indians fled and could not be rallied. They were frightened, it is said, by a bad sign in the sky.

Governor Sir William Berkeley called out every twentieth man and boy of the home-guard militia, and by horse and foot and dog pursued.

Next we may see the sachem Opechancanough, in his one hundredth year, borne hither-thither in his bough litter, by his warriors, directing them how to retreat, where to fight, and when to retreat again. He suffered severely from hunger and storm and long marches, until the bones ridged his flabby skin, he had lost all power over his muscles, and his eyelids had to be lifted with the fingers before he could gaze beyond them.

Governor Berkeley and a squadron of horsemen finally ran him down and captured him. They took him, by aid of his litter-bearers, to Jamestown.

He was a curious sight, for Jamestown. By orders of the governor he was well treated, on account of his great age, and his courageous spirit. The governor planned to remove him to England, as token of the healthfulness of the Virginia climate.

But all this made little difference to Opechancanough.

He had warred, and had lost; now he expected to be tortured and executed. He was so old and worn, and so stern in his pride of chiefship, that he did not care. He had been a sachem before the English arrived, and he was a sachem still. Nobody heard from his set lips one word of complaint, or fear, or pleading. Instead, he spoke haughtily. He rarely would permit his lids to be lifted, that he might look about him.

His faithful Indian servants waited upon him. One day a soldier of the guard wickedly shot him through the back.

The wound was mortal, but the old chief gave not a twinge; his seamed face remained as stern and firm as if of stone. He had resolved that his enemies should see in him a man.

Only when, toward the end, he heard a murmur and scuff of feet around him, did he arouse. He asked his nurses to lift his eyelids for him. This was done. He coldly surveyed the people who had crowded into the room to watch him die.

He managed to raise himself a little.

"Send in to me the governor," he demanded angrily.

Governor Berkeley entered.

"It is time," rebuked old Opechancanough. "For had it been my fortune to have taken Sir William Berkeley prisoner, I should not have exposed him as a show to my people."

Then Opechancanough died, a chief and an enemy to the last.

CHAPTER IV

KING PHILIP THE WAMPANOAG (1662–1676)

THE TERROR OF NEW ENGLAND

WHILE in Virginia the white colonists were hard put to it by the Powatans, the good ship *Mayflower* had landed the Puritan Pilgrim Fathers on the Massachusetts Bay shore to the north, among the Pokanokets.

The Po-kan-o-kets formed another league, like the league of the Powatans. There were nine tribes, holding a section of southeastern Massachusetts and of water-broken eastern Rhode Island.

The renowned Massasoit of the Wam-pa-no-ag tribe was the grand sachem. In Rhode Island, on the east shore of upper Narragansett Bay was the royal seat of Montaup, or Mount Hope, at the village Pokanoket.

Great was the sachem Mas-sa-so-it, who ruled mildly but firmly, and was to his people a father as well as a chief.

Of his children, two sons were named Wamsutta and Metacomet. They were renamed, in English, Alexander and Philip, by the governor of this colony of Plymouth.

Alexander was the elder. He had married Wetamoo, who was the young squaw sachem of the neighboring village of Pocasset, to the east. Philip married her sister, Woo-to-ne-kau-ske.

When late in 1661 the sage Massasoit died, Alexander became grand sachem of the Pokanoket league.

Now the long reign of Massasoit had been broken. With him out of the way, certain hearts, jealous of the Wampanoags and their alliance with the English, began to stir up trouble for the new sachem. They reported him as planning a revolt against Plymouth Colony.

There may have been some truth in this. The Puritans were a stern, strict people, who kept what they had seized, and who constantly added more. To them the Indians were heathens and inferiors; not free allies, but subjects of the king of England.

Before the landing of the Pilgrims in the Indians' territory, sailing ships, touching at the New England shore, had borne Indians away into slavery. Since the landing of the Pilgrims, the Pequots had been crushed in battle, and Captain Miles Standish had applied knife and rope to other Indians.

So some doubts as to the wisdom of Massasoit's treaty with the English began to spread through the Pokanokets.

The Plymouth officers ordered Alexander to appear at court and answer the charges against him. When he delayed, Major Josiah Winslow was sent to get him. The major took ten armed men, and proceeded for Mount Hope. On the way he found Alexander and party in a hunting lodge, their guns leaning outside.

The major seized the guns. With pistol in hand he

KING PHILIP

Courtesy of The American Bureau of Ethnology.

demanded that Alexander come with him, or die. Alexander claimed that he was a sachem and free ruler, not a dog. He "fell into a raging passion." He had a proper pride, and a fierce temper.

He agreed to go, as a sachem attended by his own followers. The charge against him never was pressed, because his rage and shame at the insult threw him into a fever, from which he soon died.

He had reigned only a few months. In this year 1662 Philip or Metacomet took his place as grand sachem of the Pokanokets. The death of his brother grieved him. Wetamoo, the young widow, said that Alexander had been poisoned by his captors, the English. The story counted, and the fate of Alexander was not a pleasant story, to the Pokanokets.

Philip saw trouble ahead. His neighbors the Narragansetts had long been at outs with the English. In his father's reign their old chief Mi-an-to-no-mah had been handed over by the Puritans of Connecticut to Chief Uncas of the Mohegans for execution in the Indian way. The Narragansetts were friendly with the Pokanokets; they rather looked upon Philip as their adopted leader.

His lands were rapidly going, the English were rapidly spreading, the Puritan laws and religion were being forced upon him. It was galling that he, a king by his own right, should be made a subject of another king whom he had never seen.

The New England colonists could not forget how the Virginia colonists had been surprised and killed by the Powatans. They watched King Philip closely. In

1671 he was said to be complaining that certain of them were trespassing on his hunting grounds. This led to the report that his people were holding councils, and were repairing their guns and sharpening their hatchets, as if for war.

So King Philip, like his brother King Alexander, was summoned to the Puritan court, to be examined. He had not forgotten the treatment of Alexander. He went, but he filled half the town meeting-house with his armed warriors.

There he denied that war was planned against the English. He was persuaded to sign a paper which admitted his guilt and bound him to deliver up all his guns.

He decided not to do this latter thing. To give up his guns would leave him bare to all enemies.

He was made to sign other papers, until little by little the Pokanokets seemed to have surrendered their rights, except their guns. The white people, and not Philip, ruled them.

Then, in the first half of 1675 the affair of John Sassamon occurred.

John Sassamon was an educated Indian who had returned to the Wampanoags, after preaching. He spoke English, and was used by King Philip at Mount Hope as secretary. He thought that he had found out war plans, and he carried the secrets to Plymouth.

The Indian law declared that he should die. In March his body was discovered under the ice of a pond of Plymouth Colony. His neck had been broken.

To the Pokanoket idea, this had been legal execution

ordered by the sachem. The English called it a murder. They arrested three of King Philip's men. These were tried in court before a jury of twelve colonists and five Indians. They were found guilty. Two were hanged, the third was shot.

That was the end of peace. Miantonomah of the Narragansetts had been handed over by the colonists to the law of the Mohegans, but when the Pokanokets tried a similar law against a traitor, they had been punished. King Philip could no longer hold back his young men.

He had been working hard, in secret, to enlist all the New England tribes in a league greater than the league of Opechancanough, and by one stroke clean New England of the white colonists. The time set was the next year, 1676. The Narragansetts had promised then to have ready four thousand warriors.

But when the word from the English court was carried to Pokanoket, that the three prisoners were to be killed, and that Philip himself was likely to be tried, the warriors of the Wampanoags broke their promise to wait.

They danced defiantly. They openly sharpened their knives and hatchets upon the stone window-sills of settlers' houses, and made sport of the English.

A sudden cold fear spread through New England. A blood-red cloud seemed to be hovering over. Signs were seen in the sky—a great Indian bow, a great Indian scalp, racing horsemen; a battle was heard, with boom of cannon and rattle of muskets and whistling of bullets. The pious Puritans ordered a fast day, for public prayer, in the hope that God would stay the threatened scourge.

Upon that very day, June 24, 1675, the war burst into flame. At the town of Swansea, Massachusetts, near the Rhode Island border, and the nearest settlement to Mount Hope, a Wampanoag was wounded by an angered colonist. The Indians were glad. They believed that the party whose blood was shed first would be victors. The colonists returning from town meeting were fired upon; that day seven were killed and several wounded. King Philip's young men had acted without orders.

When King Philip heard, he wept. He was not yet ready for the war, but now he had to fight. He had at hand sixty Wampanoag men of fighting age; all the Pokanoket league numbered six hundred warriors. Against these could be mustered thousands of the colonists, whose ninety towns extended through Massachusetts, and Connecticut, and into present Rhode Island. Therefore he must act swiftly, or his cause was lost. All depended upon his appeal to the inland tribes on the north.

The powerful Narragansetts, his neighbors on the west, were not prepared, and sent no warriors at once; but certain of the other tribes did respond with gun and hatchet and fire.

Before the colonists could rally under a skillful leader, the forces of King Philip were successful. He had plenty of guns and ammunition. Town after town in Plymouth Colony of southeastern Massachusetts was laid in ashes by fierce surprise attacks. The scene shifted to western Massachusetts. The Nipmucks of the Connecticut River, there, aided in the dreadful work.

Throughout the summer and fall of 1675 all settled Massachusetts rang with the war-whoops of the Pokanokets and their allies. King Philip proved himself a master in Indian warfare to strike, and run, and strike again. In this one brief space he earned his title, the Terror of New England, not only because of his first successes, but also because during the span of more than a year no Englishman recognized his voice in battle, and only once was his face seen by his enemies.

Long after the war his name was used for frightening children.

"King Philip is coming!" And the naughtiest child would quiet and seek his mother's skirt.

Although tortures and brutal killings were committed, King Philip himself opposed this. Many stories are told of his kindness to captives. He showed fully as much mercy as the colonists did.

Some tribes had failed to help. The Mohegans under Uncas enlisted with the English, which was expected. The "praying Indians," as the Christianized Pokanokets were known, also either stayed aloof, or else were used as scouts against their people. The New Hampshire Indians refused to take up the hatchet, and the Narragansetts still hung back.

King Philip's own home of Pokanoket or Mount Hope had of course early been seized by the English troops. They had planned to keep him from escaping to the mainland in the north. But he easily moved his men out, by way of the narrow neck that connected with the mainland.

Now he was a roamer, until in this winter of 1675 he decided to stay among the Narragansetts, in southern Rhode Island, and renew his league.

To compel the Narragansetts to deliver over the King Philip people, an army of fifteen hundred was raised by Massachusetts, Plymouth and Connecticut colonies.

South Rhode Island was then an Indian wilderness, heavily timbered and deep with swamps. Near present South Kingston, in the Narragansett country, upon a meadow upland amidst a dense swamp Philip had built a fort containing five hundred wigwams. He had built well.

The only entrance from the swamp was defended by a high log fence or series of palisades. In addition, around a space of five acres he had laid a thick hedge of felled trees. A single log bridged the water separating the fort from the drier land beyond. The wigwams were made bullet-proof by great stores of supplies piled against their walls, inside.

It was reported that he had three thousand persons in the fort—these being his Pokanokets, and many Narragansett men, women and children. The place was called Sunke-Squaw.

Treachery it was that broke the power of King Philip. An Indian named Peter sought the English and offered to show them how to get in. After a long march amidst bitter cold and driving snow, they arrived at one o'clock in the afternoon of December 19. They were short of provisions, and very weary. For a time matters went ill with them. Again and again their attacking parties were swept from the single log that Peter the traitor had showed to them. A number of officers and men had fallen, before, pressing hard, with night at hand, a party succeeded in entering the fort.

Here the hot fight passed from wigwam to wigwam. Some of the English were killed by balls from their own soldiers. Through all the swamp the battle raged.

"They run, they run!" sounded the loud cries, from the English within the fort. Their comrades on the outside hastened—scrambling, wading, straddling the log or knee-deep in the half frozen mire.

Indian women and children and warriors had taken refuge in the wigwams. Torches were applied, burning them or driving them out to be shot down. Officers tried to prevent the burning of the wigwams, in order to save the provisions, but the fire spread.

So by night the fort was in ruins. The Indians were killed, captured or fleeing. Seven hundred had been killed by bullet and sword, three hundred more perished by cold and hunger and wounds; how many old men, women and children had burned to death, no one knew. But a third of the Narragansett nation had been slain or taken captive, and of the Pokanokets only a remnant was left.

Eighty killed, was the report of the Connecticut troops alone. There were one hundred and fifty men grievously wounded. As the soldiers had destroyed the fort and its provisions, they had no shelter. Through a furious snowstorm they made a miserable night march of eighteen miles before even the wounded could be attended to.

King Philip was now a fugitive, but he was by no means done fighting. He removed to the interior of Massachusetts—it is said that he traveled clear to the Mohawks of New York, and asked their aid in this war against the English. He did not get it.

From January on into the summer of 1676 the war-whoop, the gun-shot and the torch again terrified the colonies. Aided by a few allies, King Philip was making his last great effort. He carried the war to within twenty miles of Boston. Of ninety towns in New England, thirteen had been burned; six hundred buildings had been leveled in smoke, and six hundred arms-bearing colonists killed.

"These were the most distressing days that New England ever beheld," reads a record. "All was fear and consternation. Few there were, who were not in mourning for some near kindred, and nothing but horror stared them in the face."

Presently Captain Benjamin Church, as noted in New England as Kit Carson is in the West, was upon the sachem's trail. He was a skilled Indian-fighter; he knew King Philip's haunts, and all the Indian ways.

There was no let-up by Captain Church. Some captives he turned into scouts, so that they helped him against their former chief; the more dangerous he shot or hanged. To the English notion, these hostile Indians were rebels against the government and deserved no mercy. Other captives, especially women and children, were sent to the West Indies as slaves.

Soon King Philip's allies began to desert him. They saw no hope of lasting victory; they accused King Philip of persuading them into a useless war, and either scattered or went over to the English.

Among the deserters was Queen Awashonks, squaw sachem of the Sogkonate tribe of the Pokanoket league. Her country lay in the southeast corner of Rhode Island. When Philip had heard that the Sog-ko-nates were helping Captain Church to trail him down, he is said to have smiled never again.

Chief Canonchet, great leader of the Narragansetts, was captured and executed. Thus another nail was driven into King Philip's fate.

Of Queen Wetamoo's three hundred warriors, twenty-six remained; they were betrayed by one of their own number, and captured, and Wetamoo was drowned in flight.

These deaths saddened Philip, but the many desertions blackened his horizon and he knew that he was doomed.

By midsummer he was fleeing from spot to spot, with Captain Church hard after. He had only a handful of Pokanokets and scarcely more Narragansetts with him. Although frequently attacking, he himself was never sighted. The English accused him of hiding in cowardly fashion, but he well knew that with his death or capture the war would be ended. Only the name King Philip supported it still.

Toward the close of July he had been forced south,

to his own Wampanoag country of Mount Hope and Pocasset. In a sally north into southern Massachusetts he was surprised, on Sunday, July 30, and his uncle killed and his sister taken prisoner.

The next morning there came in haste from Plymouth the doughty Captain Church, aided by Queen Awashonks's men. Where a tree had been felled for a bridge of escape across the Taunton River thirty miles south of Boston, he espied, on the opposite bank, an Indian sitting alone upon a stump.

The captain aimed and would have fired, but his Indian companion said: "No. I think him one of our own men." The Indian upon the stump slowly turned his head; the captain saw that he was King Philip with his hair cut short.

At the fall of the gun hammer King Philip leaped from the stump, and plunging down a steep bank, was gone.

Captain Church crossed the river in pursuit, but did not catch him.

The next day he came upon the beaten sachem's forlorn camp. There he captured Philip's wife, Woo-to-ne-kau-ske, and their little boy of nine years.

The end of King Philip was very near. His relatives, even his sister-in-law, Wetamoo, had died; his friends had deserted him; his remaining family were in the hands of his enemies.

"You now have made Philip ready to die, for you have made him as poor and miserable as he used to make the English," Captain Church's Indian scouts praised. "You have now killed or taken all his relations. This bout has almost broken his heart, and you will soon have his head."

The head of King Philip was indeed the prize. His escape north was barred by a "great English army"; his flight southward into Rhode Island was limited by the sea. His "kenneling places" (as they were styled perhaps because of the dog's life that he was leading) were constantly betrayed, and his force of true-hearts was melting like the snows. But he received no offer of mercy. None was sent, and he asked for none.

He doubled and twisted in vain, and tried an ambush. Captain Church easily side-stepped this; and with only thirty English and twenty Indian scouts, in two days killed or captured one hundred and seventy-three more of the Philip people. Assuredly, King Philip was growing weak. He might have listened to terms, but in those stern days terms were not made with rebels, especially with troublesome Indians who were assumed to be children of Satan.

Captain Church, urged on by the Plymouth government, closed in farther. Now died two of King Philip's remaining captains. Sam Barrow, "as noted a rogue as any among the enemy," was captured, and sentenced at once to death, by Captain Church. He was an old man, but a hatchet was sunk into his head.

Chief Totoson, with his eight-year boy and old wife, escaped and reached Agawom, his former home. His little son fell sick; his own heart "became a stone within him, and he died." His old wife threw some brush and leaves over his body, and soon she, also, died. Thus was the Totoson family disposed of.

Only old Annawan, Philip's greatest captain, was left with him. They two, and their miserable band of men, women and children, sought last refuge at the abandoned Mount Hope. Here they were, back again, defeated, with nowhere else to turn.

On the morning of August 10 Captain Church was home, also, visiting his wife. He lived on the island of Rhode Island, in Narragansett Bay and separated by only a narrow strait from Mount Hope, on the north.

There he had word, in much haste, that one of King Philip's men was waiting, to guide him to a swamp where the sachem might be killed.

The name of the King Philip man was Alderman, in English. His brother had proposed to King Philip that they all surrender, and King Philip had struck him dead. So revenge burned in Alderman's heart, and he turned traitor. He was of the Queen Wetamoo people, but had deserted her, also.

Upon getting word of King Philip's whereabouts, so near at hand, Captain Church kissed his wife goodby, and gladly mounted his horse again—hoping, he said, "by tomorrow morning to have the rogue's head."

This night Alderman guided the captain's force truly. They had not far to go—only a dozen or so miles up the Mount Hope peninsula, to the narrow neck. The captain was well acquainted with the exact spot: a little isle of dry land in the midst of the swamp.

On the morning of August 12 he had his men arranged silently. Captain Golding was given the "honor of beating up Philip's headquarters." With a picked party, crawling on their bellies, he entered, to surprise the little isle, and drive out the game.

Throughout the swamp the other men were placed, two (a white man and an Indian) by two, behind trees, "that none might pass undiscovered." When the enemy should be started in flight, then all the attacking party were to make a great noise. Every figure moving without noise was to be fired upon by the ambuscade.

There were not quite enough men to complete the circle of the ambuscade. However, Captain Church took his aide, Major Sanford, by the hand, and said: "Sir, I have so placed the men that it is scarce possible Philip should escape them." There was no thought of sparing King Philip's life. He was an outlaw.

Just as the captain finished his hopeful speech, a gun-shot echoed through the misty gray. Captain Golding's men had come upon one Indian, and had fired, and then had poured a volley into the sleeping camp.

Again from the harried band rose the cry "Awannux! Awannux! (English! English!)," and into the swamp they plunged.

Caleb Cook and Alderman the guide had been stationed together behind a tree. At the first gun-shot, says the Captain Church story, King Philip "threw his petunk (shot pouch) and powder-horn over his head, catched up his gun, and ran as fast as he could scamper, without any more clothes than his small-breeches and stockings."

And here he came, directly for the tree. The two behind it let him come "fair within shot." Then Caleb took the first fire upon him. But the gun only flashed in the pan. He bade the Indian fire away, and Alderman did so true to purpose; sent one musket bullet through King Philip's heart, and another not above two inches from it. The gun had been loaded with two balls.

King Philip "fell upon his face in the mud and the water, with his gun under him." He was dead, at last, on the soil of his long-time home land from which he had sallied to do battle in vain.

"By this time," reads the Captain Church story, "the enemy perceived that they were waylaid on the east side of the swamp, and tacked short about. One of the enemy, who seemed to be a great, surly old fellow, hallooed with a loud voice, and often called out, 'I-oo-tash, I-oo-tash.' Captain Church called to his Indian, Peter, and asked him who that was that called so? He answered, that it was old Annawan, Philip's great captain, calling on his soldiers to stand to it and fight stoutly. Now the enemy finding that place of the swamp which was not ambushed, many of them made their escape in the English tracks."

When the pursuit had quit, Captain Church let his men know that King Philip had been killed, and they gave three cheers.

Then the captain ordered the body to be pulled out of the mud. So some of the Indians "took hold of him by his stockings, and some by his small breeches (being otherwise naked) and drew him through the mud to the upland; and a doleful, great, naked, dirty beast he looked like," according to their opinion.

"Forasmuch as you have caused many an Englishman's body to be unburied, and to rot above ground, not one of your bones shall be buried," pronounced Captain Church. And he ordered an old Indian, who acted as executioner, to behead and quarter King Philip.

But before he struck with the hatchet, the old Indian also made a little speech, to the body.

"You have been a very great man," he said, "and have made many a man afraid of you; but so big as you are, I will now chop you up."

And so he did.

King Philip was known not only by his face, but by a mangled hand in which a pistol had burst. His head and his crippled hand were awarded to Alderman, who had betrayed him; Alderman was told to exhibit them through New England, if he wished, as a traveling show. He gained many shillings in fees.

The four quarters of King Philip were hung to the branches of a tree. The head was stuck upon a gibbet at Plymouth for twenty years. The hand was kept at Boston. Caleb Cook traded with Alderman for King Philip's gun; and King Philip's wife and little boy were sold as slaves in the West Indies.

Now the Terror of New England had been subdued. He had been leading such a sorry life, of late, that no doubt he was glad to be done, and to have fallen in his stride and not in chains. His age is not stated.

Thus peace came to the colony of Plymouth in Massachusetts, and King Philip had few left to mourn for him, until, after a season, even some of the English writers, their spirit softened, began to grant that he might have been as much a patriot as a traitor.

In another century, the colonists themselves rebelled against a government which they did not like.

CHAPTER V

THE SQUAW SACHEM OF POCASSET (1675-1676)

AND CANONCHET OF THE BIG HEART

WHEN King Philip had planned his war, he well knew that he might depend upon Wetamoo, the squaw sachem of Pocasset.

After the death of the luckless Alexander, Wetamoo married a Pocasset Indian named Petananuit. He was called by the English "Peter Nunnuit." This Peter Nunnuit appears to have been a poor sort of a husband, for he early deserted to the enemy, leaving his wife to fight alone.

Wetamoo was not old. She was in the prime of life, and as an Indian was beautiful. Not counting her faithless husband, only one of her Pocassets had abandoned her. He was that same Alderman who betrayed and killed King Philip.

In the beginning Queen Wetamoo had mustered three hundred warriors. She stuck close to King Philip, and fought in his ranks. She probably was in the fatal Narragansett fort when it was stormed and taken, on December 19, 1675. The English much desired to seize her, for her lands of Pocasset "would more than pay all the charge" of the war. She was considered as being "next unto Philip in respect to the mischief that hath been done."

But she was not taken in the fort among the Narragansetts. She fled with King Philip her brother-in-law, and warred that winter and spring, as he did, against the settlements in Massachusetts.

Truly a warrior queen she was, and so she remained to the last, ever loyal to the losing cause of her grand sachem, and to the memory of Alexander.

With Philip she was driven southward, back toward her home of Pocasset, east of Mount Hope. By the first week in August of 1676, she had only twenty-six men left, out of her three hundred.

Then there came to the colonists at Taunton, which lay up the river Taunton from Pocasset, another deserter, with word that he could lead them to the little Wetamoo camp, not far southward.

Twenty armed English descended upon her, August 6, and easily overcame her camp. She alone escaped, in flight. She had no thought of surrendering herself into slavery.

In making her way to Pocasset, she "attempted," reads the tale, "to get over a river or arm of the sea near by, upon a raft, or some pieces of broken wood; but whether tired and spent with swimming, or starved with cold and hunger, she was found stark naked in Metapoiset [near present Swansea of southern Massachusetts, at the Rhode Island line], not far from the water side, which made some think she was first half drowned; and so ended her wretched life."

No respect was paid to her. Her head was cut off and hoisted upon a pole in the town of Taunton, as revenge for the similar beheading of some English bodies, earlier in the war. When, in Taunton, the Pocasset captives saw the head—"They made a most horrid and diabolical lamentation, crying out that it was their queen's head."

Here let us close the melancholy story of the warrior queen Wetamoo, who as the companion-in-arms of her sachem sought to avenge her husband's death, as well as to save her country from the foreigner. However, Wetamoo and Philip together dragged the once mighty Narragansetts down. This brings to the surface the tale of Canonchet, the big-hearted.

The Narragansetts were a large and warlike people, and hard fighters. Their country covered nearly all present Rhode Island; the city of Providence was founded in their midst, when the great preacher Roger Williams sought refuge among them. They conquered other tribes to the north and west. When King Philip rose in 1675 they numbered, of themselves, five thousand people, and could put into the field two thousand warriors.

In the beginning, under their noble sachem Can-on-i-cus, they were friendly to the English colonists. While Roger Williams lived among them they stayed friendly. They agreed to a peace with Sachem Massasoit's Pokanokets, who occupied the rest of Rhode Island, east across Narragansett Bay. They marched with the English and the Mohegans to wipe out the hostile Pequots.

Canonicus died, and Mi-an-to-no-mah, his nephew, who had helped him rule, became chief sachem. Miantonomah was famed in council and in war. The colonies suspected him, as they did Alexander, son of Massasoit. They favored the Mohegans of the crafty sachem Uncas. When Miantonomah had been taken prisoner by Uncas, at the battle of Sachem's Plain in Connecticut, 1643, the United Colonies of Connecticut, Massachusetts and Plymouth directed that the Mohegans put him to death, as a treaty breaker.

Accordingly Uncas ordered him killed by the hatchet, and ate a piece of his shoulder.

Possibly Miantonomah deserved to die, but the hearts of the Narragansetts grew very sore.

It is scarcely to be wondered at that they favored the Pokanokets rather than the English, when King Philip, who also had suffered, called upon them to aid in cleaning the land of the white enemy. "Brothers, we must be as one, as the English are, or we shall soon all be destroyed," had said Miantonomah, in a speech to a distant tribe; and that looked to be so.

Ca-non-chet, whose name in Indian was Qua-non-chet (pronounced the same), and Nan-un-te-noo, was son of the celebrated Miantonomah. He was now chief sachem of the Narragansetts, and the friend of King Philip.

He was a tall, strongly built man, and accused by the English of being haughty and insolent. Why not? He was of proud Narragansett blood, from the veins of a long line of great chiefs, and the English had given his father into the eager hands of the enemy.

Presently, he was asked to sign treaties that would make him false to the memory of Miantonomah and double-hearted toward the hopeful King Philip.

The papers engaged the Narragansetts not to harbor any of King Philip's people, nor to help them in any way against the English, nor to enter a war without the permission of the English. He was to deliver the Philip and Wetamoo people, when they came to him.

Canonchet was not that kind of a man. He had no idea of betraying people who may have fled to him for shelter from a common enemy. A few of his men feared. It was suggested to him that he yield to the colonies, lest the Narragansetts be swallowed up by the English. He replied like a chief, and the son of Miantonomah.

"Deliver the Indians of Philip? Never! Not a Wampanoag will I ever give up! No! Not the paring of a Wampanoag's nail!"

The venerable Roger Williams, his friend, the friend of his father and the friend of the long-dead Canonicus, had advised him to stay out of the war.

"Massachusetts," said Roger Williams, "can raise thousands of men at this moment; and if you kill them, the king of England will supply their place as fast as they fall."

"It is well," replied Canonchet. "Let them come. We are ready for them. But as for you, Brother Williams, you are a good man; you have been kind to us many years. We shall burn the English in their houses, but not a hair of your head shall be touched."

The colonies did not wait for Canonchet to surrender the King Philip people. The treaty had been signed on October 28, and on November 2 an army from Connecticut, Massachusetts and Plymouth was ordered out, to march against the Narragansetts, and seize King Philip and Queen Wetamoo, and punish Canonchet.

It was known that Queen Wetamoo was with Canonchet, but not certainly that King Philip had "kenneled" there. At any rate, down marched the English, their Mohegan and Pequot allies, all piloted by one Peter who might have been the husband of Wetamoo herself, but who probably was a Narragansett traitor.

Canonchet stood firm. To his notion, he was not obliged to surrender anybody, while the English held his brother and three other Narragansetts. Besides—"Deliver the Indians of Philip? No! Not the paring of a Wampanoag's nail!"

On the afternoon of December 19, this year 1675, the bold English and their allies struck the great fortified village at Sunke-Squaw. Out from the heat and smudge of the blazing wigwams fled Philip and Wetamoo and Canonchet, with their shrieking people, into the wintry swamp where the snowy branches of the cedars and hemlocks were their only refuge. Canonchet had lost a third of his nation; large numbers surrendered to the English; but, like his friend Philip, with his warriors who remained true he carried the war to the English themselves. And a terrible war it was.

In March Captain William Peirse was sent out with seventy stout men to march from Plymouth and head off the raging Narragansetts. Plymouth had heard that the haughty young sachem Canonchet was on his way to Plymouth, at the van of three hundred warriors.

Captain Peirse made his will and marched southward, to the Pawtucket River not far above Providence. Canonchet's spies had marked him, and Canonchet was ready.

On March 26, which was a Sunday, Captain Peirse saw upon the other side of the river a party of Indians limping as if worn out and trying to get away. Therefore he crossed, near the Pawtucket Falls, in glad pursuit—and "no sooner was he upon the western side, than the warriors of Nanuntenoo, like an avalanche from a mountain, rushed down upon him; nor striving for coverts from which to fight, more than their foes, fought them face to face with the most determined bravery!"

There were Narragansetts still upon the east side of the river, also, to cut off retreat. The captain, fighting desperately, with his men ranged in two ranks back to back, sent a runner to Providence, only six or eight miles, for assistance; but so quickly was the work done, by Canonchet, that of all the English force, only one Englishman escaped, and not above a dozen of the scouts.

"Captain Peirse was slain, and forty and nine English with him, and eight (or more) Indians who did assist the English."

Canonchet lost one hundred and forty, but it was a great victory, well planned and well executed. Captain Peirse had been a leader in the storming of the Narragansett fort at Sunke-Squaw, the last winter; that is one reason why the Canonchet warriors fought so ravenously, to take revenge.

On the day after the dreadful battle, from Connecticut, southwest, there marched a larger force of English and friendly Indians, to close the red trail of the Sachem Canonchet. He was feared as much as King Philip was feared.

Canonchet did not proceed against Plymouth. With thirty volunteers he had set out south for the Mount Hope region itself, in order to gather seed corn. The abandoned fields of the English along the Connecticut River waited. They ought to be planted to Indian corn.

On his way back to the Connecticut River with his seed corn, near the close of the first week in April he made camp almost upon the very battle ground above Providence, where yet the soil was stained by the blood of March 26.

He did not know that now the enemy were upon his trail indeed; but at the moment a company of fifty English under Captain George Denison of Southerton, Connecticut, and eighty Indians—the Mohegans led by Chief Oneka, son of Uncas, the Pequots by Cas-sa-sin-na-mon, the Niantics (formerly allies of the Narragansetts) by Cat-a-pa-zet—were drawing near.

Three other companies were in the neighborhood.

This day Canonchet was lying in his blanket, telling to a party of seven warriors the story of the battleground. The other warriors were scattered through the forest. Two sentries had been placed upon a hill.

Not far away the Captain Denison party already had killed one warrior, and had seized two old squaws. The squaws confessed that Nanuntenoo was yonder, the Indian scouts picked up the fresh trail, the Denison men hastened at best speed.

In the midst of his story, Canonchet saw his two sentinels dash headlong past the wigwam, "as if they wanted for time to tell what they had seen." At once he sent a third man, to report upon what was the matter. This third man likewise suddenly made off at full pace, without a word. Then two more he sent; of these, one, returning breathless, paused long enough to say that "all the English army was upon him!"

"Whereupon, having no time to consult, and but little time to attempt an escape, and no means to defend himself, he began to fly with all speed. Running with great swiftness around the hill, to get out of sight upon the opposite side, he was distinguished by his wary pursuers," and they were hot after him.

In fact, running hard around the hill, Canonchet well-nigh ran into the Niantics of Chief Catapazet, who were coming down right over the hill. He swerved, at the view-halloo, and lengthened his stride. Some of the English had joined the chase. Canonchet tore like a deer for the river.

They had not recognized him, for he was wearing his blanket. But so hotly they pressed him, that he needs must cast aside his blanket. This revealed to them his fine lace-embroidered coat, which had been given to him as a bribe, at Boston last October. Now they knew that he was a chief, and a personage, and they yelled louder, and ran faster.

Presently Canonchet stripped off his lacy coat, and dropped it. And soon loosening his belt of wampum, he dropped that also. By this chief's belt they knew that he was the great Canonchet, and faster still they ran.

However, he was out-footing all except one Indian. That Indian was a Pequot named Monopoide—the best runner of all, and better than Canonchet himself.

With only a single pursuer to be feared, Canonchet turned sharply and leaped into the river, to cross by a strange trail. As he splashed through, wading and plunging, seeing escape close before him if he could gain the opposite bank, he stumbled upon a stone. Falling forward he not only lost valuable time but soused his gun.

"At that accident," he afterward said, "my heart and bowels turned within me so that I became like a rotten stick, void of strength."

Before he might stand straight and fix his useless gun, with a whoop of triumph the lucky Pequot, Monopoide, was upon him; grabbed him by his shoulder within thirty rods of the shore.

The Pequot was not a large man, nor a strong warrior. Canonchet was both, and might yet have fought loose, to liberty. But he had made up his mind to quit. He offered no trouble; the guns of the pursuing party were covering him again, and he obeyed the orders.

He did not break his silence until young Robert Staunton, first of the English to reach him, asked him questions. This was contrary to Indian usage. Canonchet looked upon him disdainfully.

"You much child. No understand matters of war. Let your brother or chief come; him I will answer."

Robert's brother, John Staunton, was captain of one of the Connecticut companies that had been sent out to find the Narragansetts; but Canonchet was now turned over to Captain Denison.

He was offered his life if he would help the English. This brought from him a glare of rebuke.

He was offered his life if he would send orders to his people to make peace.

"Say no more about that," he replied. "I will not talk of peace. I do not care to talk at all. I was born a sachem. If sachems come to speak with me, I will answer; but none present being such, I am obliged, in honor to myself, to hold my tongue."

"If you do not accept the terms offered to you, you will be put to death."

"Killing me will not end the war. There are two thousand men who will revenge me."

"You richly deserve death. You can expect no mercy. You have said that you would burn the English in their houses. You have boasted that you would not deliver up a single Wampanoag, nor the paring of a Wampanoag's nail."

"I desire to hear no more about it," replied Canonchet. "Others were as eager in the war as myself, and many will be found of the same mind. Have not the English burned my people in their houses? Did you ever deliver up to the Narragansetts any of the Narragansetts' enemies? Why then should I deliver up to them the Wampanoags? I would rather die than remain prisoner. You have one of equal rank here with myself. He is Oneka, son of Uncas. His father killed my father. Let Oneka kill me. He is a sachem."

"You must die."

"I like it well. I shall die before my heart is soft, or I have said anything of which Canonchet shall be ashamed."

Even his enemies admired him. The English compared him to some old Roman.

He was not killed here. Forty-three of his people, men and women, had been taken by the troops and scouts; a number of these were given over to death by the scout Indians. But Canonchet was borne in triumph to Stonington, Connecticut.

In order to reward the friendly Indians, the Pequots were permitted to shoot him, the Mohegans to behead and to quarter him, the Niantics to burn him. As a return favor, the Indians presented the head of Canonchet, or Nanuntenoo, to the English council at Hartford, Connecticut.

In the above fashion perished, without a plea, "in the prime of his manhood," Canonchet of the Big Heart, last Grand Sachem of the Narragansetts. Presently only the name of his nation remained.

CHAPTER VI

THE BLOODY BELT OF PONTIAC (1760-1763)

WHEN IT PASSED AMONG THE RED NATIONS

SOON after the Mohawks broke the peace with the French and Algonkins in Canada, and in 1647 killed Piskaret the champion, they and the others of the Five Nations drove the Hurons and Algonkins into flight.

The Hurons, styled in English Wyandots, fled clear into Michigan and spread down into northern Ohio.

Of the Algonkins there were three nations who clung together as the Council of the Three Fires. These were the Ottawas, the Ojibwas and the Potawatomis.

The Ottawas were known as the "Trade People" and the "Raised Hairs." They had claimed the River Ottawa, in which was the Allumette Island upon which Piskaret and the Adirondacks had lived.

The Ojibways were known as the "Puckered Moccasin People," from the words meaning "to roast till puckered up." Their tanned moccasins had a heavy puckered seam. The name Ojibwa, rapidly pronounced, became in English "Chippeway." As Chippeways and Chippewas have they remained.

The Potawatomis, whose name is spelled also Pottawattamis, were known as the "Nation of Fire." They had lived the farthest westward of all, until the Sioux met them and forced them back.

The Ottawas were recorded by the early French as rude and barbarous. The Chippewas, or Ojibwas, were recorded as skillful hunters and brave warriors. The Potawatomis were recorded as the most friendly and kind-hearted among the northern Indians.

Of these people many still exist, in Canada and the United States.

When England, aided by her American colonies, began to oppose France in the New World in 1755, the Three Fires helped the French. They were then holding part of present Wisconsin and all of Michigan.

Now in the fall of 1760 France had lost Canada. She was about to surrender to England all her forts and trading posts of the Upper Mississippi basin, from the Great Lakes to the Ohio River.

In November Major Robert Rogers, a noted American Ranger, of New Hampshire birth, with two hundred hardy American woodsmen in twelve whaleboats, and with a herd of fat cattle following the shores, was on his way from Montreal, by water, to carry the English tongue and the British flag to the French posts of the Great Lakes.

He had passed several posts, and was swinging around for Detroit, when a storm of sleet and rain kept him in camp amidst the thick timber where today stands the city of Cleveland, Ohio.

Here he was met by a party of Indians from the west, bearing a message.

"You must go no farther," they said. "Pontiac is

PONTIAC, THE RED NAPOLEON

From a painting

coming. He is the king and lord of this country you are in. Wait till he can see you with his own eyes."

That same day in the afternoon Chief Pontiac himself appeared. Major Rogers saw a dark, medium tall but very powerful Indian, aged near fifty years, wearing not only richly embroidered clothes but also "an air of majesty and princely grandeur."

Pontiac spoke like a great chief and ruler.

"I have come to find out what you are doing in this place, and how you dare to pass through my country without my permission."

Major Rogers replied smoothly.

"I have no design against you or your people. I am here by orders from your new English fathers, to remove the French from your country, so that we may trade in peace together."

And he gave the chief a pledge of wampum. Pontiac returned another belt.

"I shall stand in the path you are walking, till morning," was all that he would say; and closed the matter for the night.

During the storm of the next few days he smoked the pipe of peace with the major, and promised safe passage for him, to Detroit.

Thus Major Rogers was the first of the English Americans to be face to face with one of the master minds of the Indian Americans.

This Pontiac was head chief not alone of the Ottawas, but of the Chippewas and Potawatomis. Rumor has declared that he was born a dark Catawba of that fierce fighting nation in South Carolina, who frequently journeyed north to fall upon the northern tribes. But his father probably was an Ottawa, his mother an Ojibwa.

By reason of his strong mind, and his generalship in peace and in war, he was accepted as a leader throughout all the Great Lakes country. The name and fame of Pontiac had extended far into the south and into the east. It is said that he commanded the whole Indian force at the bloody Braddock's Field south of Pittsburg, when on July 9, 1755, the British regulars of General Sir William Braddock, aided by the colonial militia of Major George Washington, were crushed and scattered by the French and Indians.

Before that he had saved the French garrison of Detroit from an attack by hostile Foxes.

Having talked with Major Rogers, Pontiac sent runners to notify the villages that the English had his permission to march through the country. He himself went on with the party. He astonished the major by his shrewd questions—as to how the English waged war, how their clothing was made, how they got iron from the ground, for their weapons.

He even stated that he was willing to form an alliance with the king of England and to call him uncle; but that he must be allowed to reign as he pleased in his own country, or "he would shut up the way and keep the English out."

Puzzled and stung by the news that their fathers, the French, had been beaten in war, a great number of Ottawas, Potawatomis, Chippewas, Sacs and Wyandots gathered at old Detroit, to witness the surrender.

They could not understand why the French should march out and lay down their arms to such a small company of English. Evidently these English were gifted with powers that made their enemies weak.

For a brief space all went well, while the Indians of Pontiac's country watched, to see what kind of men these English should prove to be.

But the name of the English already was bad. These Northern tribes well knew what had occurred in Virginia and in New England. The Powatans, the Pokanokets, the Narragansetts and other peoples had been wiped out, their lands seized. The English were bent upon being masters, not allies.

There was found to be a great difference in the methods of the French, and these English.

The French treated chiefs as equals, and tribes as brothers and children; lived in their lodges, ate of their food, created good feeling by distributing presents, interfered little with ancient customs, traded fairly, and forebade whiskey.

The English despised the Indians, lived apart, demanded rather than asked, were stingy in trading, and cheated by means of liquor.

"When the Indians visited the forts, instead of being treated with attention and politeness, they were received gruffly, subjected to indignities, and not infrequently helped out of the fort with the butt of a sentry's musket or a vigorous kick from an officer."

Pontiac and his people soon saw this. The French-Canadian traders still at large took pains to whisper, in cunning fashion, that the great French king was old and had been asleep while the English were arming; but that now he had awakened, and his young men were coming to rescue his red children. A fleet of great canoes was on its way up the St. Lawrence River, to capture the Lakes, and the French and the Indians would again live together!

The Three Fires and their allies the Sacs and the Wyandots longed for the pleasant company of their French brothers. In his village on the Canada border just across the river from Detroit, Pontiac watched these "Red Coats" for two years and found, as he thought, nothing good in them or their cheating traders and he resolved to be rid of them all.

With the eye of a chief and a warrior he had noted, also, that they were a foolish people. As if despising the power of the Indian, they garrisoned their posts with only small forces, although many of these posts were lonely spots, far separated by leagues of water and forest from any outside aid. Messages from one to another could be easily stopped.

The French were being allowed to remain and to move about freely. The peace treaty between the French and the English had not yet been signed. No doubt the French would join the Indians in driving the invaders from this country so rich in corn and fish and game.

Out of his brooding and his hate, Pontiac formed his plan. It was a plan like the plan of Opechancanough and King Philip, but on a larger scale. He worked at it alone, until he was prepared to set it in motion.

Then, late in the year 1762, he sent to the eastward

his runners bearing to the Senecas a red-stained tomahawk and a Bloody Belt.

They carried the message:

"The English mean to make slaves of us, by occupying so many posts in our country. Let us try now, to recover our liberty, rather than wait until they are stronger."

From the Senecas the Bloody Belt was passed to the Delawares of western New York and eastern Pennsylvania; from the Delawares to the Shawnees of western Pennsylvania and eastern Ohio; from the Shawnees it was passed westward to the Miamis, and the Wyandots of Indiana.

Several thousands of miles had the Bloody Belt traveled, when in March, of 1763, it was caught and stopped by Ensign Holmes, the young commander at old Fort Miami near the present city of Fort Wayne, Indiana.

He sent it back to Detroit, far northward, with a note of warning for Major Gladwyn the commander. He believed that with the stoppage of the belt he had checked the plan. Major Gladwyn, in turn, reported to his superiors that this "was a trifling matter which would blow over."

The belt may have been stopped, but not the word of Pontiac. It traveled on, until from Lake Superior of the Canada border down to Kentucky all the tribes between the Alleghanies and the Mississippi River were only waiting for the Day.

Vague rumors brought in by traders and friendly scouts floated hither-thither—rumors of mysterious remarks, of secret councils, of a collecting of arms and powder, and a sharpening of knives and hatchets, even among tribes remote from the posts.

But the garrisons were not reinforced. The soldiers idled and joked, the Indians came and went as usual, gates were not closed except at night.

A Delaware prophet was reported to be preaching death to the Red Coats. Unrest seethed, and yet could not be traced to any source. On April 27, unknown to a single one of the English at the Great Lakes, a hundred strange chiefs gathered within a few miles of Detroit itself, to confer with Pontiac.

In the midst of the forest he addressed them. Here, seated in a large circle, were Ottawas, Ojibwas, Sacs, Potawatomis, Wyandots, Senecas, Miamis, Shawnees, Foxes, Delawares, Menominis—all intent for the words of Pontiac.

His speech was full of fire and eloquence. He was an orator. He reminded his brothers of their treatment by the English, and of their better treatment by the French—their friends who had been ousted. He told them that now was the time to rise, when the war canoes of their French father were on the way to re-people the land with happiness.

A prophet had been born among the Delawares, said Pontiac. The Great Spirit had appeared to this prophet in a dream, and had demanded why the Indians suffered the white strangers to live in this land that he had provided with everything for the Indian's use.

Let the Indians return to the customs of their ancestors—fling away the blankets, the coats, the guns, the fire-water, and use again the skins, the bows, and the native foods, and be independent. "As for these English, these dogs dressed in red, drive them from your hunting grounds; drive them! And then when you are in distress, I will help you."

The day was named by Pontiac. It should date from the change of the moon, in the next month (or about May 7). At that time should begin the work, by all the tribes, of seizing every English fort and trading post in the Great Lakes country and west of the Alleghany Mountains. The tribes nearest to each should attend to the matter—strike when they heard that he had struck Detroit.

The date and the plan were approved. The council broke up. As silently as they had come, the chiefs went home; some by water, some afoot, and no white man knew of the meeting!

Detroit was the largest and most important of the English posts. Pontiac himself would seize this by aid of his Ottawas, some Potawatomis and Wyandots. To the Chippewas and the Sacs was given over the next important fur-trade station, that of Mich-il-i-mac-ki-nac, north.

CHAPTER VII

THE BLOODY BELT OF PONTIAC (1763–1769)

HOW AN INDIAN GIRL SAVED FORT DETROIT

OLD Fort Detroit was a stockade twenty feet high, in the form of a square about two-thirds of a mile around. It enclosed a church and eighty or one hundred houses, mainly of French settlers with a sprinkling of English traders.

In the block-houses at the corners and protecting the gates, light cannon were mounted. The garrison consisted of only one hundred and twenty men of the Eightieth Foot. In the village there were perhaps forty other men.

On both sides of the river lay the fertile farms of the French settlers. Back of the farms on the east or Canadian side, and about five miles from Detroit, was the teeming village of Pontiac's Ottawas. Potawatomis and Wyandots also lived near. At Pontiac's call there waited more than a thousand warriors.

The set time approached. On May 1 Pontiac and forty chiefs and warriors entered the fort, and danced the calumet, a peace dance, for the pleasure of the officers. Pontiac said to Major Gladwyn that he would return, at the change of the moon, May 7, or in one week, to hold a council with him, and "brighten the chain of peace with the English."

The major agreed. He was a very foolish man, for a chief. Having returned to his village, Pontiac called a different kind of a council, there—a war council of one hundred chiefs. They were to have their people cut off the ends of muskets that should be carried concealed under the blankets. Sixty chiefs and warriors should go with him into the council chamber at the fort; the others should linger in the streets of the town and at the fort gates.

He would speak to the major with a belt, white on the one side, green on the other. When he turned the belt and presented it wrong end first, let every warrior kill an English soldier, beginning with the officers. At the sound let every warrior outside the council use gun and hatchet.

On May 5 a French settler's wife crossed the river to buy maple-sugar and deer-meat at the Ottawa village. She saw the warriors busy filing at their gun-barrels—shortening the guns to scarce a yard of length. This was a curious thing to do. When she went back to the post she spoke about it.

"That," said the blacksmith, "explains why those fellows have been borrowing all my files and hack-saws. They wouldn't tell me what for. Something's brewing."

When Major Gladwyn was informed, still he would not believe. But the fur-traders at the post insisted that when an Indian shortened his gun, he meant mischief. The opinion of fur-traders carried no weight with Major Gladwyn, the British officer.

The next evening Catharine, a pretty Ojibwa girl

who lived with the Potawatomis, came to see him in his quarters. She was his favorite. She had agreed to make him a pair of handsome moccasins, from an elk hide. Now she brought the moccasins, and the rest of the hide.

Usually she had been much pleased to look upon and talk with the handsome young major in the red clothes. This time her face was clouded, she hung her head, and spoke hardly at all. Her eager girlishness had vanished. The major's delight with the moccasins failed to cheer her up.

Trying to win her smiles, he told her the moccasins were so beautiful that he wished to give them to a friend. Would she take the elk-hide away with her, and make another pair of moccasins for himself?

She finally left, with strangely slow step, and backward glances. At sunset, when the gates of the fort were to be closed, the guard found her still inside. As she would not go, the sergeant took word to the major.

"She won't talk with me, sir," he reported.

"Send her in and I will talk with her," ordered the major.

Catharine came, downcast, silent, and timid.

"Why have you not gone before the gates are shut, Catharine?"

She hesitated.

"I did not wish to take away the skin that is yours."

"But you did take it away, as far as the gate."

She hesitated more.

"Yes, that is so. But if I take it outside I can never return it."

"Why not?"

"I cannot tell. I am afraid."

"You can talk freely. Nothing that you say shall go to other ears. If you bring me news of value you will be well rewarded, and no one shall know."

Catharine loved the major. Presently she told him of the mind of Pontiac, and the deed planned for to-morrow morning.

A cold fear clutched the heart of Major Gladwyn. He recalled the shortened guns, he recalled the Bloody Belt, he recalled the date made with him for a big council on the morrow. At last he rather believed.

So he sent away the trembling Catharine, that she might go to her village. He held a council with his officers.

Here they were, with only one hundred and twenty soldiers, and less than three weeks' provisions, cut off by one thousand, two thousand, three thousand merciless Indian warriors, and by the French settlers and traders who probably would be glad to have the English killed.

"The English are to be struck down, but no Frenchman is to be harmed," had said Catharine.

That looked bad indeed.

This night guards were doubled along the parapets, and in the block-houses. The major himself walked guard most of the night. From the distant villages of the Ottawas, the Wyandots, and the Potawatomis drifted the clamor of dances—an ugly sound, full of meaning, now.

Precisely at ten o'clock in the morning a host of

bark canoes from the Ottawa side of the Detroit River slanted across the current, and made landing. Pontiac approached at the head of a long file of thirty chiefs and as many warriors. They walked with measured, stately tread. Every man was closely wrapped in a gay blanket.

They were admitted through the gate of the fort, but it was closed against the mass of warriors, women and children who pressed after.

As Pontiac, with his escort, stalked for the council room, his quick glances saw that the soldiers were formed, under arms, and moving from spot to spot, and that a double rank had been stationed around the headquarters.

In the council chamber he noted, too, that each officer wore his sword, and two pistols!

"Why," asked Pontiac, of Major Gladwyn, "do I see so many of my father's young men standing in the street with their guns?"

"It is best that my young men be exercised as soldiers, or they will grow lazy and forget," answered the major.

Ha! Pontiac *knew.* Somehow his plans had been betrayed; his game was up, unless he chose an open fight.

His chiefs and warriors sat uneasily. They all feared death. By Indian law they ought to be killed for having intended to shed blood in a calumet council.

Pontiac started his talk. He acted confused, as though he was not certain what course to pursue.

Once he did seem about to offer the belt wrong end first, as the signal—and Major Gladwyn, still sitting, slightly raised his hand. Instantly from outside the door sounded the clash of arms and the quick roll of a drum, to show that the garrison was on the alert. The officers half drew their swords.

Pontiac flushed yet darker. He stammered, and offering the belt right end first, closed his talk, and sat down again.

Major Gladwyn made a short reply. He said that the English were glad to be friends, as long as their red brothers deserved it; but any act of war would be severely punished.

That was all. The major let the Indians file out again. Pontiac *knew*.

He was too great a leader, in the Indian way, to be balked by one defeat. He actually proposed another council; he actually persuaded the foolish major to send out to him two officers, for a peace talk. One of the officers barely escaped from captivity, the other never came back.

Then Pontiac boldly besieged Detroit, in white race fashion—the closest, longest siege ever laid by Indians against any fort on American soil.

His two thousand Indians swarmed in the forest, held the fences and walls and buildings of the fields, peppered the palisade with bullets and arrows, shot fire into the town; captured a supply fleet in the river, ambushed sallying parties, cut to pieces a column of reinforcements.

The siege lasted six months. The orders to attack

went out. On May 16 Fort Sandusky, at Lake Erie in northern Ohio, was seized by the Wyandots and Ottawas, during a council.

On May 25, Fort St. Joseph of St. Joseph, Michigan, on Lake Michigan across the state from Detroit, was seized in like manner by the Potawatomis. On May 27, Fort Miami, near present Fort Wayne of Indiana, commanded by Ensign Holmes who had discovered the Bloody Belt, was forced to surrender to the Wyandots. Ensign Holmes himself was decoyed into the open, and killed.

On June 4, populous Michilimackinac of northern Michigan was pillaged. The Chippewas and Sacs celebrated the King's Birthday, in honor of the English, with a great game of lacrosse in front of the post. Michilimackinac *did not know that Detroit was being besieged!* The gates were left open, the officers gathered to witness the game. The ball was knocked inside the palisades, the players rushed after—and that was the end of Michilimackinac.

On June 15 the little fort of Presq' Isle, near the modern city of Erie on the Lake Erie shore of northern Pennsylvania, was attacked. It was captured in two days, by the Ottawas and Potawatomis from Detroit.

On June 18, Fort Le Bœuf, twelve miles south of it, was burned. Just when Fort Venango, farther south, fell to the Senecas, no word says, for not a man of it remained alive. June 1, Fort Ouatanon, below Lafayette on the Wabash River in west central Indiana, had surrendered.

Niagara in the east was threatened; Fort Legonier, forty miles southeast of Pittsburg in Pennsylvania, was attacked by the Delawares and Shawnees, but held out; the strong Fort Pitt (now Pittsburg), with garrison of over three hundred soldiers and woodsmen, was besieged by the united Delawares, Shawnees, Wyandots and Mingo Iroquois.

A second Bloody Belt had been dispatched by Pontiac from Detroit; as fast as it arrived, the allies struck hard. Of twelve fortified English posts, eight fell. Not only that, but the fiery spirit of Pontiac had aroused twenty-two tribes extending from Canada to Virginia, and from New York to the Illinois. A hundred English traders were murdered in camp, and on the trail. A thousand English are supposed to have been killed. Five hundred families of northern Virginia and of western Maryland fled for their lives.

While this work was going on, and the frontier settlements shuddered, and feared the morrow, Pontiac was sternly sticking to his siege of Fort Detroit.

The French around there complained to him that his men were robbing them of provisions, and injuring the corn-fields.

"You must stand that," rebuked Pontiac. "I am fighting your battles against the English."

He gave out receipts, for the supplies as taken. These receipts were pieces of bark, pictured with the kind of supplies taken, and signed with the figure of an otter—the totem of the Ottawas. After the war every receipt was honored, by payment.

Only his Ottawas were still fighting Detroit, when

on October 30, this 1763, there arrived, from the French commander on the lower Mississippi, a peace belt and a messenger for Pontiac.

He had been told that peace had been declared between the French and the English, but he had not believed. Now he was told again, by word direct, that the king of France and the king of England had signed peace papers; the country was English, his father the king of France could not help him. He must stop his war, and "take the English by the hand."

Weeks before this, the Indians to the south had withdrawn; his other allies were fading into the forest. So, sullen and disappointed, he, too, withdrew. His sun had set, but he tried to follow it southwestward.

Before he gave his hand to the English he did attempt another war. The tribes of the Illinois hesitated, in council.

"If you do not join my people," thundered Pontiac, "I will consume you as the fire eats the dry grass of the prairies!"

The plot failed, but the Illinois did not forget his insulting words. In April, 1769, while leaving a council with the Illinois beside the Mississippi River, and wearing a blue-and-silver uniform coat given to him years before by the brave General Montcalm of the French, he was murdered by a Kaskaskia of the Illinois nation, in the forest which became East St. Louis.

The Kaskaskia had been bribed by an English trader, with a barrel of whiskey, to do the deed. There died Pontiac. He was buried, it is said, on the site of the present Southern Hotel in St. Louis City.

The Illinois suffered from this foul crime. All of Pontiac's loyal people—the Ottawas, the Potawatomis, the Sacs, the Foxes, the Chippewas—rose against them and swept them from the face of the earth.

Now what of Catharine, who saved Detroit from Pontiac? She saved Detroit, but Fort Detroit did not save *her*. Pontiac was no fool; he very quickly had suspected her. He well knew that Major Gladwyn was her friend, and that she had taken the moccasins in to him.

She was seized by the chief, beaten almost lifeless with a lacrosse racquet, and condemned to the meanest of labor. After the siege, Major Gladwyn made no effort to rescue her or reward her. At last, when an old and miserable woman, she fell into a kettle of boiling maple sap, and died.

CHAPTER VIII

LOGAN THE GREAT MINGO (1725–1774)

AND THE EVIL DAYS THAT CAME UPON HIM

DURING the French-and-Indian war with England, and during the war waged by Pontiac, there was one prominent chief who did not take up the hatchet. His name was the English one of John Logan. He was a Mingo, or Iroquois, of a Cayuga band that had drifted south into east central Pennsylvania.

There Chief Shikellemus, his father, had settled and had proved himself a firm friend of the whites. Old Shikellemus invited the Moravian missionaries to take refuge on his lands. He spoke good English. He acted as agent between his people and the Province of Pennsylvania. He was hospitable and shrewd, and ever refused to touch liquor because, as he said, he "did not wish to become a fool."

His house was elevated on stilts, as protection against the "big drunks."

About 1725, a second son was born to him and his wife, and named Tah-gah-jute, meaning "His-eye-lashes-stick-out," or, "Open-eyes." In admiration of his good friend James Logan, of Philadelphia, secretary of Pennsylvania, and sometimes acting governor,

Chief Shikellemus gave little Tah-gah-jute the English name of Logan.

As "John Logan" he was known to the settlers.

The wise and upright Shikellemus died—"in the fear of the Lord." His people scattered wider. Logan his son moved westward, to the Shawnee and Delaware country of Pennsylvania.

Here he married a Shawnee girl. He set up housekeeping and traded venison and skins with the white settlers, for powder, ball, and sugar and flour.

The tide of white blood was surging ever farther into the west, and the Indians' hunting grounds. Many of the Indians grew uneasy. Pontiac's Bloody Belt passed from village to village, but the weary and nervous traveler was always welcome at the cabin of Logan, "friend of the white man."

A white hunter, Brown, trailing bear in the Pennsylvania timber, laid aside his rifle and stooped to drink at a spring. Suddenly he saw mirrored in the clear water the tall figure of an armed Indian, watching him. Up he sprang, leaped for his gun, leveled it —but the Indian smiled, knocked the priming from his own gun, and extended his hand.

This was Logan—"the best specimen of humanity I ever met with, red or white," wrote Brown. "He could speak a little English, and told me there was another white hunter a little way down the stream, and guided me to his camp."

Other stories of Logan's kindnesses to the whites in his country are told. In the latter part of 1763, a party of white settlers had broken in upon the refuge of twenty Conestoga Iroquois, in southern Pennsylvania, and killed every one. The Conestogas were kin to the other Mingos; but Logan made no war talk about it.

Simon Kenton, one of the most famous scouts of Daniel Boone's time in Kentucky and Ohio, says that his form was "striking and manly," his countenance "calm and noble."

Although Logan started out to walk the straight path of peace, sore days were ahead of him. He moved westward again in 1770, erected a cabin at the mouth of Beaver Creek, on the Ohio side of the Ohio River about half way between Pittsburg of Pennsylvania and Wheeling of West Virginia.

His cabin was kept wide open. Everybody spoke well of Logan. He removed once more. The new cabin, "home of the white man," was built on the Sciota River of central Ohio, among the Shawnees of Chief Cornstalk's tribe. He and Chief Cornstalk were close friends. They both stood out for peace. But Cornstalk had been a war chief also, during the Pontiac up-rising. He and his warriors had obeyed the Bloody Belt. His name, Cornstalk, meant that he was the support of the Shawnee nation.

Now the evil days of Logan were close at hand.

Since the treaty signed with the twenty-two tribes of Pontiac, in 1765, there had been general peace between the red men and the white men in America. This peace was not to continue.

For instance, Bald Eagle, a friendly old Delaware chief, who frequently came in, by canoe, to trade for tobacco and sugar, was killed, without cause, by three white men, in southern Pennsylvania. They propped him, sitting, in the stern of his canoe, thrust a piece of journey-cake, or corn-bread, into his mouth, and set him afloat down the stream. Many settlers who knew him well saw him pass and wondered why he did not stop for a visit. Finally he was found to be dead, and was brought ashore for burial.

There were bad Indians, too, who murdered and stole. For this, the good Indians suffered. Western Pennsylvania and eastern Ohio were a wild and lawless country.

Up to 1774 these tit-for-tats had not brought on war. But the French of Canada and the Great Lakes country still secretly urged the Indians to drive out the settlers. The Americans were becoming annoyed by the harsh laws of the English king. There were English officials who desired an Indian war. That would give the Colonists something else to think about.

Lord Dunmore, royal governor of Virginia, was one of these officials. He had claim to land extending into Pennsylvania; Fort Pitt, at present Pittsburg, was garrisoned by Virginia troops, and he wanted to keep them there, to help his land schemes.

April 25, 1774, he issued a proclamation calling upon the commander at Fort Pitt to be ready to repel the Indians. The commander called on the border settlers.

There was great excitement. Almost at once the peace chain that Logan had received from his father Shikellemus was broken. He and his wife and relatives, and a number of Shawnees and Delawares, were encamped along Yellow Creek. This emptied into the

Ohio River a few miles below Beaver Creek, his former home.

On the very day after the commander at Fort Pitt had issued his notice to the border people to arm, from Wheeling, on the Ohio in West Virginia, Captain Michael Cresap led a party of militia and frontiersmen to hunt Indians.

They promptly killed two friendly Shawnees at Pipe Creek, fourteen miles below Wheeling. The Shawnees had no time in which to make resistance. The next Indians who were attacked, fired back; one white man was wounded. Among the Indians killed in these two meetings was a relative of Logan.

Captain Cresap started north to wipe out Chief Logan's camp. He well knew that as soon as the word of the killings reached the camp, trouble might break. On the way his heart failed him. He was a hot-headed man, he hated Indians—but he balked at shooting women and children. So he turned aside, with his party.

There were white men not so particular as he. On Baker's Bottom, opposite the mouth of Yellow Creek, lived Joshua Baker, whose principal business was that of selling rum to the Indians. In the same settlement lived Daniel Greathouse—"a ruffian in human shape," and an enemy to all Indians.

Greathouse, too, was inspired to "strike the post," in the worst Indian fashion. He gathered thirty-two whites, and hid them in Baker's house. He feared that the Logan camp had heard of the Cresap killings, so he crossed over the river, to investigate.

A friendly squaw warned him to go back, or he might be harmed, for the camp was very angry. Back he went. Because he was afraid to attack the camp with his thirty-two men, he invited the Indians over, to drink "peace" with him. He was a rum seller, himself.

On April 30, they came. First a canoe containing six warriors, Logan's sister, another woman, and a little girl. The warriors were made drunk, and all but the little girl were butchered.

Across the river Logan heard the shooting. He sent two men in a canoe to find out what was the matter. They were killed. A larger canoe was sent. It was ambushed and the survivors fled back to the camp.

Now Logan learned that his sister and brother had been murdered. They were the last of his blood relatives. That was his reward for having remained the friend of the white man. That was his reward for having opened his cabin to the white wayfarer. He went bad, himself. He saw only red, and he vowed vengeance. A bitter wrath turned his heart sour. He felt that he must grasp the hatchet, buried so long ago by his father Shikellemus.

The war spirit blazed high among whites and reds on the frontier. The whites accused the Indians of many thoughts and deeds—some false, some true. The Indians accused the whites of many deeds—mainly true. Block-houses were hastily erected, for the protection of settlers. Governor Dunmore of Virginia called out troops in earnest. "Dunmore's War" as well as "Cresap's War" was this named.

The Shawnees, the Delawares, the Mingo Cayugas,

the Wyandot Hurons, held councils in their Scioto River country of central Ohio. Belts were sent to the Miamis on the west and the Senecas on the east. There were debates upon striking the Long Knives, as the Virginians were called.

These Long Knife Americans had crossed the rivers and the mountains, were possessing themselves of Ohio, and even of Kentucky; much blood had been shed, and the wiser heads among the tribes did not know exactly what to do about it.

The great Cornstalk, loved chief of the Shawnees, and now fifty years in age, lifted his voice for peace. He could see no good in a war against the Americans. Logan, gnawed by his own wrongs, remained apart and said little. But the Americans struck first.

Hoping to keep the Indians at home, in June four hundred border men were ordered by Governor Dunmore of Virginia to attack the villages in Ohio. They marched west across country until in southern Ohio they destroyed two Shawnee towns.

The light-skinned Shawnees were known as the fiercest, most stubborn fighters among all the Algonquins between the Alleghanies and the Mississippi River. Now their hot natures burst. Chief Cornstalk yielded.

"It is well," he said. "If you go to war, then I will lead you. If we fight at all, we must fight together."

But of the Indians it was Logan who first struck the Long Knives. With only seven warriors he suddenly appeared in Virginia itself. This was Long Knife country. Here, July 12, he fell upon William Robinson, Thomas Hellen and Coleman Brown, three settlers who were gathering flax in their field.

Brown died under the first volley; Hellen and Robinson ran hard. Hellen was an old man, and easily caught, but William Robinson was young and strong. Dodging and legging, he had almost reached the timber. Hearing loud shouting, with English words, behind him, and fearing a rifle bullet, he turned his head and lunged full tilt into a tree. Down he dropped, stunned.

After a bit he came to. He was lying, securely tied, hands and feet. Logan was sitting quietly beside him, waiting for him to waken. The old man Hellen had not been harmed, either. Logan's party took their two captives to Logan's town in Ohio—treated them kindly on the way.

"What will be done to us at your town?" asked Robinson.

"You will be made to run the gauntlet," answered Logan. "But if you listen to my words, you will not be hurt. You must break through the lines and run to the council house. When you are in the council house, you will be safe. That will end the gauntlet."

Approaching the Mingo and Shawnee towns, Logan uttered a terrific scalp-halloo, as signal of success. Warriors hastened out. The gauntlet was formed. This was two lines of warriors, squaws and children, armed with sticks, clubs and switches. Through the long, narrow, living aisle the two prisoners had to make their way.

Remembering Logan's advice, Robinson charged aside, broke through, and raced for the council house. All out of breath, he reached it ahead of his howling pursuers. No Indian dared to attack him there. It was sanctuary.

Poor old Mr. Hellen failed. The lines were stout, the clubs and switches blinded him; before he had reached the council house a war-club struck him helpless. He might have been beaten to death had not Robinson bravely grabbed him and dragged him in.

He had won his life, and was adopted into an Indian family. Now the Indians were angry with Robinson. They decided to burn him at the stake.

"Have no fear. You shall not die," asserted Logan.

But matters looked bad. He was tied to the stake. While he stood there, with the squaws howling around him, he heard Logan speak, appealing for his life.

"The most powerful orator I've ever listened to," afterward said Robinson. "His gestures and face were wonderful!"

The warriors still called for fire. The torch was ready, when Logan sprang angrily forward. With his own hatchet he cut the ropes, and marching the white captive through the mob landed him in the lodge of an old squaw. Few chiefs would have dared an act like this, to save merely a white man, and an enemy.

However, Logan was not yet done. Thirteen of his people, he claimed, had been killed by the whites; and thirteen white scalps should pay. Just before he set out on the war-path again, he brought to William Robinson a goose-quill and some gun-powder.

He bade Robinson sharpen the quill, and with gun-powder-and-water for ink write a letter.

Captain Cresap:
What did you kill my people on Yellow Creek for? The white people killed my kin at Conestoga, a great while ago, and I thought nothing of that. But you killed my kin again on Yellow Creek, and took my cousin prisoner. Then I thought I must kill, too; and I have been three times to war since; but all the Indians are not angry, only myself.

July 21, 1774. CAPTAIN JOHN LOGAN.

This note was carried clear down into western Virginia, as if to show how far Logan could reach. It was found tied to a war-club and left at a plundered settler's cabin.

Logan never would believe but that Michael Cresap had killed the warriors and women at Yellow Creek. When Captain Cresap heard of this note, and that he was blamed, he said that he would like to sink his tomahawk in Daniel Greathouse's head!

Chief Logan was not long in getting his thirteen scalps.

"Now," he announced, "I am satisfied. My relations have been paid for. I will sit still."

He was not to sit still yet. The hands of the Shawnees grasped the hatchet very firmly. Forty scalps at a time had been hung in the Shawnee lodges, but the spirits of their fathers and the ashes of their towns called for more. The Delawares had not taken payment enough for the scalp of old Bald Eagle. The Senecas remembered that many years ago eight of their warriors were attacked by one hundred and fifty Long Knife soldiers. The Mingos had not forgotten the massacre of the Conestogas. The Wyandots were red, and hated the white face in the east.

These nations formed the league of the Northern Confederacy, to defend themselves. Cornstalk the Shawnee was chosen head chief.

CHAPTER IX

CORNSTALK LEADS THE WARRIORS (1774-1777)

HOW HE AND LOGAN STROVE AND DIED

AT the last of September a Shawnee scout ran breathless into the Chief Cornstalk town. He brought word that far across the Ohio River, in northwestern (now West) Virginia, he and his comrade had met a great column of Long Knives, advancing over the mountains, as if to invade the Indian country. His comrade had been killed. He himself had come back, with the word.

Taking eleven hundred warriors—the pick of the Shawnees, the fighting Delawares, the Wyandots, the Mingo Cayugas and the Mingo Senecas—Chief Cornstalk marched rapidly down to give battle.

There really were two American columns, on their way to destroy the Shawnee and Mingo towns in interior Ohio.

The Division of Northern and Western Virginia, twelve hundred men, had mustered at Fort Pitt (Pittsburg, Pennsylvania), in the territory disputed by Virginia and Pennsylvania. It was under command of Lord Dunmore himself, governor of Virginia for the king of England.

The Division of Southern and Eastern Virginia, fifteen hundred men, had mustered at Lewisburg, West

Virginia. It was under command of General Andrew Lewis, a valiant soldier.

The Lord Dunmore division was to march south, the General Lewis division was to march west; the two were to join forces at Point Pleasant, where on the border of West Virginia the Big Kanawha River empties into the noble Ohio.

Cornstalk moved fast. He had as aides Logan of the Cayugas, Chi-ya-wee of the Wyandots, Scop-pa-thus of the Senecas, young Red Hawk of the fighting Delawares, his own son El-li-nip-si-co—noted chiefs, all. Among the Shawnee sub-chiefs was Puck-ee-shin-wah, father of a boy named Tecumseh who grew to the greatness of Pontiac.

The General Lewis division had arrived first at the mouth of the Big Kanawha. On the evening of October 9, from the opposite side of the Ohio, Cornstalk's and Logan's men sighted them there, in camp.

Fresh news had come to Cornstalk. He had learned of the other division, under Lord Dunmore. He had learned that the column across from him was equal to his own force, and that another detachment of it was hurrying on its trail.

In a council of the chiefs and principal warriors he proposed that he go over, in person, and treat for peace. But all his men voted him down.

"Very well," he replied. "If you are resolved to fight, then fight you shall. We must not delay. It is likely that we shall have hard work tomorrow, but if any warrior attempts to run away, I will kill him with my own hand."

This night the warriors ferried the Ohio, above the camp, by means of seventy-eight rafts. They worked hard, and formed for battle at daybreak.

"We will make a line behind the Long Knives," ordered Cornstalk, "and drive them forward like bullocks into the two rivers."

Most of the Virginians were asleep in their tents, when, before sunrise, two of their hunters, seeking deer for breakfast, found the Indian army, already in battle array, and covering, as one of the hunters excitedly reported, "four acres of ground."

But these Virginians were no fools. Of the eleven hundred here, wellnigh every man had been a buckskin borderer, deadly with rifle, tomahawk and knife, and up to all Indian tricks. They were fairly drilled, too, as militia. A number of the officers had fought under Major George Washington, when on the fatal Braddock's Field, in 1755, the American Rangers had tried to save the day from the French, and from Pontiac's whooping warriors.

They all had marched for five weeks across one hundred and sixty miles of trackless mountain country, driving their pack-horses and their herds of beef cattle; now they rallied briskly to save their lives. It was nip and tuck.

From before sunrise until sunset raged the great battle of Point Pleasant, or the Big Kanawha. It was the first pitched battle between simon-pure Americans —but the Revolution was near and after this the Americans were to do their own fighting.

The lines were over a mile long, rarely more than

twenty yards apart, frequently less than six yards apart, and sometimes mingling. The armies were equal.

Both sides fought Indian fashion, from behind trees and brush. Rifle met rifle, tomahawk met tomahawk, knife met knife. The air was filled with whoops and cheers. Able chiefs faced able chiefs—on the white American side there were leaders who soon became more famous in the Revolution and in the history of the new nation.

It was a long-famous battle. A ballad written upon it was frequently sung, on the frontier:

Let us mind the tenth day of October,
Seventy-four, which causéd woe;
The Indian savages they did cover
The pleasant banks of the O-hi-o.

The battle beginning in the morning,
Throughout the day it lashéd sore,
Till the evening shades they were returning
Upon the banks of the O-hi-o.

Seven score lay dead and wounded.
Of champions that did face their foe,
By which the heathens were confounded,
Upon the banks of the O-hi-o.

Col. Lewis and noble captains
Did down to death like Uriah go.
Alas, their heads wound up in napkins,
Upon the banks of the O-hi-o.

O bless the mighty King of Heaven
For all his wondrous works below,
Who hath to us the victory given,
Upon the banks of the O-hi-o.

Logan was seen here, there, everywhere. So was Cornstalk. His mighty voice was heard above the din, like the voice of old Annawan when King Philip had been surprised. "Be strong! Be strong!" he appealed to his warriors. With his tomahawk he struck down a skulker. That had been his promise, in the council.

All this October day the battle continued. In single encounters, man to man, valorous deeds were done.

Cornstalk proved himself a worthy general. When his line bent back, before the discipline of the Long Knives, it was only to form an ambush, and then the whites were bent back. He had early placed his warriors across the base of the point, so that they held the whites in the angle of the two rivers. They dragged logs and brush to position, as breast-works. "We will drive the Long Knives into the rivers like so many bullocks."

That was not to be. Two of General Lewis's colonels had fallen; the Indian fire was very severe and accurate; but after vainly trying to feel out the end of the red line, the general at last succeeded, toward evening, in sending a company around.

Chief Cornstalk thought that this company, appearing in his rear, was the absent part of the division. Lest he be caught between two fires, he swung about and skillfully withdrew.

The battle slackened, at dusk. This night he safely removed his army across the Ohio again, that they might avoid the Lord Dunmore division and protect their towns in Ohio.

Nearly all the Indian bodies found, and nearly all the Virginians killed and wounded, were shot in the head or the breast. That was the marksmanship and the kind of fighting!

The Long Knives lost seventy-five men killed and one hundred and fifty wounded. They lost two great chiefs: Colonel Charles Lewis, the brother of the general, and Colonel John Field—both Braddock men; six captains and as many lieutenants were killed, also.

The Indians said that had they known how to clean their rifles, they would have done better. Cornstalk and Logan lost the sub-chief Puck-ee-shin-wah, but only forty or fifty others in killed and wounded. But when they hastened for their towns they found them in danger from the Lord Dunmore column.

Governor Dunmore sent Chief White-eyes, of the Delawares, who had not joined in the war, to ask Chief Cornstalk for a talk. Chief White-eyes returned with no answer, for the Cornstalk chiefs were in bitter council.

Cornstalk addressed them:

"You would not make peace before Point Pleasant; what is your voice now, when the Long Knives are pressing on in two columns?"

There was no reply.

"We cannot save our villages," he continued. "If your voice is for war, let us first kill our women and children. Then let us warriors go out and fight like men until we, too, are killed."

Still no reply. Cornstalk dashed his hatchet into the council post.

"You act like children," he thundered. "I will go and make peace, myself."

And leaving his hatchet sticking in the post, go he did.

Logan had not been here. He was away, down in Virginia, scouting with his Mingos, and delivering his note to Captain Cresap. On October 21 he arrived with scalps.

He refused to meet the governor.

"Tell the governor that I am a warrior, not a councillor," he bade.

His sore heart was not yet healed. His Mingos were for war. The Revolution was brewing, and Governor Dunmore was anxious to be about his own affairs. So he sought out Logan with two messengers, Scout Simon Girty, and Trader John Gibson, who spoke the Mingo tongue. They returned with Logan's stubborn answer, written out by John Gibson:

> I appeal to any white to say, if ever he entered Logan's cabin hungry, and he gave him not meat; if ever he came cold and naked, and he clothed him not.
>
> During the course of the last long, bloody war [the French and Indian and the Pontiac war] Logan remained idle in his cabin, an advocate for peace. Such was my love for the whites, that my countrymen pointed as they passed, and said, "Logan is the friend of the white men."
>
> I had even thought to have lived with you, but for the injuries of one man. Col. Cresap, the last spring, in cold blood, and unprovoked, murdered all the relatives of Logan; not even sparing my women and children.
>
> There runs not a drop of my blood in the veins of any living creature. This called on me for revenge. I have sought it. I have killed many. I have fully glutted my vengeance. For my country, I rejoice at the beams of peace. But do not harbor a thought that

mine is the joy of fear. Logan never felt fear. He will not turn on his heel to save his life. Who is there to mourn for Logan? Not one!

Trader Gibson reported that while making this speech, Logan wept. The sad-hearted chief probably did not put his words in exactly this order, but they made a great sensation. Soon they were being repeated throughout all the Ohio River country, and east of the Alleghanies, in towns, cabins and camps.

"Who is there to mourn for Logan?" would ask some voice, in the circle. And another voice would reply, with deep feeling: "Not one!"

President Thomas Jefferson included the speech in a book that he published—"Notes on Virginia," and said that he challenged the orations of the world to produce anything better.

It was copied into other books. School-children memorized it, for "speaking day"; grown people used it, in contests; and for one hundred years it was the favorite platform piece. Thus Logan lived in the white man's words.

Still Logan did not come in to the peace talk held with Governor Dunmore, southeast of present Circleville in south central Ohio. The Shawnees and Delawares said:

"Logan is like a mad dog. His bristles are up; they are not yet fallen, but the good talk may smooth them down."

He stayed close in his cabin, up the Scioto River, and Cornstalk spoke for the Shawnees, Delawares and Wyandots. It was another great address.

"I have heard the first orators of Virginia—Patrick Henry and Richard Henry Lee," declared Colonel Benjamin Wilson, of Dunmore's men, "but never have I heard one whose powers surpassed those of Cornstalk on that occasion."

Cornstalk told of the wrongs suffered by the Indians, in their hunting grounds; how they were losing the lands of their fathers, and were being cheated by the white men. He asked that nobody be permitted to trade, on private account, with the Indians, but that the Government should send in goods, to be exchanged for skins and furs, and that no "fire water" should enter into the business, for "from fire water there comes evil."

Then he buried the hatchet. He never dug it up. When the Revolution broke, in 1776, and the British agents urged the Indians to strike the post again and help their great father, the king, Cornstalk held firm for friendship with the Americans.

In the spring of 1777, he and young Red Hawk the Delaware, and another Indian came down to the American fort that had been built on the battle field of Point Pleasant at the mouth of the Big Kanawha of the West Virginia border.

"My Shawnees are restless," he warned. "The current sets so strongly against the Americans, that I fear my people will disobey me and float with the stream."

Captain Matthew Arbuckle was the commander of the fort. He kept the Cornstalk party as hostages for the good behavior of the Shawnees. Cornstalk did not object, but spent much time in talking with the officers, and in kindly drawing maps of the Ohio country, for them.

One day in a council he said:

"When I was young and went to war, I often thought, each might be my last adventure, and I should return no more. I still lived. Now I am in the midst of you, and if you choose, you may kill me. I can die but once. It is alike to me, whether now or hereafter."

Those brave words were not forgotten. This same day somebody shouted loudly from the opposite side of the Ohio. It was the young Chief Ellinipsico. He had not known what had happened to his father, and had traveled many miles, seeking him.

Cornstalk called him over. There was much rejoicing in the reunion; they loved each other dearly.

On the very next day two soldiers, named Hamilton and Gilmore, went over the Kanawha River, to hunt. The majority of the Ohio Indians were now helping the British. Some of the hostile warriors, lurking in West Virginia, fired on the two men and killed Gilmore.

Instantly the cry arose among the soldiers at the fort, that Ellinipsico had planned the ambush. Ellinipsico denied it. He said that he had come alone, on purpose to find his old father.

But that made no difference. Captain John Hall and squad were returning in a canoe bearing the body of Gilmore.

"Let us go and kill those Indians in the fort!"

Captain Arbuckle and Private Stuart tried in vain to force them back. In their cabin, of the fort, the

Chief Cornstalk party had been told by a white woman that they were in danger. They now heard the Captain Hall men approaching. Young Ellinipsico grew frightened, but his father steadied him.

"My son," said Cornstalk, "the Great Spirit has seen fit that we should die together, and has sent you here to that end. It is his will, and let us submit—it is all for the best."

He faced the door, and stood calmly waiting. Without a word or a struggle he fell dead, pierced through the front by seven bullets. Ellinipsico was now calm, also. He did not even stand, and thus he died, not moving. He was a worthy son of Cornstalk. Young Red Hawk was a Delaware and, hoping to be spared, he crept into the fire-place chimney. But he was dragged out, to death. The fourth Indian fought with his hands, and was cut to pieces.

The murderers of the generous, noble-hearted Cornstalk were never punished, but they certainly were not admired. The white men who had met him in war and in peace mourned him as much as the red men did. And from that day the Shawnee nation "became the most deadly foe to the inhabitants of the frontiers." Who may blame them?

Meanwhile Logan was living in misery, but he was soon to follow Chief Cornstalk. His end was far less happy. He had not been much heard from lately. After he had refused to meet the Long Knives in a peace talk, the troops had destroyed some of his villages. He and a band of his Mingos retreated northward toward the Great Lakes.

The Mingos aided the British, but Logan pursued fire-water more frequently than he did war. He never got over his grief. It had bitten him too deeply, and had poisoned his thoughts. Still, the good in him cropped out.

When in 1778 the famous American scout Simon Kenton had been captured by the Shawnees, he was taken, by the torture trail, to the village in northern Ohio where Logan was living.

He had little hopes, but Logan walked over to him.

"Well, young man," said Logan in good English, "these other young men seem very mad at you."

"Yes, sir; they certainly are," frankly answered Simon Kenton. Already one arm had been almost cut from his shoulder, by an axe.

Logan gravely smiled. "Well, don't be disheartened. I am a great chief. You are to go to Sandusky; they speak of burning you there, but I will send two runners tomorrow to speak good for you."

That was the real spirit of Logan. The two runners were sent, and Simon felt much encouraged. During the next day he was well treated in the village. He and Logan talked together freely.

In the evening the two runners returned. They went straight to Logan's lodge, but no word came to Kenton. Now he feared again. He feared more, when in the morning Logan himself approached him, said only, "You are to be taken at once to Sandusky," gave him a piece of bread and whirling on his heel strode gloomily away.

Evidently the power of Logan had weakened, the

Shawnees had not listened, and Sandusky, north on the Sandusky River, was waiting with the stake.

So Simon Kenton journeyed unwillingly onward, to be saved, at the last moment, by the British. But Logan had done his best. After this he drank harder, until his mind was injured. He had flashes of good, and he had longer flashes of bad. He seemed bent upon doing as much harm to himself as he could.

Then, in 1780, one day at Detroit he thought that while drunk he had killed his Shawnee wife. He imagined that he was being arrested; and in the fight that he made he was shot dead by his own nephew, on the road between Detroit and Sandusky.

Many mourned Cornstalk. "Who was there to mourn Logan"—the "friend of the white man?"

"Not one!"

But the name "Logan" was worn, like a badge of honor, by others in the Mingo people.

CHAPTER X

LITTLE TURTLE OF THE MIAMIS (1790-1791)

HE WINS GREAT VICTORIES

DURING the Revolution, by which the United States became an independent nation, the great majority of the Indian tribes within reach took active part on the side of the British.

The Iroquois fought out of friendship, they said; the tribes farther west fought in the hope of keeping the settlers out of the Kentucky, Ohio and Indiana country.

For some years after the war, which closed in 1782, there was a dispute between the United States and England over the carrying out of certain terms in the treaty of peace. Until the matter was settled, the British kept Detroit and other American frontier posts.

This encouraged the Indians. They had been much astonished and alarmed to find that the Americans had "laid the king on his back." Now that the British had lost the fight, what would happen to *them?*

But the British agents and traders still in the Indian country urged them on to make good their boast that "no white cabin should smoke beyond the Ohio." It was reported that the king was only resting, and that the Americans yet had no right to any land west of the Ohio River.

So the Miamis, the Potawatomis, the Ottawas, the Shawnees, the war Delawares, the Chippewas, the Kickapoos, the Wyandots, the Senecas, refused to meet the Americans in council or to bury the hatchet. They formed a league of defense.

The Miamis were the central nation. "People who live on the peninsula" was their Chippewa name—for they were Algonquins from the Chippewa and Ottawa country north of the Great Lakes. "Twanh-twanh," the cry of the crane, was their own name. Miamis, from the Chippewa word Omaumeg, were they called in English.

They had been described by early travelers as a pleasant-faced, lively, very polite people, slow of speech, swift of foot, fond of racing, and obedient to their chiefs.

Their present home was in the Wabash River valley of northern Indiana, up as far as the modern city of Fort Wayne. They claimed this country and also all of western Ohio, where they formerly had lived. The Shawnees and the Wyandots of Ohio had moved in behind them, they said, and were merely tenants upon their lands.

Little Turtle, or Mich-i-kin-i-kwa, had become their chief. He had been born on the Eel River near Fort Wayne in 1752. Therefore now at the close of the Revolution he was thirty years old. He had not been born a chief, nor even a Miami. To be sure, his father was chief and a Miami, but his mother was a Mohegan of the Delawares. By Indian law he had ranked as only a warrior and a Mohegan. An Indian was known by his mother.

As a boy of eleven or twelve he had been stirred by the Pontiac war, in which the Miamis had joined. As a warrior he had campaigned with the British under General Burgoyne who surrendered at Saratoga.

So by his deeds and his experience in field, camp and council he was a veteran and had won the chieftainship of the twelve hundred Miamis.

Although his name was Little Turtle, he had nothing little in his make-up. On the contrary, he was of good size, strong and dignified, with a long face and full high forehead—not the face or forehead of a Miami. He seems to have been rather sarcastic, and unpopular.

Those were bloody days while the new United States was trying to extend across the Ohio River. A treaty was made with the Cherokees and Chickasaws of the South, and with the Six Nations of the North; one was supposed to have been made with these Ohio country tribes, also.

These Indians said that they would do nothing for peace until they had talked with their British "father" at Detroit. They were not sure that the king had really surrendered their lands beyond the Ohio.

They asserted that their treaty, by which they had sold their lands, had not been signed by the proper chiefs.

In the seven years since the end of 1782, some two thousand American settlers and traders had been killed or captured, along the Ohio River; twenty thousand horses had been stolen. The rifle was more necessary than the ax and plough.

The Miami villages on the northern border between Ohio and Indiana formed the base for the many war parties.

So in 1790, President George Washington and Congress ordered General Arthur Saint Clair, the governor of this Northwest Territory, to clear the land for the smoke of the white cabins.

Little progress had been made by the white settlements, across the Ohio River. There were only two of any note: Marietta, named for the French queen Marie Antoinette; and the newer Cincinnati, christened in 1790 by Governor Saint Clair himself. There were several smaller ones, struggling to live.

The governor called for regulars and militia. General Josiah Harmar, the commander-in-chief of the United States army, was detailed in charge. On October 3 he started from Fort Washington, at Cincinnati, with three hundred and twenty regulars of the First Infantry, and eleven hundred and thirty-three militia of Kentucky and Pennsylvania, to destroy the towns of Little Turtle the Miami.

Little Turtle of course soon knew all about this. His spies infested the region. He rallied his bands. The Indians whom he commanded—Ottawas, Potawatomis, Chippewas, Shawnees, Senecas, Delawares, Miamis, and so forth—were the same nations that had obeyed the Bloody Belt of Pontiac. He had able aides, too; the skilled Buc-kon-ga-he-las of the Delawares,

Blue-jacket of the Shawnees, and others—great fighters, every one.

White men, also, were helping him. There were three, especially: Simon Girty, Matthew Elliott, and Alexander McKee, who was part Indian. They were three traitors who had deserted from the American garrison at Fort Pitt, in 1778, and had spread false reports among White-eyes' Delawares, and elsewhere.

Serving the enemies of their country, they had continued to live among the Shawnees and Wyandots, and in their savagery were worse than the Indians. Their names are red on the pages of history.

In Chief Little Turtle's main village, sometimes called "Girty's Town," located a few miles southeast of present Fort Wayne, Indiana, there was another white man—a young man. His name had been William Wells, but now was Black Snake. The Indians had captured him when a little boy in Kentucky; he had grown up with the Miamis, had married Chief Little Turtle's sister, and was rated as a Miami warrior. But his heart was not bad.

General Josiah Harmar, commander-in-chief of the United States army, was a year younger than Chief Little Turtle, commander-in-chief of the Indian army. They both were veterans of the Revolution, had good fighters under them, and might be thought well matched. But the general got threshed.

Little Turtle waited for him to come on, and plagued his march with parties of scouts who in the swamps and thickets cut off his foraging squads.

The general had tough going, for two weeks. When

on October 17 he arrived at Girty's Town, he found it abandoned and burning, to deprive him of more supplies.

Then General Harmar made his first mistake. He detached thirty of the First Infantry regulars, under Captain John Armstrong, and one hundred and fifty of the militia, under Colonel John Hardin of Kentucky, to follow the retreating Indians and perhaps destroy the next village.

He played into the hands of Little Turtle, who had over a thousand warriors. Colonel Hardin and Captain Armstrong had marched scarcely six miles, when in an open place they were completely ambushed. A swarm of Indians suddenly poured in a heavy fire from the brush on all sides; rose, and charged with tomahawk and knife.

This was too much for the militia, who were poorly drilled. Away they pelted, trying to reach the main army. But the well-drilled regulars stood stanch, and met the tomahawk with the bayonet, in the hope of forcing a passage.

The Little Turtle warriors cared nothing about the militia, and let them go. The few regulars did not last long. Every soldier except two officers and two privates was killed.

Of these two officers, in the break-up Ensign Asa Hartshorne of Connecticut fortunately stumbled over a log and lay concealed until he might escape.

Captain Armstrong crouched to his neck in a swampy pond, and stayed there all night, while only two hundred yards from him the enemy held a war-dance over the bodies of the slain. They had whipped the trained soldiery, who had fought bravely.

The next day, with all his army General Harmar advanced upon the Miami towns. Little Turtle had ordered them burned. The general destroyed the cornfields and the fruit-trees; and seeing no Indians to fight, turned back for Fort Washington.

He had gone about ten miles, when scouts brought word that the Indians were gathering in their towns again. The general made a second mistake. Colonel Hardin, stung by the way in which his militia had acted, begged for another chance. Instead of going, himself, General Harmar again detached some of the militia—six hundred this time—and sixty of the regulars under Major John P. Wyllys of Washington's old Continentals. He told Colonel Hardin to find the Indians.

The colonel found them, on the morning of October 22. His only fear had been that they would run off and not give him his revenge. But he had not counted the strategy of Little Turtle.

When the first few Indians were sighted, Colonel Hardin made careful and scientific preparation. He attacked. The Indians did run off, with the happy, shouting militia in full hue and cry after. The regulars followed slowly. When a gap of two miles had opened, as if from the very earth out sprang Little Turtle's whole remaining force, a thousand, and the hapless regulars were in the same plight as before.

The militia fought their way back, too late. The battle on the field had become hand-to-hand. Both sides were brave; but when a soldier thrust with his bayonet, two tomahawks were there, to crash into his skull.

Major Wyllys was killed; so was Lieutenant Ebenezer Frothingham; fifty of the rank and file fell. Only eight men escaped. Of the militia, a major, two captains, and over ninety others died.

After he had been joined by the survivors, General Harmar resumed his march to Fort Washington. He claimed a victory, because he had destroyed the Indians' winter supplies; but he had lost one hundred and eighty-three soldiers killed, and forty wounded, and the Indians not more than fifty warriors.

The victory and the field of battle were left to Little Turtle. General Harmar had proved to be a commander whose orders were "Go" instead of "Come," and Colonel Hardin had not known how to fight Indians.

However, Little Turtle realized that the Americans had other officers, and that General Washington was not a man to back down. There would be another army.

So he spent much of the winter in visiting various tribes and enlisting them. He went as far north as Ontario of Canada, and there appealed to the Missisauga nation of Algonquins. He traveled west to the Illinois River. He was a second Pontiac.

General and Governor Saint Clair himself was the officer appointed by President Washington to lead the next expedition against the Little Turtle army. He was a gallant old Continental, aged fifty-seven and gray-haired. As a young officer in a Scotch regiment he had come over to America with a British army, in 1758, to fight the French and Indians. After that war he had become a true American citizen of Pennsylvania, and as colonel and major-general had served with the Buff-and-Blue in the war for American independence.

He had been unlucky in his campaigns, but nobody ever doubted his courage. General Washington thought highly of him, and now took pains to say, in person, to him, before the start was made:

"Beware of a surprise. You know how the Indians fight. So I repeat—beware of a surprise."

General Saint Clair had been promised three thousand men, but when early in September of this year 1791 he left Fort Washington, he had only two thousand men. Still, it was a strong army, comprising the greater portion of the whole army of the United States. There were the First and Second Infantry, half a battalion (two companies) of the regular artillery, a company of mounted riflemen volunteers, and six hundred Kentucky militia.

Major-General Richard Butler of Pennsylvania, and of the Continental army in the Revolution, was field officer in command; and a number of the other officers had been trained under Washington. But the Second Regiment was new, the last spring, and largely of recruits; and the Kentucky militia had not wanted to come.

Part of them deserted, on the way out. The First Regiment was sent to catch them. This left fourteen hundred men, to march on into the Indian country. General Saint Clair was so crippled with the rheumatism and the gout that he could scarcely mount a horse.

Twenty miles north of Fort Washington he halted long enough to erect Fort Hamilton—Hamilton, Ohio; twenty miles farther he erected Fort Saint Clair; and twenty miles farther, Fort Jefferson, near the present city of Greenville, Ohio.

He was following up along the Indiana-Ohio line, to strike the Miami villages. By the night of November 3 he had arrived within about fifty miles of Little Turtle's principal town. The place on the modern map is Fort Recovery, northern Ohio, close to Indiana.

Little Turtle was ready. He had twelve hundred men. Buckongahelas the Delaware, and Blue-jacket the Shawnee were helping him. So was a Missisauga chief who had been drilled under British officers. So was Simon Girty the white-Indian savage. So were a number of Canadians and French half-breeds, from Canada and from the Illinois country. And so, it is stated, were several British officers from Detroit, who wished to see their old foes, the Continentals, licked. Their red coats were noticed in the battle, next day.

General Saint Clair was a good soldier, and planned well. He had planted a string of supply depots behind him. He had made a practice of sounding the reveille two hours before day-break, every morning in camp, and keeping the men at parade until almost sunrise, to guard against a surprise. He tried to be thorough.

This afternoon of November 3 he had selected an excellent camp ground, from which a few Indians had fled at his approach. It was high, compact, and protected by a creek. He stationed his main body in two lines about seventy yards apart, facing in opposite directions.

His scouts had reported that the Indians were collecting in force about twelve miles distant. His intention was, to fortify the camp, so that the knapsacks and other baggage might be left there; and as soon as the delayed First Regiment came in, to push right on and attack.

Little Turtle's scouts also had been active. They had surveyed the marches and the camps, had measured the infantry, artillery and cavalry—and had been alarmed by the showing. Here was an old general and some big captains, wise in the art of war.

Now what to do?

Little Turtle called a grand council of all the chiefs, red and white. They debated whether to attack the camp, or to try an ambush in the field. Little Turtle favored attacking the camp. An ambush would be expected by the old general, but an attack upon a strongly guarded camp would not be expected. A maxim of war says: "Never do what the enemy expects you to do."

The Missisauga chief sided with Little Turtle. He was a tall, stout, fierce fellow, very swarthy and severe looking. He wore hide leggins and moccasins; a long blue shirt, a brocade vest, an overcoat instead of a blanket, and a turban studded with two hundred silver brooches. In either ear were two bangles, twelve inches long, formed of silver medals and quarter-dollars; in his nose were three nose-jewels of painted silver.

He was respectfully listened to as a wise captain, and he and Little Turtle carried the day.

"But the gray-haired general is always ready for a surprise attack."

"All right. Wait until the hour when he is not ready. Then strike."

Under the direction of Commander-in-Chief Little Turtle, in the darkness this night the Indian army stole forward and was posted with as much skill as any white army.

The Miamis held the center; the Wyandots, the Delawares and the Senecas held the right; the Ottawas, the Potawatomis, the Shawnees, and others, held the left.

They were ready. They could hear the challenges of the alert sentries, at the gray-hair's camp. Two hours before day-break they heard the drums beating the reveille. The soldiers of the gray-hair were on the watch.

The light in the east broadened. Securely hidden, the Little Turtle army waited. They might see the dim tents of the militia advance-guard, camped a quarter of a mile this side of the creek.

Beyond, where the main camp was under arms, the smoke of the fires began to thicken.

Toward the time of sunrise the soldiers grew tired of standing in ranks. The dawn-hour for surprise by Indians had passed. Trumpet and drum-roll sounded for "Break ranks." Having stacked their guns the soldiers gladly made for their tents, or squatted around the breakfast fires.

Another day had begun, without event.

Little Turtle allowed fifteen minutes or so, for the soldiers to settle and doze. Then he gave the signal, a half hour before sunrise.

General Saint Clair was lying sick in his tent. There burst a distant rifle shot; it was instantly followed by a crackling volley, as from half a thousand rifles—and an answering heavier volley from the muskets of the militia.

Struggling to don his blanket-coat he limped out, his gray queue ragged. The camp sprang to arms, for officers and men knew their business; but here came the militia like a drove of stampeded cattle, legging frantically for shelter from a horde of whooping, darting Indians. The militia dived through the lines of the regulars, into the very center of the camp, and for a short period all was chaos.

It was a furious fight. Re-forming their lines, the regulars stood well. They checked the charge by a thunderous volley from the long-barreled flint-lock muskets—the same as used at Brandywine, Princeton and Yorktown.

The strategy of Little Turtle and his chiefs was excellent. They shifted the attack from point to point. They attacked both lines at once. They took advantage of every cover, and constantly appeared closer. They killed every horse and every gunner of the artillery posted in the center.

Of the Second Infantry, all the officers fell except

two. General Butler hastened bravely up and down the one line, encouraging the troops; General Saint Clair limped heroically up and down the other line. Eight bullets pierced his clothing—a lock of his hair was shorn off. General Butler was shot twice; and while he was sitting, mortally wounded, an Indian rushed in and tomahawked him.

General Saint Clair's army was being shot to pieces. He ordered bayonet charges; but when these had cleared a little space, the Indians re-appeared, thicker than ever. Their fire, it is recorded, "was tremendous."

The camp was entered, and pillaged. Some two hundred and fifty women, among them the general's dashing daughter, had come with the army; and these suffered terribly.

After three hours' battle, the general ordered a final charge, to open a way. Pressing behind the bayonets, the weary troops commenced a retreat of twenty-nine miles to Fort Jefferson.

The general, on a poor pack-horse, insisted on bringing up the rear. Out of his less than fourteen hundred soldiers, thirty-eight officers and six hundred men were killed or missing; twenty-one officers and two hundred and forty-two men were wounded. Fifty of the women had died. It was as bad as the defeat of General Braddock's army, in 1755. For a year and a half the field was covered with bleaching bones.

Little Turtle, the Missisauga chief and Simon Girty the white savage had directed the attack. After a pursuit of four miles, seeing that the soldiers were on the run and throwing away guns, knapsacks, and all, they called the chase off.

It had been victory enough. They had captured seven pieces of cannon, two hundred cattle, many horses; they returned to the villages with one hundred and twenty scalps strung on one pole, and with three pack-horses piled high with kegs of liquor.

Their own loss was stated to be fifty-six. Surely this was a great triumph for Commander-in-Chief Little Turtle.

CHAPTER XI

LITTLE TURTLE FEARS THE BIG WIND (1792–1812)

AND IT BLOWS HIM INTO PEACE

PRESIDENT WASHINGTON was almost beside himself when he got the frank report from General Saint Clair. Another American army—as good a selection as had opposed the British themselves in many a battle of the Revolution—had been fairly outwitted and fairly defeated, by Indians.

General Anthony Wayne was appointed to try next. "Mad Anthony," soldiers and citizens had styled him, because of his head-long valor in the Revolution. He was a good man for the job, if he did not act too fast and get ambushed.

He took his time. The army of the United States was reorganized into the Legion of the United States. He was placed in command.

There were four Sub-legions, or corps, each composed of artillery, dragoons, infantry and riflemen. The enlisted men wore round caps like helmets.

The badge of the First Sub-legion was white binding, with short plumes of white wool and black horse-hair.

The badge of the Second Sub-legion was red binding, with short plumes of red wool and white horse-hair.

The badge of the Third Sub-legion was yellow binding, with yellow wool and black horse-hair.

The badge of the Fourth Sub-legion was green binding, with green wool and white horse-hair.

"Another defeat will be ruinous to the reputation of the United States," had said President Washington. With this in mind, General Wayne declared for drilling his troops hard, at Legionville, below Pittsburg. Infantry, artillery and cavalry were kept busy at target practice, broad-sword practice, and battle formations.

In the spring of 1793 he moved down to Fort Washington at Cincinnati. On August 8, he marched north, with two thousand troops the equal of any troops in the world, to invade the country of the Miamis.

Meanwhile there had been fighting, but the warriors of Little Turtle showed no signs of letting up. A message from the British had told them that war with the United States was due this year, and that the Indians were expected to hold their ground.

Now the great warrior "Mad Anthony" was advancing. Him, the Indians much respected. His reputation was known. They had named him "Black Snake," and "Big Wind" or "Whirlwind." From the methods with which he made his marches—his men deployed in open order, his dragoons sweeping the flanks, his scouts before, and every night's camp pitched early and surrounded by a log breast-works—they saw that he was wise.

He established more forts. He erected a new one near the site of Fort Jefferson at Greenville, Ohio; and spent the winter there. He built Fort Recovery on the skull-dotted field where General Saint Clair had been routed. There the Wayne men defeated the Little

Turtle men. The Indians spent two nights in carrying off their dead and wounded. But the British from Detroit had come southward and built another fort for themselves—Fort Maumee—at the Maumee River Rapids, in northwestern Ohio, south of modern Toledo.

That was a rallying-place for the allied Indians, and encouraged them. The "Big Wind" continued, laying waste the villages and fields. He built Fort Defiance in the very heart of the Miami country, and proceeded down the Maumee River toward the British fort.

Within seven miles of the British fort he built Fort Deposit. He had two thousand Legionaries, and eleven hundred mounted Kentucky riflemen; Little Turtle's army was being driven back upon the British fort, and must fight or quit.

So far, the "Big Wind" had proved himself the master.

By this time Little Turtle had lost his brother-in-law, "Black Snake" or William Wells, whose blood was the white blood, and who could no longer fire upon his race.

When he had heard that another American army was on its way, he had led Little Turtle apart.

"I now leave your nation for my own people," he had said. "We have been friends. We are friends yet until the sun is an hour higher. From that time we are enemies. Then if you wish to kill me, you may. If I want to kill you, I may."

William Wells plunged into the forest, and found

General Wayne. He became a valuable scout with the United States column.

From Fort Deposit General Wayne sent word to the Miamis that they must make peace at once, or be attacked. Little Turtle called a council. Some of his men were dubious.

"It is no use fighting that man. His eye is never shut," they complained.

Little Turtle himself was dubious. The council debated upon whether to try another "Saint Clair" surprise, or to choose their ground, and wait.

Blue-jacket the Shawnee was for fighting.

"Listen," spoke Little Turtle. "We have beaten the enemy twice, under separate generals. We cannot expect the same good fortune always. The Americans are led now by a chief who never sleeps. The night and the day are alike to him. During all the time that he has been marching upon us we have watched him close but we have never been able to surprise him. Think well of it. Something whispers to me that we could do well to treat with him."

Somebody accused Little Turtle of being afraid, at last. That was enough. He objected no more, and the council decided to form battle array and wait, at Presq' Isle, near the British fort. Blue-jacket took charge.

It was good ground for defense. Another "Big Wind" had passed through the timber, and laid the trees crisscross in great confusion. Amidst this maze Little Turtle, Blue-jacket, Simon Girty, and the other leaders stretched three lines of warriors and half-breeds, in a front two miles long. Their left rested at the river, their right was protected by a thicket, the British fort was behind them.

The British commander had said that he would open his gates to them, if they were again driven back.

The "Big Wind," who never slept, had not delayed. This morning of August 20, 1794, he marched right onward, in battle array. At noon he struck the Fallen Timbers, at Presq' Isle.

Now he was "Mad Anthony," again. He made short work of the Little Turtle army of fifteen hundred. He sent his Kentucky mounted riflemen against their right flank; he sent his dragoon regulars against their left flank; he sent his regular infantry in a bayonet charge straight through their center. They were not to fire a shot until the Indians had broken cover; then they were to deliver a volley and keep going so hard that the enemy would have no time to reload.

For once, Little Turtle's warriors did not stand. They feared this mad general. The trained infantry Legionaries moved so fast that they outfooted the cavalry; and they alone drove the warriors helter-skelter back through the timber, to the very walls of the British fort.

There the mounted riflemen and the dragoons smote with their "long knives," or broad-swords—for the gates of the fort were *not* opened, and the walls proved only a death-trap.

The Battle of Fallen Timbers was over in about an hour. The Americans lost thirty-eight killed, one hundred and one wounded. The loss of the Miamis and their allies numbered several hundred. Nine Wyandot chiefs had been slain.

Their warriors were scattered, their villages and corn-fields were destroyed, the British had not helped them, United States forts occupied their best ground from the Ohio River right through north to Lake Erie, and the long war had ended.

The Miamis and eleven other nations signed a treaty of peace, at Greenville, in August of the next year, 1795.

"I am the last to sign," said Little Turtle, "and I think I will be the last to break it."

Ever after this, Little Turtle lived at peace with the Americans.

The United States built him a house on his birthplace at the Eel River twenty miles from Fort Wayne, Indiana. He tried to adopt civilization and bring his people to agriculture and prosperity.

He was opposed by jealous chiefs, who envied him his house and accused him of having been bought by the Americans. But he was wiser than they.

He had been the first of the great chiefs to frown upon the torture of captives; give him a good mark for that. Now he frowned upon liquor. With Captain William Wells, his friend, he appeared before the Kentucky legislature, and asked for a law against selling liquor to the Indians. In the winter of 1801–1802 he asked to be vaccinated, at Washington, and took some of the vaccine back with him, for his people.

He frequently visited Philadelphia. There he met the famous Polish patriot Kosciusko. They had many talks. Kosciusko presented him with a fine pair of pistols and a valuable otter-skin robe.

Chief Little Turtle died July 14, 1812, while on a visit at Fort Wayne. The notice in a newspaper said:

"Perhaps there is not left on this continent, one of his color so distinguished in council and in war. His disorder was the gout. He died in a camp, because he chose to be in the open air. He met death with great firmness. The agent for Indian affairs had him buried with the honors of war."

His portrait, painted by a celebrated artist, was hung upon the walls of the War Department at Washington.

CHAPTER XII

THE VOICE FROM THE OPEN DOOR (1805–1811)

HOW IT TRAVELED THROUGH THE LAND

IN the battle of the Fallen Timbers, when General "Big Wind" broke the back of the Ohio nations, two young warriors fought against each other.

One was Lieutenant William Henry Harrison, aged twenty-one, of the Americans. The other was Sub-chief Tecumseh, aged twenty-six, of the Shawnees.

They were the sons of noted fathers. Benjamin Harrison, the father of Lieutenant Harrison, had been a famous patriot and a signer of the Declaration of Independence in 1776. Puck-ee-shin-wah, the father of Tecumseh, also had been a patriot—he had died for his nation in the battle of Point Pleasant, in 1774, when Chief Cornstalk fought for liberty.

At the Fallen Timbers, Lieutenant Harrison was an aide to General Wayne; young Tecumseh was an aide to Blue-jacket. The two did not meet, but their trails were soon to join.

The name Tecumseh (pronounced by the Indians "Tay-coom-tha") means "One-who-springs" or "darts." It was a word of the Shawnees' Great Medicine Panther clan, or Meteor clan; therefore Tecumseh has been known as "Crouching Panther" and "Shooting Star."

He was born in 1768 at the old Shawnee village of Piqua, on Mad River about six miles southwest of present Springfield, Ohio. His mother may have been a Creek or Cherokee woman, who had come up from the South with some of the Shawnees. The Shawnees were a Southern people, once. The mother's name was Me-tho-a-tas-ke.

Tecumseh had five brothers and one sister. Two of his brothers were twins, and at least two, besides his father, fell in battle while he was still young.

He had not been old enough to go upon the war trail with his father and Head Chief Cornstalk; but his elder brother Chee-see-kau went, and fought the Long Knives at Point Pleasant. When he came back he took little Tecumseh in charge, to train him as a warrior.

When Tecumseh was nineteen, he and Chee-see-kau, with a party of other braves, went upon a long journey of adventure south to the Cherokee country of Tennessee. It is said that the mother, Me-tho-a-tas-ke, already had left, to return to the Cherokees. Likely enough the two brothers planned to visit her.

They swung far into the west, to the Mississippi, and circled to the Cherokees. Here Chee-see-kau was killed, while helping the Cherokees fight the whites.

He was glad to die in battle—"I prefer to have the birds pick my bones, rather than to be buried at home like an old squaw."

Tecumseh stayed in the South three years, fighting to avenge his brother, who had been a father to him, and whose spirit still urged him to be brave. He got home to Ohio just in time. In league with the Little

Turtle Miamis, War Chief Blue-jacket's Shawnees had defeated the American general Harmar, and every warrior was needed.

Tecumseh had left as a young brave; he returned as a young chief. He was sent out with a party to spy upon the march of the gray-haired general, Saint Clair. He did good work, but he missed the big battle. But he was at the Fallen Timbers.

Here, in the excitement when the American infantry came scrambling and cheering and stabbing, through the down trees, he rammed a bullet into his rifle ahead of the powder, and had to retreat.

"Give me a gun and I will show you how to stand fast," he appealed, to the other Indians. He was given a shot-gun. The white soldiers were too strong, his younger brother Sau-wa-see-kau was killed at his side, and he must fall back again.

This hurt his heart. When the treaty with General Wayne was signed, the next year, he did not attend. Blue-jacket, his chief, afterwards sought him out and told him all about it: that the Indians had surrendered much land.

For some years the peace sun shone upon the Ohio country. Tecumseh was careful to cast no red shadow. He bore himself like an independent chief; gathered his own band of Shawnees, married a woman older than himself, lived among the Delawares, and spent much time hunting. He became known for his ringing speeches, in the councils; no Indian was more eloquent.

He was handsome, too—a true prince: six feet tall and broad shouldered, of active and haughty mien, quick step, large flashing eyes, and thin, oval Indian face, with regular features. His face was the kind that could burn with the fire of his mind.

In 1800 the Northwest Territory of which General Saint Clair had been the first governor was divided. The name Northwest Territory was limited to about what is now the state of Ohio; all west of that, to the Mississippi River, was Indiana Territory.

Captain William Henry Harrison, who had resigned from the army, was appointed governor and Indian commissioner, of Indiana Territory. He moved to Vincennes, the capital, on the lower Wabash. Chief Tecumseh was living eastward on the White River. Their trails were pointing in. Two master minds were to meet and wrestle.

The name of one of the two twins, brothers of Tecumseh, was La-la-we-thi-ka, meaning "Rattle" or "Loud Voice." He was not handsome. He was blind in the right eye and had ugly features. He was looked upon as a mouthy, shallow-brained, drunken fellow, of little account as a warrior. His band invited Tecumseh's band to unite with them at Greenville, in western Ohio where General Saint Clair's Fort Jefferson and General Wayne's Fort Greenville had been built.

Then, almost immediately, or in the fall of 1805, "Loud Voice" arose as the Prophet.

While smoking his pipe in his cabin he fell backward in a pretended trance, and lay as if dead. But before he was buried, he recovered. He said that he had been to the spirit world. He called all the nation to meet him at Wapakoneta, the ancient principal village of the Shawnees, fifty miles northeast, and listen to a message from the Master of Life.

The message was a very good one. It was a great deal like the message of the Delaware prophet, as used by Pontiac. The Indians were to cease white-man habits. They must quit fire-water poison, must cherish the old and sick, must not marry with the white people, must cease bad medicine-making (witch-craft) and tortures; and must live happily and peacefully, sharing their lands in common.

As for him, he had been given power to cure all diseases, and to ward off death on the battle-field.

He changed his name to Ten-skwa-ta-wa—the "Open Door," but is generally styled the Prophet. His words created intense excitement. Shawnees, Delawares and other Indians came from near and far to visit him. Tecumseh was very willing. It was a great thing to have a prophet for a brother—and whether this was a put-up job between them, is to this day a mystery. But they were smart men.

The Prophet enlarged his rant. To the whites he proclaimed that he, the Open Door, Tecumseh, the Shooting Star, and the other twin brother all had come at one birth. He asserted that their father had been the son of a Shawnee chief and a princess, daughter of a great English governor in the South.

Anybody whom he accused of witch-craft was put to death. They usually were persons that he did not like. The Delawares and Shawnees killed old chiefs who were harmless, and friends of the settlers.

Although the Open Door's teachings seemed to be for

peace and prosperity among the Indians, they brought many Indians together, and aroused much alarm among the settlers of Ohio and Indiana Territory. Moreover, the gatherings at Greenville were upon ground that had been sold to the United States, under the treaty after the battle of the Fallen Timbers.

Governor Harrison sent a message to the Delawares, in the name of the Seventeen Fires—the United States.

"Who is this pretended prophet who dares to speak for the great Creator? If he is really a prophet, ask of him to cause the sun to stand still, the moon to alter its course, the rivers to cease to flow, or the dead to rise from their graves!"

And—

"Drive him from your town, and let peace and harmony prevail amongst you. Let your poor old men and women sleep in quietness, and banish from their minds the dreadful idea of being burnt alive by their own friends and countrymen."

The Delawares listened, even the Shawnees were sickening of the witch-craft fraud—but the Prophet seized upon an opportunity.

In this 1806 an eclipse of the sun was due, and he knew, beforehand. Perhaps he was told by British agents, for the war of 1812 was looming, and there was bad feeling between the two white nations.

"The American governor has demanded of me a sign," he proclaimed. "On a certain day I will darken the sun."

And so he did.

His fame spread like a wind. Runners carried the

news of him and of his power through tribe after tribe. He made long journeys, himself. In village after village, from the Seminoles of Florida to the Chippewas of the Canada border, from the Mingos of the Ohio River to the Blackfeet of the farthest upper Missouri, either he or some of his disciples appeared.

They bore with them a mystic figure, the size of the body of a man, all wrapped in white cloth and never opened. This they tended carefully. They bore with them a string of white beans, said to be made from the Prophet's flesh.

They preached that dogs were to be killed; lodge fires were never to go out; liquor was not to be drunk; wars were not to be waged, unless ordered by the Prophet. Each warrior was obliged to draw the string of beads through his fingers; by this, he "shook hands" with the Prophet, and swore to obey his teachings.

It was rumored that within four years a great "death" would cover the entire land, and that only the Indians who followed the Prophet would escape. These should enjoy the land, freed of the white men.

Tecumseh bowed before his talented brother, and had his own dreams; dreams of a vast war league against the Americans. The Prophet was in control of eight or ten thousand warriors.

The Prophet's band at Greenville increased to four hundred—Shawnees, Delawares, Wyandots, Chippewas, and others; a regular hodge-podge.

Captain William Wells, who was the Indian agent at Fort Wayne, asked them to have four chiefs come in, to listen to a message from their Great Father, the President.

On a sudden Tecumseh took the lead, as head chief.

"Go back to Fort Wayne," he ordered of the runner, a half-breed Shawnee, "and tell Captain Wells that my fire is kindled on the spot appointed by the Great Spirit above; and if he has anything to say to me, he must come here. I shall expect him in six days from this time."

Captain Wells then sent the message. The President asked the Indians to move off from this ground which was not theirs. He would help them to select other ground.

Tecumseh replied hotly, in a speech of defiance.

"These lands are ours; no one has a right to remove us, because we were the first owners. The Great Spirit above knows no boundaries, nor will his red people know any. If my father, the President of the Seventeen Fires, has anything more to say to me, he must send a big man as messenger. I will not talk with Captain Wells."

"Why does not the President of the Seventeen Fires send us the greatest man in his nation?" demanded the Prophet. "I can talk to him; I can bring darkness between him and me; I can put the sun under my feet; and what white man can do this?"

This month of May, 1807, fifteen hundred Indians had visited the Prophet. They came even from the Missouri River, and from the rivers of Florida. A general up-rising of the tribes was feared.

Governor Harrison worked, sending many addresses. He could not stem the tide set in motion by the Prophet and kept in motion by Tecumseh.

"My children," appealed Governor Harrison, "this business must be stopped. You have called in a number of men from the most distant people to listen to a fool, who speaks not the words of the Great Spirit, but those of the devil and of the British agents. My children, your conduct has much alarmed the white settlers near you. They desire that you will send away those people, and if they wish to have the impostor with them they can carry him. Let him go to the Lakes; he can hear the British more distinctly."

"I am sorry that you listen to the advice of bad birds," answered the Prophet, of the one eye and the cunning heart. "I never had a word with the British, and I never sent for any Indians. They came here themselves, to hear the words of the Great Spirit."

Tecumseh also made speeches, at the councils. Once he spoke for three hours, accusing the whites of having broken many treaties. Some of his sentences the interpreter refused to translate, they were so frank and cutting. The teachings of the Prophet his brother were apparently all for peace, and against evil practices such as drinking and warring; and Governor Harrison could only wait, watchfully. But he did not like the signs in the horizon. There were too many Indians traveling back and forth.

The war of 1812 with Great Britain was drawing nearer. The Sacs and Foxes of the Mississippi country had accepted presents from the British. Governor

Harrison was warned that the Prophet and Tecumseh had been asked to join.

In the summer of 1808 the Prophet moved his town to the north bank of the Tippecanoe River, on the curve where it enters the upper Wabash River in northern Indiana. He still had a following of Shawnees, Chippewas, Potawatomis, Winnebagos, and so forth.

This was Miami land, shared by the Delawares. They objected. But the Prophet's Town remained.

In 1809 the United States bought from the Miamis a large piece of territory which included this land. The Prophet's people refused to move off. The Great Spirit had told them that the Indians were to hold all property in common; therefore no tribe might sell land without the consent of all the tribes.

Tecumseh was absent, on a visit to other tribes. He asked the Wyandots and the Senecas to come to Prophet's Town on the Tippecanoe. But the Wyandots and the Senecas had no wish to offend the United States again. They remembered that the British had not opened the gates of the fort to them, when the "Big Wind" was blowing them backward—"You are painted too much, my children," they accused the British of saying—and they were wary of Tecumseh.

He asked the Shawnees of the upper country, also, to join him and the Prophet. But they declined to meddle. Old Black Hoof, a chief whose memory extended back ninety years, advised against it.

The Prophet was more clever than Tecumseh. The Wyandots were the keepers of the great belt which had bound the Ohio nations together in Little Turtle's day.

The Prophet asked them if they still had it, and if they, the "elder brothers," would sit still while a few Indians sold the land of all the Indians.

They replied they were glad to know that the belt had not been forgotten. Let the Indians act as one nation. They passed the belt to the Miamis—and the Miamis were forced to obey.

Governor Harrison was told that there were eight hundred warriors at the Prophet's Town, and that Vincennes was to be attacked.

News of Tecumseh came from here, there, everywhere. He seemed to be constantly traveling, carrying the words of the Prophet his brother. *Something was going on,* underneath the peace blanket. Governor Harrison and others of the whites read the puzzle in this wise:

The peace blanket spread by the Prophet to cover all red nations and make them one, concealed a hatchet, as the blanket of Pontiac concealed a gun. The Indians were to be increased and strengthened by right living and good habits, until fitted to stand on their feet without aid. Then, all together, as one nation, they could strike for their country, from the Ohio River west to the Missouri.

Tecumseh was to be the Pontiac who would lead them. It was a scheme so wonderful, so patient and so shrewd, that the Western whites might well gasp before it.

The governor and Tecumseh had never met. The Prophet had been in Vincennes several times, to explain that he preached only peace—which was true.

But the town at the Tippecanoe was getting to be a nuisance. Horse-thieves and murderers used it as a shelter, and the authority of the United States was defied. A messenger sent there by the governor was threatened by the Prophet with death.

The message was sent to warn the brothers that the Seventeen Fires were surely able to defeat all the Indians united, and that if there were complaints, these should be taken directly to the President. Tecumseh replied:

"The Great Spirit gave this great island to his red children. He placed the whites on the other side of the big water. They were not contented with their own, but came to take ours from us. They have driven us from the sea to the lakes; we can go no farther. They say one land belongs to the Miamis, another to the Delawares, and so on; but the Great Spirit intended it as the property of us all. Our father tells us we have no right upon the Wabash. The Great Spirit ordered us to come here, and here we will stay."

However, Tecumseh said that he remembered the governor as a very young man riding with General Wayne, and he would go to Vincennes and talk with him. He probably would bring thirty of his men.

"The governor may expect to see many more than that," added the Prophet.

Tecumseh brought not thirty, but four hundred warriors, painted and armed. Attended by a small guard, the governor stood to receive him on the broad columned porch of the official mansion. Tecumseh, with forty braves, approached, and halted. He did not like the porch; he asked that the council be held in a grove near by.

"Your father says that he cannot supply seats enough there," answered the interpreter.

"My father?" retorted Tecumseh, his head high. "The sun is my father, the earth is my mother, and on her bosom will I repose!"

In the grove he made a ringing, fiery speech. He accused the United States of trying to divide the Indians, so as to keep them weak. He blamed the "village" or "peace" chiefs for yielding, and said that now the war chiefs were to rule the tribes. He warned the governor that if the lands along the Wabash were not given back to the Indians, the chiefs who had signed the sale would be killed, and then the governor would be guilty of the killing. He threatened trouble for the whites if they did not cease purchasing Indian land.

"It is all nonsense to say that the Indians are all one nation," reproved Governor Harrison, who was as fearless as Tecumseh. "If the Great Spirit had intended that to be so, he would not have put six different tongues into their heads. The Miamis owned these lands in the beginning, while the Shawnees were in Georgia. You Shawnees have no right to come from a distant country, and tell the Miamis what shall be done with their property."

Tecumseh sprang up and angrily interrupted.

"That is a lie! You and the Seventeen Fires are cheating the Indians out of their lands."

The warriors leaped up, as if to attack. The few whites prepared for defense.

"You are a man of bad heart," thundered the governor, to Tecumseh. "I will talk with you no more. You may go in safety, protected by the council-fire, but I want you to leave this place at once."

Other councils were held. Tecumseh stood as firm as a rock, for what he considered to be the rights of the Indians. He was very frank. He said that if it were not for the dispute about the land, he would continue to be the friend of the Seventeen Fires. He would rather fight with them than against them. He had no love for the British—who clapped their hands and sicked the Indians on as if they were dogs. As for making the Indians one nation, had not the Seventeen Fires set an example when they united? It was true, he said, that now all the Northern tribes were one. Soon he was to set out, and ask the Southern tribes to sit upon the same blanket with the Northern tribes.

The governor knew. From Governor William Clark of Missouri he had received a letter telling him that friendship belts and war belts were passing among the nations west of the Missouri River, calling them to an attack on Vincennes. The Sacs of the upper Mississippi had sent to Canada for ammunition.

From Chicago had come word that the Potawatomis and other tribes near Fort Dearborn were preparing.

Governor Harrison had suggested that the two brothers travel to Washington and talk with the President about lands. He himself had no power to promise that treaties should not be made with separate nations. He also said, to Tecumseh:

"If there is war between us, I ask you to stop your Indians from abusing captives, and from attacking women and children."

Tecumseh promised, but he went out upon his trip. Before he left, he asked that nothing should be done regarding the land, before he came back; a large number of Indians were on the way to settle there, and they would need it as a hunting-ground! If they killed the cattle and hogs of the white people, he would fix up everything with the President, on his return.

So in August of 1811 he left, taking twenty warriors. With the fire-brand of tongue and the burning mystery of his presence he kindled the nations of the South. He spoke in the name of the Great Prophet. He urged them all to join as one people and dam back the white wave that was seeking to swallow them.

He told them that the Prophet had stationed a "lamp" in the sky, to watch them for him—and sure enough, a comet flamed in the horizon. To a Creek chief in Alabama he said:

"You do not mean to fight. I know the reason. You do not believe that the Great Spirit has sent me. You shall know. I go from here to Detroit; when I arrive there I will stamp on the ground with my foot and shake down all your houses."

In December occurred an earthquake which destroyed New Madrid town on the Mississippi in southern Missouri, and was felt widely. The ground under the Creek nation trembled. The Creeks covered their heads and cried aloud:

"Tecumseh has got to Detroit!"

Courtesy of The Field Museum.

An Indian Brave

That was so. In December Tecumseh really had got to Detroit. But he had stamped his foot before time, and he had not made the earth to tremble. He had stamped in wrath not at the Creeks, but at his own people.

When he had left for the North he was ready to strike, at any moment, with five thousand warriors of North, South and West. When he arrived home, he found that his plans were shattered like a bubble; he had no Prophet, and the former Prophet had no town!

CHAPTER XIII

BRIGADIER GENERAL TECUMSEH (1812–1813)

THE RISE AND FALL OF A STAR

IN Vincennes, the white chief, Governor William Henry Harrison, had grown tired of the insults and defiance from the Prophet. He took nine hundred regulars and rangers, to visit the Prophet's Town, himself, and see what was what.

He camped within a mile of the sacred place, on a timber island of the marshy prairie seven miles northeast of the present city of Lafayette, Indiana. During the darkness and early daylight of November 7, this 1811, he was attacked by the Prophet's warriors. He roundly whipped them in the hot battle of Tippecanoe.

The Prophet had brewed a kettle of magic, by which (he proclaimed to his warriors) he had made one half of the American army dead, and the other half crazy. During the attack he sat upon a high piece of ground, and howled a song that should keep his warriors invisible and turn the bullets of the white men.

But something was wrong with the kettle, and something was wrong with the song; for the Americans fought hard when surprised, and none seemed to be dead; and of the one thousand Shawnees, Winnebagos, Chippewas, Kickapoos, forty were killed by the bullets and many more wounded.

Of the Americans, thirty-seven were killed and one hundred and fifty-two wounded. They pressed on to the town, and burned it in spite of the Great Spirit.

"You are a liar!" accused a Winnebago, of the Prophet. "You said that the white people were dead or crazy, when they were all in their senses and fought like demons!"

When Tecumseh arrived with his good news, the Indians were scattered. In his camp the "Prophet" was being hooted at by even the children. Tecumseh was so enraged with his brother for not having somehow kept the peace until the time for war was ripe, that he seized him by the hair of the head and shook him until his teeth rattled.

To Governor Harrison, Tecumseh announced that he was well-minded for the visit with the President.

"If you go, you must go alone, without any company of warriors," replied the governor.

"I am a great chief, and I will not go in such a shameful fashion," said Tecumseh. So he went to Canada instead.

Now the game was up. The Prophet had proved to be no prophet from the Great Spirit. The Indians felt cheated, and were not afraid to speak boldly.

Councils were held by twelve tribes, together. Band opposed band. The Delawares, the Miamis, the Kickapoos, most of the Wyandots, were for peace with the Americans, and for letting the British alone. So were the Potawatomis; they accused the Prophet of leading them falsely.

Captain Elliott, the traitor and British agent, threatened to have the Wyandots arrested for their talk.

The band of Canadian Wyandots touched the British war-hatchet; so did Tecumseh and the Prophet. The war between the white people had commenced.

Between-the-logs brought a message to the Canadian Wyandots, from Head Chief Crane, of all the Wyandots. They were to come back to their hunting-grounds.

Round-head of the hostile Wyandots spoke.

"Tell the American commander it is our wish that he should send more men against us. We want to fight in good earnest."

The British agent Captain Elliott spoke. "Tell my wife, your American father, that I want her to cook the provisions for me and my red children more faithfully than she has done. If she wishes to fight with me and my children, she must not burrow in the earth like a ground-hog. She must come out and fight fairly."

Between-the-logs answered valiantly, in behalf of Chief Crane the wise man:

"Brothers! I entreat you to listen to the good talk I have brought. If you doubt what I have said about the force of the Americans, you can send some of your people to examine it. The truth is, your British father tells you lies and deceives you.

"And now, father, I will bear your message to my American father. You compare the Americans to ground-hogs. I must confess that a ground-hog is a hard animal to fight. He has such sharp teeth, such a stubborn temper, and such unconquerable spirit, that he is truly a dangerous animal, especially when in his own hole. But, father, you will have your wish. Before many days you will see the ground-hog floating on yonder lake, paddling his canoe toward *your* hole; and then you may attack him to suit yourself!"

This council was held at Brownstown, beside Lake Erie, south of Detroit. Nobody cared anything about the Prophet—he was no warrior. But an invitation was sent to Tecumseh, in Canada, across the Detroit River.

"No," he answered. "I have taken sides with the king, my father, and my bones shall bleach upon this shore before I will recross that stream to join in any good words council."

The Wyandots privately told Between-the-logs that the most of them were being held prisoners by the British; but that they accepted the belt from Head Chief Crane, and would return to the Americans as soon as possible. And they did.

Tecumseh, however, had made up his mind. He was an honest enemy. There never was anything half-way about Tecumseh. His promised army of five thousand warriors had shrunk to less than one hundred; only thirty of these were with him, but he set about getting more.

The Prophet his brother was down at the Fort Wayne agency in Indiana. "Open Door" had partly explained away his failure in the battle of Tippecanoe. His wife, he said, had touched his medicine and spoiled its power, before the battle, and he had not known.

Tecumseh sent a rider with word for the Prophet to

remove all the Indian women and children to the Mississippi, and to bid the warriors strike Vincennes. He himself would join, if he lived, in the country of the Winnebagos—which was Wisconsin.

Delawares, Senecas, Chief Crane's Wyandots and the majority of the Shawnees themselves refused to rise against the Americans. The other Indians waited for stronger signs. But they did not need to wait long.

Tecumseh's star became fixed in the sky—he won the first battle of the war and won it for the British. Commanding seventy Indians and forty soldiers he whipped an American force at Brownstown.

In a second battle there, although the Americans were not captured it was Tecumseh again who held his position longest. As reward, he was promoted to brigadier general in the army of the king.

The Americans surrendered Michilimackinac. The American big chief, General Hull, retreated out of Canada.

Runners from Brigadier General Tecumseh spread the news. The Indians waited no longer. The Potawatomis rose, the Miamis rose, the Ottawas and Winnebagos and Kickapoos rose. Sioux of Minnesota and Sacs of Illinois hastened forward. General Tecumseh ruled.

To the Miamis and Winnebagos was assigned the task of taking Fort Harrison near present Terre Haute of Indiana; to the Potawatomis and Ottawas, aided by Tecumseh and some English, was assigned the task of taking Fort Wayne.

But the Shooting Star's old foe, William Henry Harrison, was out upon the war trail again. He lifted the siege of Fort Wayne. The attack upon Fort Harrison also failed. From now on he and Tecumseh fought their fight, to a finish.

This fall and winter of 1812 Tecumseh traveled once more. From Canada he journeyed south across a thousand miles of forest, prairie and waters clear to the Indians of Georgia, Tennessee and Alabama. He did not now come with word from any Prophet, to make the red people one nation and a better nation.

He came as a British officer, to bid the Southern Indians join the king's standard, and fight the Americans into the sea while he and the English did the same work in the north.

He distributed bundles of red sticks for them to count—one stick a day. With the last stick, they were to strike.

The Creeks and Cherokees were persuaded, and strike they did. A bloody trail they made, which many rains did not wash clean.

Back to the war in the spring of 1813, Tecumseh brought into camp six hundred fresh warriors from the Wabash. Now two thousand fighting men obeyed his orders alone. His command frequently out-numbered the British command. He was not a general in name only; he knew military strategy—"he was an excellent judge of position," admitted the British officers. He was consulted in the war councils.

The British thought much of him; the Americans were obliged to think much about him. But the star of Harrison also was marching on. The two stars came together, in the trail.

Tecumseh with his Indians, and the British General Proctor with his soldiers besieged the troublesome American general at Fort Meigs, near by the battle field of Fallen Timbers. So again the two rival chiefs were face to face.

An American detachment was surprised and captured. The Indians commenced to kill and torture. General Proctor looked on. Tecumseh heard and rushed to the scene. He had given his word to General Harrison, two years ago, and he was furious at the insult to his honor.

Defending the prisoners with knife and tomahawk, he sprang for the British general.

"Who dares permit such acts?"

"Sir, your Indians cannot be controlled."

"Begone!" roared Tecumseh. "You are unfit to command; go and put on petticoats."

After that he openly despised General Proctor.

He sent a note in to his American foeman:

"General Harrison: I have with me eight hundred braves. You have an equal number in your hiding place. Come out with them and give me battle. You talked like a brave when we met at Vincennes, and I respected you; but now you hide behind logs and in the earth, like a ground-hog. Give me answer. Tecumseh."

But General Harrison knew his business, and carried on to the successful end.

That end was not far distant. General Tecumseh and General Proctor together failed to take Fort Meigs.

General Proctor ordered a retreat. General Harrison followed on the trail. General Tecumseh hated to retreat. At every step he was abandoning Indian country.

The retreat northward to Canada continued. Tecumseh was fighting the battle of his people, not of the English; he wished to go no farther.

He proposed to his warriors that they leave for another region, and let the Americans and British fight their own war.

"They promised us plenty of soldiers, to help us. Instead, we are treated like the dogs of snipe-hunters; we are always sent ahead to rouse the game."

"You got us into this war by your promises," retorted the Sioux and the Chippewas. "You have no right to break us."

Any appeal to Tecumseh's honor was certain to win; he stuck. Then American ships under Commodore Oliver Hazard Perry fought British ships under Commodore Barclay, on Lake Erie, and gained a great victory.

From an island near shore the Tecumseh warriors peered eagerly, to the sound of the heavy guns.

"A few days since you were boasting that you commanded the waters," had said Tecumseh, to General Proctor. "Why do you not go out and meet the Americans? They are daring you to meet them; you must send out your fleet and fight them."

Now, after the battle, the British general asserted:

"My fleet has whipped the Americans, but the vessels are injured and have gone to Put-in Bay, to refit. They will be here in a few days."

Tecumseh was no fool. He had before caught the general in a lie. Here at Fort Malden opposite Detroit he challenged him in a hot speech.

Father! Listen to your children. You have them now all before you.

The war before this, our British father gave the hatchet to his red children, when our old chiefs were alive. They are now dead. In that war our father was thrown flat on his back by the Americans, and our father took them by the hand without our knowledge. We are afraid that our father will do so again.

Summer before last, when I came forward with my red brothers, and was ready to take up the hatchet in favor of our British father, we were told not to be in a hurry—that he had not yet decided to fight the Americans.

Listen! When war was declared, our father stood up and gave us the tomahawk, and told us that he was then ready to strike the Americans—that he wanted our aid—and that he would surely get us our lands back, which the Americans had taken from us.

Listen! When we were last at the Rapids [Fort Meigs] it is true that we gave you little assistance. It is hard to fight people who live like ground-hogs.

Father, listen! Our ships have gone out; we know they have fought; we have heard the great guns; but we know nothing of what happened. Our ships have gone one way, and we are much astonished to see our father tying up everything and preparing to run away the other, without letting his red children know what it is about.

You always told us to remain here, and take care of our lands; it made our hearts glad to hear that was your wish. You always told us you would never draw your foot off British ground. But now, father, we see you are drawing back, and we are sorry to see our father doing so without seeing the enemy. We must compare our father's action to a fat dog, that carries its tail upon its back, but when frightened, drops it between its legs and runs off.

Father, listen! The Americans have not yet defeated us by land; neither are we sure that they have done so by water.

We wish to remain here, and fight the enemy, should they appear. If they defeat us, we will then retreat with our father.

At the battle of the Rapids [Fallen Timbers] last war, the Americans certainly defeated us; and when we returned to our father's fort at that place, the gates were shut against us. Now instead of that, we see our British father making ready to march out of his garrison.

Father! You have got the arms and ammunition which our great father sent for his red children. If you have an idea of going away, give them to us, and you may go and welcome. Our lives are in the hands of the Great Spirit. We are resolved to defend our lands, and if it be his will, we wish to leave our bones upon them.

General Proctor writhed under this speech, but he had to swallow it. He might have done better by taking council with Tecumseh and attacking the Americans at the instant of their landing on the Canadian shore. The Indians would have fought very hard, even yet, for him. But he ordered the retreat again, he burned Fort Malden, and marched inland up the Thames River of southwestern Ontario.

Tecumseh went unwillingly. His Indians were down-hearted. General Harrison crossed from Detroit, and pursued. Tecumseh felt the sting.

"We are now going to follow the British," he said to Jim Blue-jacket, son of old Chief Blue-jacket, "and I believe we shall never return."

He rode with General Proctor in a buggy, and suggested several places that looked good for making a stand.

Once General Proctor agreed. It was indeed an excellent spot, where a large creek joined the Thames.

"We will here defeat General Harrison or leave our bones," he declared.

That was a talk right to Tecumseh's liking.

"When I look upon these two streams they remind me of the Wabash and the Tippecanoe of my own country," he said hopefully.

But after Tecumseh had gladly arranged his warriors, General Proctor decided to leave them as a rear guard and to march on with his soldiers. The Americans brought up ten cannon, and Tecumseh was wounded in the left arm, and the Indians had to retreat, also.

On the fourth of October, which was a few days afterward, at another good place Tecumseh said that he would go no farther into Canada. This was British soil, not Indian soil. Unless the Americans were whipped and the trail home was opened, how were his Indians ever to help the other Indians fight?

On the morning of the next day, October 5, 1813, he and General Proctor made their battle plans.

"Shall we fight the Americans, father?" asked Sagaunash, or Billy Caldwell. He was half English and half Potawatomi, and acted as Tecumseh's secretary, to translate Shawnee into French or English.

Tecumseh was gloomy. He had no faith in the British general.

"Yes, my son. Before the sun sets we shall be in the enemy's smoke. Go. You are wanted by Proctor. I will never see you again."

He posted his men. Then he addressed his chiefs.

"Brother warriors! We are about to enter a fight from which I shall not come out. My body will remain." He handed his sword and belt to a friend.

"When my son becomes a great warrior, and able to use a sword, give him this."

Then Tecumseh stripped off his red uniform coat, bearing the gold epaulets of a British brigadier general. He was to fight as an ordinary Indian, in buckskin hunting-shirt.

There were nine hundred British soldiers and one thousand Indians. They were well stationed. The left flank, British, was protected by the deep Thames River; the right flank, Indian, was protected by a soft swamp. The Americans of General Harrison came on. They numbered three thousand: one hundred and twenty United States regulars, the rest Kentucky volunteer infantry with one regiment of mounted riflemen under bold Colonel Richard M. Johnson of Kentucky.

Tecumseh would have given a great deal to whip this doughty General Harrison who had come out of his "hole" at last. There were old scores between them. But, as Between-the-logs had warned, "a ground-hog is a very difficult animal."

General William Henry Harrison of Virginia knew how to fight when in his "hole," or fort—and he knew how to fight when out of his "hole," and he knew Indian fighting as well as white fighting.

Here were three brigadier generals—Harrison, Tecumseh, and Proctor.

But the battle was soon over. General Proctor had made the mistake of posting his soldiers in open order. General Harrison's eye was quick to note the weakness. He let the Indians alone, for a few minutes, and sent the right of the mounted backwoodsmen in a charge against the British.

The horses broke clear through, wheeled—and the deed had been done. The British soldiers threw aside their guns, to surrender; General Proctor dashed furiously away in his buggy.

Headed by Colonel Johnson himself, the left companies of the mounted riflemen now charged upon Tecumseh. The infantry followed.

The Indians had small chance, but they fought well. Tecumseh waited until they could see the flints in the American rifles. Then he fired, raised the Shawnee war-whoop, they all fired, and rushed with their tomahawks to the encounter.

Yes, they fought well. Their close volley had killed many Americans. The horse leader, who was Colonel Johnson, had been wounded; the horse soldiers were fighting on foot, because the swamp had entangled the horses' legs. The American infantry barely stood fast, under the first shock.

Tecumseh's voice had been heard constantly, shouting for victory—as before him old Annawan the Wampanoag and Cornstalk the other Shawnee had shouted. Suddenly the voice had ceased.

A cry arose instead: "Tecumseh is dead! Tecumseh is dead!" And at that, as a Potawatomi afterward explained, "We all ran."

Some people said that Tecumseh had charged with the tomahawk upon the wounded Colonel Johnson, and that Colonel Johnson had shot him with a pistol, just in time. Some people denied this. Colonel Johnson himself said that he did not know—he did not pause to ask the Indian's name, and did not stay to examine him! There was quite an argument over the honor—but Tecumseh did not care. He was lying dead, in his simple buckskin, and for a time was not even recognized.

A gaudily dressed chief was mistaken for him, until friendly Indians with General Harrison stated that the great Tecumseh had a ridge on his thigh, from a broken bone.

By this he was found, after nightfall. He was brought to the camp-fires, where a circle of the Kentuckians gathered about him, to admire his fine figure and handsome face. He had been a worthy foeman.

So Tecumseh quit, at last. He never could have lived to see the white men pushed across the Ohio, and all the red men occupying the West as one nation. That was not written of his star, or any other star.

But he left a good reputation. He had been of high mind and clean heart, and he had fought in the open. The British adjutant-general at Montreal issued public orders lamenting his death and praising his bravery. The British throne sent his young son, Puck-e-sha-shin-wa, a sword, and settled a pension upon the family, in memory of the father.

The Prophet received a pension, too. He stayed in Canada until 1826, when he moved down among the Shawnees of Ohio again. He long out-lived his greater brother, and died in the Shawnee village in present Kansas, in 1837. He posed as a prophet to the very last.

As for General William Henry Harrison, who had broken them both—borne onward by his nickname "Old Tippecanoe" he became, in 1841, ninth President of the United States; and on his reputation of having "killed Tecumseh," Colonel Johnson already had been a vice-president.

CHAPTER XIV

THE RED STICKS AT HORSESHOE BEND (1813–1814)

AND THE WONDERFUL ESCAPE OF CHIEF MENEWA

AS fast as Tecumseh and the Open Door, or their messengers, traveled, they left in their trail other prophets. Soon it was a poor tribe indeed that did not have a medicine-man who spoke from the Great Spirit.

When Tecumseh first visited the Creeks, in Georgia and Alabama, they were not ready for war. They were friendly to the whites, and were growing rich in peace.

The Creeks belonged to the Musk-ho-ge-an family, and numbered twenty thousand people, in fifty towns. They had light complexions, and were good-looking. Their women were short, their men tall, straight, quick and proud.

Their English name, "Creeks," referred to the many streams in their country of Georgia and eastern Alabama. They were also called "Muskogee" and "Muscogee," by reason of their language—the Musk-ho-ge-an.

They were well civilized, and lived almost in white fashion. They kept negro slaves, the same as the white people, to till their fields, and wait upon them; they wore clothing of calico, cotton, and the like, in bright colors. Their houses were firmly built of reed and cane, with thatched roofs; their towns were orderly.

With the Chickasaws and the Choctaws, their neighbors in western Alabama and in Mississippi, they were at war, and had more than held their own.

White was their peace color, and red their war color. And when Tecumseh gave them the red sticks, on which to count the days, he did nothing new. The war parties of the Creeks already were known as Red Sticks.

This was their custom: that a portion of their towns should be White Towns, where peace ceremonies should be performed and no human blood should be shed; the other portion should be Red Towns, where war should be declared by erecting a red-painted pole, around which the warriors should gather. The war clans were Bearers of the Red, or, Red Sticks.

The first visit by Tecumseh, in 1811, carrying his Great Spirit talk of a union of all Indian nations, failed to make the Creeks erect their red poles. Even the earthquake, that Tecumseh was supposed to have brought about by the stamping of his foot, failed to do more than to frighten the Creeks.

But they caught the prophet fad. Their pretended prophets began to stir them up, and throw fear into them. In 1802 the United States had bought from the Creeks a large tract of Georgia; the white people were determined to move into it. Alarmed, the Creeks met in council, after Tecumseh's visit, and voted to sell no more of their lands without the consent of every tribe in the nation. Whoever privately signed to sell land, should die. All land was to be held in common, lest the white race over-run the red. That was a doctrine of the Shawnee Prophet himself, as taught to him by the Great Spirit.

When Tecumseh came down from Canada, in the winter of 1812, on his second visit, the Creeks were ripening for war. Their Red Sticks party was very strong. The many prophets, some of whom were half negro, had declared that the whites could be driven into the sea. The soil of the Creek nation was to be sacred soil.

Traders had been at work, promising aid, and supplying ammunition, in order to enlist the Creeks upon the British side.

So in the Red Towns the Red Sticks struck the painted poles; the peace party sat still in the White Towns, and was despised by the Reds as white in blood as well as in spirit.

The hope of the Creeks was to wipe the white man's settlements from the face of Mississippi, Georgia and Tennessee. Alabama, in the middle, would then be safe, also. But the Choctaws, the Chickasaws, the Cherokees, refused to join. The White Sticks themselves listened to the words of their old men, and of Head Chief William MacIntosh; they said that they had no feud with the United States.

Commencing with President Washington, the United States had treated the Creeks honestly; the Creek nation had grown rich on its own lands.

The Red Sticks went to war—and a savage war they waged; the more savage, because by this time, the spring of 1813, all the Creeks were not of pure blood.

They had lived so long in peace, in their towns, that their men and women had married not only among the white people but also among the black people; therefore their blood was getting to be a mixture of good and bad from three races.

Head Chief William MacIntosh was the peace chief. He was half Scotch and half Creek, and bore his father's family name. He joined the side of the United States.

The war chiefs were Lam-o-chat-tee, or Red Eagle, and Menewa. They, too, were half-breeds.

Chief Red Eagle was called William Weatherford, after his white trader father who had married a Creek girl. He lived in princely style, on a fine plantation, surrounded with slaves and luxury.

Menewa was second to Chief MacIntosh. His name meant "Great Warrior"; and by reason of his daring he had earned another name, Ho-thle-po-ya, or Crazy-war-hunter. He was born in 1765, and was now forty-eight years old. He and Chief MacIntosh were rivals for favor and position.

Menewa was the head war chief—he frequently crossed into Tennessee, to steal horses from the American settlers there. A murder was committed by Indians, near his home; Georgians burned one of his towns, as punishment. Chief MacIntosh was accused of having caused this murder, in order to enrage the white people against Menewa; and when MacIntosh stood out for peace, Menewa stood out for war.

He and Chief Weatherford led the Red Sticks upon the war trail; but greater in rank than either of them was Monahoe, the ruling prophet, of Menewa's own band. He was the head medicine-chief. He was the Sitting Bull of the Creeks, like the later Sitting Bull of the Sioux.

Out went the Red Sticks, encouraged by Monahoe and the other prophets. Already the white settlers had become alarmed at the quarrel between the MacIntosh bands and the Menewa bands. When two Indian parties fight, then the people near them suffer by raids. All Alabama, Mississippi and Georgia prepared for defense.

There were killings; but the first big blow with the Creek hatchet, to help the British and to drive the Americans into the sea, was struck in August against Fort Mimms, at the mouth of the Alabama River in southwestern Alabama above Mobile.

With all the cunning of the three bloods, the warriors waited until sand enough had drifted, day by day, to keep the gate of the fort from being quickly closed. Then, at noon of August 30, they rushed in. The commander of the fort had been warned, but he was as foolish as some of those officers in the Pontiac war. The garrison, of regulars, militia, and volunteers, fought furiously, in vain. More than three hundred and fifty—soldiers, and the families of settlers, both—were killed; only thirty persons escaped.

Now it was the days of King Philip, over again, and this time in Tennessee, Georgia, Alabama and Mississippi, instead of in Massachusetts, Rhode Island and Connecticut. At the news of Fort Mimms, the settlers fled for protection into towns and block-houses. If the

Choctaws, the Chickasaws and other Southern Indians joined in league with the Creeks, there easily would be fifteen thousand brave, fierce warriors in the field.

However, the Choctaws and Chickasaws enlisted with the United States; Chief MacIntosh's friendly Creeks did not falter; and speedily the fiery Andy Jackson was marching down from Tennessee, at the head of two thousand picked men, to crush out the men of Menewa and Weatherford.

Other columns, from Tennessee, Georgia, Alabama and Mississippi, also were on the trail. The Creeks fought to the death, but they made their stands in vain. The United States was on a war footing; it had the soldiers and the guns and the leaders; its columns of militia destroyed town after town—even the sacred Creek capital where warriors from eight towns together gathered to resist the invader. Yes, and even the town built by direction of the prophets and named Holy Ground and protected by magic.

By the close of 1813, this Jackson Chula Harjo—"Old Mad Jackson," as the Creeks dubbed him—had proved to be as tough as his later name, "Old Hickory." But Menewa and Weatherford were tough, too. They and their more than one thousand warriors still hung out.

In March they were led by their prophets to another and "holier" ground; Tohopeka, or Horseshoe Bend, on the Tallapoosa River in eastern Alabama.

The Creek town of Oakfuskee was located below. And here, in 1735, some eighty years before, there had been a fort of their English friends. It was good ground.

Chief Prophet Monahoe and two other prophets, by song and dance enchanted the ground inside the bend, and made it safe from the foot of any white man. Monahoe said that he had a message from Heaven that assured victory to the Creeks, in this spot. If the Old Mad Jackson came, he and all his soldiers should die, by wrath from a cloud. Hail as large as hominy mortars would flatten them out.

As was well known to the Creeks, Old Mad Jackson was having his troubles. The Great Spirit had sent troubles upon him—had caused his men to rebel, and his provisions to fail, until acorns were saved and eaten. The United States could not much longer fight the British and the Indians together. Let the Creeks not give up.

The Horseshoe was rightly named, for a sharp curve of the Tallapoosa River enclosed about one hundred acres of brushy, timbered bluffs and low-land, very thick to the foot. The entrance to the neck was only three hundred yards wide. On the three other sides the river flowed deep.

Menewa was the field commander of the Red Sticks, at this place. He showed a great head—he was half white and half red, but all Creek in education. Across the neck, at its narrowest point he had a barricade of logs erected, from river bank to river bank.

The barricade, of three to five logs piled eight feet high and filled with earth and rock, was pierced with a double row of port-holes: one row for the kneeling warriors, and one for the standing warriors. The barricade was built in zigzags, along a concave curve, so that attackers would be cut down by shots from two sides as well as from in front. By reason of the zigzags it could not be raked from either end.

All around the high ground back of the barricade, trees were laid, and brush arranged so that the warriors might, if driven, pass back from covert to covert, until they reached the huts of the women and children and old men, at the river, behind. Here a hundred canoes were drawn up, on the bank, in readiness.

But the Red Sticks of Chief Menewa had no thought of flight. They were one thousand. Their prophets had assured them over and over that the medicine of the Creek nation was strong, at last; that the Great Spirit was fighting for them; that the bullets of the Americans would have no effect, and that the Americans themselves would die before the barricade was reached. The cloud would come and help the Creeks, with hail—hail like hominy mortars!

On March 24 "Old Mad Jackson," just appointed by President Madison to be major-general in the United States army, set out against "Crazy-war-hunter" Menewa at Tohopeka.

The way was difficult, through dense timber, swamps and cane-brakes. Alabama, in these days, had been only thinly settled by white people.

He had three thousand men: a part of the 39th U. S. Infantry, a thousand Tennessee militia, six hundred friendly Creeks and Cherokees. He had two cannon: a six-pounder and a three-pounder.

His chief assistant was General John Coffee of Alabama, who had formerly been his business partner. Major Lemuel P. Montgomery, a Virginian of Tennessee, commanded one battalion of the regulars. He was six feet two inches, aged twenty-eight, and "the finest looking man in the army." Young Sam Houston, who became the hero of Texas independence, was a third lieutenant. Head Chief William MacIntosh, Menewa's rival, led the Creeks. Chief Richard Brown led the Cherokees.

In the evening of March 26 bold General Jackson viewed the Red Sticks' fort, and found it very strong. He was amazed by the skill with which it had been laid out. No trained military engineers could have done better.

But his Indian spies saw everything—they saw the line of canoes drawn up in the brush along the river bank behind, at the base of the bend; and General Jackson decided to do what the Red Sticks had not expected him to do.

Early in the next morning, March 27, he detached General Coffee, with seven hundred mounted men, the five hundred Cherokees and the one hundred Creeks, to make a circuit, cross the river below the bend, and come up on the opposite side, behind the Horseshoe. This would cut off escape in canoes.

With the remainder of his soldiers he advanced to the direct attack upon the breast-works. He planted his two cannon. At ten o'clock he opened hot fire with the cannon and with muskets.

Chief Menewa's Red Sticks were ready and defiant.

They answered with whoops and bullets. Their three prophets, horridly adorned with bird crests and feathers and jingling charms, danced and sang, to bring the cloud. The balls from the cannon only sank into the damp pine logs, and did no damage. The musket balls stopped short or hissed uselessly over.

For two hours Old Mad Jackson attacked, from a distance. He had not dared to charge—the prophets danced faster, they chanted higher—the Red Sticks had been little harmed—they whooped gaily—they had faith in their Holy Ground.

But suddenly there arose behind them a fresh hubbub of shots and shouts, and the screams of their women and children; the smoke of their burning huts welled above the tree-tops. General Coffee, with his mounted men, had completely surrounded the bend, on the opposite side of the river; his Indians had swum across, had seized the canoes, had ferried their comrades over by the hundred, the soldiers were following—and now the Menewa warriors were between two fires.

At the instant, here came Mad Jackson's troops to charge the barricade.

That was a terrible fight, at the breast-works. Chief Menewa encouraged his men. The test of the Holy Ground protected by the Great Spirit and the prophets had arrived.

The battle was to decide whether the Creek nation or the American nation was to rule in Georgia and Alabama, and the Red Sticks made mighty defense. While they raged, they looked for the cloud in the sky.

So close was the fighting, that musket muzzle met musket muzzle, in the port-holes; pistol shot replied to rifle shot; and bullets from the Red Sticks were melted upon the bayonets of the soldiers.

Major Lemuel Montgomery sprang upon the top of the barricade. Back he toppled, shot through the head. "I have lost the flower of my army," mourned General Jackson, tears in his eyes.

Lieutenant Houston received an arrow in his thigh; and later, two bullets in his shoulder.

Lieutenants Moulton and Somerville fell dead.

Again and again the white warriors were swept from the barricade by the Red Sticks' arrows, spears, tomahawks and balls. Others took their places, to ply bayonets and guns—stabbing, shooting. The uproar in the rear grew greater, and many of the Red Sticks behind the breast-works were being shot in the back; the voices of the prophets had weakened; no cloud appeared in the sky, bearing to the whites death from the Great Spirit.

Beset on all sides, Chief Menewa's men began to scurry back for their timber shelters, to fight their way to the river. But no one surrendered.

Having won the barricade, and cut off the escape of the Red Sticks in the opposite direction, the white general halted the further attack. He sent a flag of truce forward, toward the jungle.

"If you will stop fighting, your lives will be spared," he ordered the interpreter to call. "Or else first remove your women and children, so they will not be killed."

But the anxious eyes of warrior and prophet had seen the Spirit cloud rising, at last, into the sky; high pealed their whoops and chants again; a volley of bullets answered the truce flag.

The white soldiers re-opened with musket balls and grape-shot. The Cherokee and Creek scouts, fighting on their side, tried to ferret out the hiding places. Alas, the cloud proved to be only a little shower, and then vanished. The Great Spirit had deserted the prophets.

The American bullets thickened. With torches and blazing arrows the jungle was set afire. Roasted from their coverts, the Red Sticks had to flee for the river. When they fled, the rifles of the Tennessee sharpshooters caught them in mid-stride, or picked them off, in the river.

Chief Menewa was bleeding from a dozen wounds. He made desperate stand, but the cloud had gone, the fire was roaring, Head Prophet Monahoe was down dead, dead; the Great Spirit had smitten him through the mouth with a grape-ball, as if to rebuke him for lying. There was only one prophet left alive. Him, Menewa angrily killed with his own hand; then joined the flight.

He plunged into the river. His strength was almost spent, and he could not swim out of reach of the sharp-shooters' bullets. The water was four feet deep. So he tore loose a hollow joint of cane; and crouching under the water, with the end of the cane stuck above the surface, he held fast to a root and breathed through the cane.

Here he stayed, under water, for four hours until darkness had cloaked land and river, and the yelling and shooting had ceased. Then, soaked and chilled and stiffened, he cautiously straightened up. He waded through the cane-brake, hobbled all night through the forest, and got away.

But he had no army. Of his one thousand Red Sticks eight hundred were dead. Five hundred and fifty-seven bodies were found upon the Horseshoe battle-field. One hundred and fifty more had perished in the river. Only one warrior was unwounded. Three hundred women and children had been captured—and but three men. The Red Sticks of the Creek nation were wiped out.

Of the whites, twenty-six had been killed, one hundred and seven wounded. Of the Cherokee and Creek scouts, twenty-three had been killed, forty-seven wounded.

Chief William MacIntosh also had fought bravely, but he had not been harmed.

The Red Sticks now agreed to a treaty of peace with the United States; and Chief Menewa, scarred from head to foot, was the hero of his band. "One of the bravest chiefs that ever lived," is written after his name, by white historians. In due time he again opposed Chief MacIntosh, and won out.

For in 1825 MacIntosh was bribed by the white people to urge upon his nation the selling of the last of their lands in Georgia. He signed the papers, so did a few other chiefs; but the majority, thirty-six in number, refused.

Only some three hundred of the Creeks were parties to the signing away of the land of the whole nation. The three thousand other chiefs and warriors said that by Creek law, which Chief MacIntosh himself had proposed, the land could not be sold except through the consent of a grand council.

As the nation owned the land, and had built better towns, and was living well and peacefully, the council decided that Chief MacIntosh must be put to death—for he was a traitor and he knew the law.

Chief Menewa was asked to consent; he ruled, by reason of his wisdom and his scars. Finally he saw no other way than to order the deed done, for the Creek law was plain.

On the morning of May 1 he took a party of warriors to the Chief MacIntosh house, and surrounded it. There were some white Georgians inside. He directed them to leave, as he had come to kill only Chief MacIntosh, according to the law.

So the white men, and the women and children, left. When Chief MacIntosh bolted in flight, he was shot dead.

The Georgia people, who desired the Creek land, prepared for war, or to arrest Menewa and his party. But the President, learning the ins and outs of the trouble, and seeing that the land had not been sold by the Creek nation, ordered the sale held up. The Creeks stayed where they were, for some years.

Menewa went to war once more, in 1836, and helped the United States fight against the Seminoles of Florida. In return for this, he asked permission to remain and live in his own country of the Creeks. But he was removed, with the last of the nation, beyond the Mississippi to the Indian Territory.

There, an old man, he died.

CHAPTER XV

BLACK-HAWK THE SAC PATRIOT (1831–1838)

THE INDIAN WHO DID NOT UNDERSTAND

THE two small nations of the Sacs and the Foxes had lived as one family for a long time. They were of the Algonquian tongue. From the northern Great Lakes country they had moved over to the Mississippi River, and down to Illinois and Iowa. Their number was not more than six thousand. They were a shave-head Indian, of forest and stream, and accustomed to travel afoot or in canoes.

The Foxes built their bark-house villages on the west side of the Mississippi, in Iowa's "great nose." They called themselves Mus-qua-kees, or the Red Earth People. They said that they had been made from red clay. Their totem was a fox; and the French of the Great Lakes had dubbed them Foxes—had asserted that, like the fox, they were quarrelsome, tricky and thievish. As warriors they were much feared. They had lost heavily.

The Sacs built opposite, on the Illinois shore, from Rock River down. They called themselves Saukees, from their word O-sa-ki-wug, or Yellow Earth People. They were larger and better looking than the Foxes, and not so tricky; but their bravery was never doubted.

These two nations together drove out the other Indians in this new country. They whipped even the Sioux, who claimed the northern Iowa hunting grounds; they whipped the Omahas, Osages and Pawnees of the west, the Mascoutins to the south, and the Illinois tribes. They were here to stay.

While the men hunted and fished and went to war, the women raised great crops of beans, squashes, melons, potatoes and Indian corn, and gathered the wild rice of the lakes.

Among the Sac leaders was Ma-ka-tai-me-she-kia-kiak—Big-black-breast, or Black-hawk. Like Little Turtle of the Miamis he had not been born a chief; but he was of the Thunder clan, the head clan of the Sacs.

His father was Py-e-sa, a warrior of the rank of braves, and keeper of the tribal medicine-bag. His grandfather was Na-na-ma-kee, or Thunder—also a brave.

Black-hawk was born in 1767, in Sauk-e-nuk, the principal Sac village, where Rock Island, Illinois, now stands, north of the mouth of the Rock River.

He won the rank of brave when he was only fifteen years old. He did this by killing and scalping an Osage warrior, on the war-trail against these head-takers. After that he was allowed in the scalp-dances.

He went against the Osages a second time. With seven men he attacked one hundred, and escaped carrying another scalp. When he was eighteen, he and five comrades pierced the Osage country across the Missouri River, and got more scalps. When he was nineteen, he led two hundred other braves against the Osages, and killed five Osages with his own hand.

By his deeds he had become a chief.

In a battle with the Cherokees, below St. Louis, his father Pyesa fell. Young Black-hawk was awarded the medicine-bag—"the soul of the Sac nation."

In the early spring of 1804 a man of the Sac band then living on the Missouri, near St. Louis, to hunt and trade, killed a white man. He was arrested. The Sacs and Foxes held a council and chose four chiefs to go to St. Louis and buy their warrior's freedom with presents. This was the Indian way.

The chiefs selected were Pa-she-pa-ho, or Stabber, who was head chief of the Sacs; Quash-qua-me, or Jumping Fish; Ou-che-qua-ha, or Sun Fish; and Ha-she-quar-hi-qua, or Bear.

They went in the summer of 1804 and were gone a long time. When they returned, they were wearing new medals, and seemed ashamed. They camped outside of Saukenuk for several days, before they reported in council. The man they had been sent to get was not with them.

Finally, in the council they said that they had signed away a great tract of land, mostly on the west side of the Mississippi above St. Louis, in order to buy the warrior's life; they had been drunk when they signed—but that was all right. However, when they had signed, the warrior was let out, and as he started to come to them, the soldiers had shot him dead.

They still were not certain just what land they had signed away. That made the council and people angry. Black-hawk called the chiefs fools. They had no right to sell the land without the consent of the council.

After this, the "Missouri band" of the Sacs kept by themselves, in disgrace.

It was too late to do anything more about the treaty. The United States had it. An Indian gets only one chance—and Head Chief Pashepaho himself had put his mark on the paper. The United States has two chances: the first, on the ground; the second, when the paper is sent to Washington.

Later it was found that Pashepaho and the others had signed away all the Sac and Fox lands *east* of the Mississippi River! That was how the treaty might be made to read. The payment for many millions of acres was $2,234.54 down, in goods, and $1,000 a year, in other goods.

But there was one pleasing clause. As long as the United States held the land, the Sacs and Foxes might live and hunt there. Any white men who tried to come in were to be arrested and put off.

At any rate, although Black-hawk raged and said that the treaty was a false treaty, it stood. The United States officials who had signed it were men of honest names, and considered that they had acted fairly. But Black-hawk never admitted that.

The United States was to erect a trading post, up the Mississippi, for the convenience of the Sacs and Foxes. In 1808 soldiers appeared above the mouth of the Des Moines River, on the west side of the Mississippi, in southeastern Iowa, and began to build.

This turned out to be not a trading post but a fort, named Fort Belle Vue, and afterward, Fort Madison.

The Sacs and Foxes, and their allies, the Potawatomis and Winnebagos, planned to destroy it, and made attacks.

Black-hawk was sore at the Americans. He listened to the words of Tecumseh and the Prophet, accepted the presents of the British agents who came to see him, and with two hundred warriors marched to help the British in the War of 1812. The British traders had been more generous with the Indians than the American traders. Now the British father at the Lakes saluted him as "General Black-hawk."

Only Black-hawk's band went. All the other Sacs and Foxes paid attention to the talk of Keokuk, the Watchful Fox, who was the Sac peace chief.

Like the great Cornstalk, he said to the people that if they were bound to go to war, they should first put all the women and children "into the long sleep, for we enter upon a trail that has no turn."

He was called a coward by the Black-hawk band; but the other Sacs and Foxes stayed where they were.

"General" Black-hawk fought beside General Tecumseh. He asserted that he was in the big battle when Tecumseh was killed. When he found that the Indians had nothing to gain in the war, he came home. He had done wrong to go at all.

Then he learned that a young man whom he had adopted as a son had been murdered, while hunting, by bad whites. They had seized him, tied him, killed him and scalped him. The young man had not been to war, and Black-hawk could see no reason for the killing. So he set forth in revenge, and fought a battle with the United States Rangers.

He remained unfriendly. It all dated back to the year 1804, and the treaty signed by Pashepaho, by which the Sacs had lost their country.

They loved this country. They especially loved Rock Island, in the Mississippi—where today is located a Government arsenal.

It was indeed a beautiful island for them. It bore grapes and nuts, and they called it their garden. In a cave there, a kind spirit dwelt, who blessed the land of the Indians. The spirit had white wings, like a swan. But in 1816 the United States built Fort Armstrong right on top of the cave, and the good spirit flew away, never to come back. The guns of the fort frightened it.

Black-hawk himself had another favorite spot, upon a bluff overlooking the Mississippi River and his village of Saukenuk. Here he liked to sit. It is still known as Black-hawk's Watch Tower.

After Fort Armstrong was built, and the United States was again at peace with the other white nations, settlers commenced to edge into this Sac country of western Illinois. Although by another treaty, which Black-hawk himself had signed, the treaty of 1804 was re-pledged by the Sacs and Foxes, this all was United States land, and no settlers had any rights to it.

The Indians were unable to put the settlers off, and trouble arose. Once Black-hawk was taken, in the forest, by settlers who accused him of shooting their hogs; they tore his gun from him, and beat him with sticks.

This was such a disgrace to him, that he painted a

black mark on his face, and wore the mark for almost ten years. Only a scalp could wipe it off.

The white trespassers kept coming in. They respected nothing. They even built fences around the corn fields of the principal Sac village, at the mouth of Rock River; they ploughed up the grave-yard there; they took possession of Black-hawk's own lodge; and when in the spring of 1828 the Black-hawk people came back from their winter hunt, they found that forty of their lodges had been burned.

Up to this time none of the land had been put on the market by the United States. But the Indian agent was trying to persuade the Sacs to move across the Mississippi, into Iowa. That was for their own good. The white settlers were using whiskey and every other means, to get the upper hand.

Chief Keokuk agreed with the agent. He was not of the rank of Black-hawk and the Thunder clan, but he had fought the Sioux, and was of great courage and keen mind and silver tongue. He was an orator; Black-hawk was a warrior.

So the Sacs split. Keokuk—a stout, heavy-faced man—took his Sacs across into the country of the Foxes. Black-hawk's band said they would be shamed if they gave up their village and the graves of their fathers.

Black-hawk visited some white "chiefs" (judges) who were on Rock Island. He made complaint. He said that he wore a black mark on his face; but that if he tried to avenge the black mark, by striking a white man, then the white men would call it war. He said that the Sacs dared not resent having their lodges burned and their corn fields fenced and their women beaten, and the graves of their fathers ploughed up.

"Why do you not tell the President?"

"He is too far off. He cannot hear my voice."

"Why do you not write a letter to him?"

"It would be written by white men, who would say that we told lies. Our Great Father would rather believe a white man, than an Indian."

The two judges said that they were sorry for the Sacs, but could do nothing.

Now in 1829 the settlers were so anxious to keep the Sac lands at the mouth of the Rock River, that the Government put these on the market. This would dispose of Black-hawk's people, for they would have no village. Whether the other lands were sold, did not matter.

It was done while Black-hawk and his men and women were hunting. On their return to plant their crops, they learned that their village and grave-yard had been sold to the whites—the most of whom were already there.

So the white people had won out. They in turn asked protection, of the Government, from "General Black-hawk" and his band. The Government listened, and ten companies of regular troops were sent to Rock Island in a steamboat, to remove the Sacs, "dead or alive," to the west side of the Mississippi.

A council was held with Black-hawk at Fort Armstrong, on Rock Island. Black-hawk rose to speak. He said that the Sacs never had sold their lands; it had been a mistake, and that they were bound to keep their village.

"Who is this Black-hawk?" retorted General Edmund P. Gaines, the commander of the troops. "Is he a chief? By what right does he appear in council?"

Black-hawk wrapped his blanket around him and strode angrily out of the council room. But the next morning he made answer.

"My father, you asked yesterday, who is Black-hawk? Why does he sit among the chiefs? I will tell you who I am. I am a Sac, my father was a Sac—I am a warrior and so was my father. Ask these young men, who have followed me to battle, and they will tell you who Black-hawk is. Provoke our people to war, and you will learn who Black-hawk is."

More troops were called, until there were twenty-five hundred. But seeing so many soldiers marching, Black-hawk took all his people and camped across the Mississippi, under a white flag.

After this Black-hawk was required to sign another treaty, which made him say that he had tried to enlist the Potawatomis, Winnebagos and Kickapoos in a war against the United States. It did not mention the fact that for a dozen and more years the whites had been warring upon him by seizing his lands and ploughing his fields and burning his lodges.

The paper also set him down below the other chiefs, who had left their lands. It set him below Keokuk, and the Fox chiefs—and this hurt him deeply. All the Sacs and Foxes laughed at the idea of Keokuk, and his lowly clan, being placed above Black-hawk and the Thunder clan.

In these years of trouble, the Black-hawk band had killed or abused no white settlers. The so-called "war," on their part, had been a war of words and fences. Now they soon were to take up the hatchet.

They had been expelled over the river in this year 1831 too late for planting crops. The white settlers declined to share with them, from the fields at the village of Saukenuk. One night some of the Sacs crossed "to steal roasting-ears from their own fields," as they said. They were shot at by the settlers, and driven off. This made more bad feeling.

Black-hawk had sent his head warrior, Nah-po-pe, or Soup, up to Canada, to ask council from the British "father" there. He had been "General Black-hawk" in the British army, and thought that he deserved help. But the United States and Great Britain had been at peace many years. The British father told Nahpope that if the Sacs never had sold their land, of course they had a right to live upon it. That was all.

On the way back, Nahpope stopped to see Wa-bo-kie-shiek, or White Cloud, who was half Sac and half Winnebago, and a great medicine-man or prophet. He had a village at his Prophet's Town, thirty-five miles up the Rock River, in Illinois.

White Cloud pretended to rival the Open Door of the Shawnees. He fell into a trance, and cut several capers, and spoke a message from the Great Spirit. Let Black-hawk go to war. The Great Spirit would arouse the Winnebagos and the Potawatomis and the

British, and the Americans would be driven away! White Cloud said this out of his own heart, which was black toward the Americans.

He invited Black-hawk to visit him and the Winnebagos and the Potawatomis, raise a summer crop and talk with the Great Spirit.

Much rejoiced, Nahpope hastened to tell the news to his chief. When Keokuk heard it, he advised Black-hawk to stay at home. The prophet White Cloud was a mischief maker and a liar.

Black-hawk was inclined to listen, and to wait until he was more certain of the other nations who might join with him. But the young men of his band were hot. Unless he did something, Keokuk would appear to be stronger than he. His people looked to him to get back their village and their grave-yard. The black mark on his face had not been wiped off.

None of Keokuk's Sacs or the Foxes would help him. So in April of 1832 he took his men and their families and started up the river from Fort Madison, Iowa, for Rock River. The warriors were on horses, the women and children in canoes.

By the last treaty that he had signed, Black-hawk had promised not to cross to the east side of the Mississippi without the permission of the United States. Now he said that he was going up the Rock River, to the country of the Winnebagos, his friends, to visit among them and plant corn and beans.

On the way up the Rock River he was ordered back, by word from General Henry Atkinson, commander at Fort Armstrong.

Black-hawk replied that he had a right to travel peacefully, the same as white persons. He was going to the Winnebago country, for the summer.

The general sent another word, that if Black-hawk did not turn around, soldiers would make him turn around.

Black-hawk replied that he was at peace and would stay at peace unless the soldiers attacked him. He told his men not to fire first.

Pretty soon he met some Winnebagos and Potawatomis. They said that their nations never had sent him any message talking war. They wished no trouble with the United States. Wabokieshiek had lied.

So Black-hawk decided to give his guests a dog-feast, and then return home. He was an old man of sixty-five, and he was too weak to fight alone. He was getting tired.

He had made camp one hundred miles up the Rock River, near Kishwaukee, a few miles below present Rockford, Illinois. By this time, early in May, all Illinois was alarmed; the regulars and militia were on his trail. They gathered at Dixon, about forty miles down the river from his camp.

Major Isaac Stillman took two hundred and seventy-five mounted militia, to scout for Black-hawk. They arrived at Sycamore Creek, within eight miles of him, and did not see his camp. But Black-hawk knew that they were there.

He sent out three young men with a white flag, to bring the American chiefs to the camp, for a council; then they would all go down-river together. He sent out five young men to follow the three, and see what happened.

Only three of the five came back. The three with the white flag had been taken prisoners, and the soldiers had chased the others and shot two.

Black-hawk prepared for war. He had but forty men with him; the rest were out hunting. Presently here came all the white soldiers, galloping and yelling, to ride over him. They were foolish—they seemed to think that the Sacs would run.

But Black-hawk was old in war. He laid an ambush—his forty warriors waited, and fired a volley, and charged with the tomahawk and knife, and away scurried the soldiers like frightened deer.

They fled without stopping forty miles to Dixon's Ferry. They reported that they had been attacked by fifteen hundred savages. They left all their camp stuff. Fourteen soldiers had been killed—but no Indians, except those sent by Black-hawk to treat for peace.

"Stillman's Run," the battle was called.

Black-hawk sat down to smoke a pipe to the Great Spirit, and give thanks. Two of the flag-of-truce party came in. They had escaped. The third young man had been shot while in the soldiers' camp.

The Black-hawk band took the blankets and provisions left in the soldiers' camp, and proceeded to war in earnest. Of what use was a white flag? They sent away their families. Some Winnebagos, hearing of the great victory, enlisted.

Now Black-hawk was much feared. General Atkinson fortified his regulars and militia, at Dixon's Ferry. More volunteers were called for, by the governor of Illinois. The Secretary of War at Washington ordered one thousand additional regulars to the scene, and directed General Winfield Scott himself, the commander of the United States army in the East, to lead the campaign.

For a little war against a few Indians there were many famous names on the white man's roll. Among the regulars were General Scott, later the commander in the war with Mexico; Colonel Zachary Taylor, who had defended Fort Harrison from Tecumseh—and probably Black-hawk—in the war of 1812, and who was to be President; Lieutenant Jefferson Davis, who became president of the Confederate States; Lieutenant Albert Sydney Johnston, who became a Confederate general; Lieutenant Robert Anderson, who commanded Fort Sumter in 1861; and among the volunteers was Captain Abraham Lincoln.

Black-hawk had about five hundred braves, mainly Sacs and Foxes, with a few Winnebagos and Potawatomis; but when twenty-five hundred soldiers were chasing him through the settlements, he stood little show.

After several skirmishes, and one or two bad defeats, his people were eating horse-flesh and bark and roots. To save them, he planned to go down the Wisconsin River, in southwestern Wisconsin, and cross the Mississippi.

He put his women and children and the old men on rafts and in canoes. They started—but soldiers fired into them, from the banks, killed some and drove the rest into the forest. Many died there, from hunger.

Black-hawk and his warriors, and other women and children, had cut across by land. When they came to the mouth of the Bad Axe River, at the Mississippi above the Wisconsin, the armed steamboat *Warrior* met them. Sioux were upon the western bank.

Black-hawk decided to surrender. He again raised the white flag, and called out to the captain of the *Warrior* that he wished a boat sent to him, so that he might go aboard and talk peace.

Perhaps the Winnebago interpreter on the *Warrior* did not translate the words right. At any rate, the captain of the *Warrior* asserted that Black-hawk was only trying to decoy him into ambush. He waited fifteen minutes, to give the Indian women and children that much time to hide; then he opened on the white flag with canister and musketry. The first cannon shot "laid out three." In all, he killed twenty-three.

Black-hawk fought back, but he could not do very much against a steamboat in the river.

So he had been unable to surrender, or to cross the Mississippi. His people were frightened, and sick with hunger and wounds. The next morning, August 2, he was working hard to get them ready to cross, when General Atkinson's main army, of four hundred regulars and nine hundred militia, fell upon him at the mouth of the Bad Axe.

The Indian women plunged into the Mississippi, with their babes on their backs—some of them caught hold of horses' tails, to be towed faster; but the steamboat *Warrior* was waiting, sharp-shooters on shore espied them, and only a few escaped, into the hands of the Sioux.

In two hours Black-hawk lost two hundred people, men and women both; the white army lost twenty-seven in killed and wounded.

This finished Black-hawk. He got away, but spies were on his trail, and in a few weeks two Winnebago traitors captured him when he gave himself up at Fort Crawford, Prairie du Chien, Wisconsin.

He expected to die. He had turned his medicine-bag over to the Winnebago chief at the village of La Crosse, Wisconsin—and he never got it back.

He made a speech to the Indian agent, General Joseph Street, at Prairie du Chien. He said:

You have taken me prisoner with all my warriors. I am much grieved, for I expected to hold out much longer and give you more trouble before I surrendered. I tried hard to bring you into ambush, but your last general understands Indian fighting.

I fought hard, but your guns were well aimed. The bullets flew like bees in the air, and whizzed by our ears like wind through the trees in winter. My warriors fell around me; I saw my evil day at hand. The sun rose dim on us in the morning, and at night it sank in a dark cloud, and looked like a ball of fire.

That was the last sun that shone on Black-hawk. His heart is dead. He is now a prisoner to the white men; they will do with him as they wish. But he can stand torture and is not afraid of death. He is no coward. Black-hawk is an Indian.

He has done nothing for which an Indian ought to be ashamed. He has fought for his people, against the white men, who have come year after year to cheat him and take away his lands.

You know the cause of our making war. It is known to all white men. They ought to be ashamed of it. The white men despise the Indians and drive them from their homes.

An Indian who is as bad as the white men could not live in our nation; he would be put to death and be eaten up by the wolves. The white men are poor teachers; they shake us by the hand, to make us drunk, and fool us. We told them to let us alone, but they followed us.

Things were growing worse. There were no deer in the forests; the springs were drying up and our women and children had no food. The spirits of our fathers arose and spoke to us, to avenge our wrongs, or die.

Black-hawk is satisfied. He will go to the land of spirits, content. He has done his duty. His father will meet him there and praise him.

He is a true Indian and disdains to cry like a woman. He does not care for himself. He cares for his nation. They will suffer. His country-men will not be scalped; the white men poison the heart. In a few years the Indians will be like the white men, and nobody can trust them. They will need many officers to keep them in order.

Goodby, my nation. Black-hawk tried to save you. He drank the blood of some of the whites. He has been stopped. He can do no more.

After this, Black-hawk had little authority among the Sacs and Foxes. They respected him, but they looked only to Keokuk for orders and advice. Keokuk was made rich by the United States, as reward; he gave out the goods and monies; he ruled, for he had followed the peace trail.

The Black-hawk prisoners were put in charge of Lieutenant Jefferson Davis, at Fort Crawford. Then they were sent down by steamboat to Jefferson Barracks, at St. Louis.

There were Black-hawk, his two sons—Nah-se-us-kuk or Whirling Thunder, and Wa-saw-me-saw or Roaring Thunder; White Cloud, the false prophet; Nahpope, the head brave; Ioway, Pam-a-ho or Swimmer, No-kuk-qua or Bear's-fat, Pa-she-pa-ho or Little Stabber; and others.

They were forced to wear ball and chain.

"Had I taken the White Beaver [who was General Atkinson] prisoner, I would not have treated a brave war chief in this manner," complained Black-hawk.

Keokuk, the successful, was kind and tried to get the prisoners freed. But they were sent on to Washington, to see the President. President Andrew Jackson understood Indians, and Black-hawk was pleased with him.

"I am a man; you are another," he greeted, as he grasped President Jackson's hand.

"We did not expect to conquer the whites," he explained. "They had too many houses, too many men. I took up the hatchet to avenge the injuries to my people. Had I not done so, they would have said, 'Black-hawk is a woman. He is too old to be a chief. He is no Sac.' "

From the last of April until June 4 the Black-hawk party was kept in Fortress Monroe, Virginia. Then the Indians were started home. They were given a long tour, to show them the power of the United States.

They stopped at Baltimore, Philadelphia, New York, Albany, Buffalo and Detroit. The white people crowded to see the famous Black-hawk and to hear him speak. He received valuable presents. He was treated like a chief indeed, and his heart was touched.

When he arrived at Fort Armstrong again, on Rock Island, where he was to be freed, his heart had somewhat failed. The village of Saukenuk had long ago been leveled in ashes; he returned, a chief without a people.

Keokuk came, to attend this council, and to receive him back into the nation. Keokuk arrived riding grandly in two canoes lashed side by side; a canopy over him and his wives with him, and medals on his breast.

That was rather different from ball and chain, and old Black-hawk's head sank upon his chest. He felt as bitter as Logan the Mingo had felt.

Before he finally settled down in a lodge built near Iowaville on the lower Des Moines River, Iowa, he made other trips through the East. Keokuk went, also —but it was "General Black-hawk" for whom the people clamored.

He died on October 3, 1838, at his home. His last speech was made at a Fourth of July banquet, at Fort Madison, Iowa, where he was a guest of honor.

"Rock River was a beautiful country. I liked my towns, my corn-fields, and the home of my people. I fought for it. It is now yours; keep it as we did. It will bear you good crops.

"I once was a great warrior. I am now poor. Keokuk put me down, but do not blame him. I am old. I have looked upon the Mississippi since I was a child. I love the Great River. I look upon it now. I shake hands with you, and I hope you are my friends."

These were some of his words.

He was seventy-one when he died; a spare, wrinkled old man with sharp, fiery face and flashing eye. He picked out his grave—at a place about half a mile from his cabin, where, he said, he had led his Sacs in a great battle with the Iowas.

All his people, and the neighboring whites, mourned him. He was buried sitting up, clad in the uniform given him at Washington, by the Secretary of War. He wore three medals, from President Jackson, ex-President John Quincy Adams, and the City of Boston. Between his knees was placed a cane presented to him by Henry Clay, the statesman; at his right side was placed a sword presented to him by President Jackson.

All his best things were buried with him. They included tobacco, food and moccasins, to last him on a three days' journey to spirit land.

The grave was covered by a board roof. A United States flag, and a post with his name and age and deeds, were erected over him. A picket fence twelve feet high was built around the grave.

He left an old wife—the only wife that he had ever taken. He thought a great deal of her. He rarely drank whiskey, he fought it among his people; he was opposed to torture; he had treated prisoners kindly; he had waged war in defense, as he believed, of his own country; and altogether he had been a good man in his Indian way.

His bones were dug up by a white doctor, and strung on a wire to decorate an office in Illinois. Black-hawk's sons did not like this, and had the bones brought back. They were stored in the historical collection at Burlington, where in 1855 a fire burned them.

Black-hawk probably did not care what became of his old bones. He was done with them. The white race had over-flowed the land that he loved, and the bones of his fathers, and he had ceased fighting.

CHAPTER XVI

THE BIRD-WOMAN GUIDE (1805–1806)

SACAGAWEA HELPS THE WHITE MEN

THIS is the story of one slight little Indian woman, aged sixteen, who opened the trail across the continent, for the march of the United States flag.

When in March, 1804, the United States took over that French Province of Louisiana which extended from the upper Mississippi River west to the Rocky Mountains, a multitude of Indians changed white fathers.

These Western Indians were much different from the Eastern Indians. They were long-hair Indians, and horse Indians, accustomed to the rough buffalo chase, and a wide range over vast treeless spaces.

To learn about them and their country, in May, 1804, there started up the Missouri River, by boats from St. Louis, the famed Government exploring party commanded by Captain Meriwether Lewis and Captain William Clark.

It was an army expedition: twenty-three enlisted men, a hunter, a squad of boatmen, Captain Clark's black servant York, and a squad of other soldiers for an escort part of the way. In all, forty-three, under the two captains.

Their orders were, to ascend the Missouri River to

its head; and, if possible, to cross the mountains and travel westward still, to the Columbia River and its mouth at the Pacific Ocean of the Oregon country.

No white man knew what lay before them, for no white man ever had made the trip. The trail was a trail in the dark.

This fall they had gone safely as far as the hewn-timber towns of the Mandan Indians, in central North Dakota; here they wintered, and met the little Bird-woman.

Her Indian name was Sa-ca-ga-we-a, from two Minnetaree words meaning "bird" and "woman." But she was not a Minnetaree, who were a division of the Sioux nation, living in North Dakota near the Mandans. She was a Sho-sho-ni, or Snake, woman, from the distant Rocky Mountains, and had been captured by the Minnetarees. Between the Minnetarees of the plains and the Snakes of the mountains there was always war.

Now at only sixteen years of age she was the wife of Toussaint Chaboneau, a leather-faced, leather-clad French-Canadian trader living with the Mandans. He had bought her from the Minnetarees—and how much he paid in trade is not stated, but she was the daughter of a chief and rated a good squaw. Toussaint had another wife; he needed a younger one. Therefore he bought Sacagawea, to mend his moccasins and greet him with a smile for his heart and warm water for his tired feet. His old wife had grown rather cross and grunty.

Chaboneau was engaged as interpreter, this winter,

and moved over to the white camp. Sacagawea proved to be such a cheerful, willing little woman that the captains and the men made much of her. And when, in February, a tiny boy arrived to her and Toussaint, there was much delight.

A baby in the camp helped to break the long dull spell of forty-below-zero weather, when two suns shone feebly through the ice-crystaled air.

A thousand miles it was, yet, to the Rocky or Shining Mountains, by the river trail. In the Mandan towns, and in the American camp, Sacagawea was the only person who ever had been as far as those mountains. They were the home of her people, but nearly three years had passed since she had been taken captive by the Minnetarees.

Could she still speak the Snake tongue? Certainly! Did she remember the trail to the country of the Snakes? Yes! Was there a way across the mountains? Yes! Beyond some great falls in the Missouri there was a gate, by which the Shoshonis came out of the mountains to hunt the buffalo on the plains. It was there that she had been captured by the Minnetarees. Would the Snakes be friendly to the white men? Yes, unless they were frightened by the white men. Would she like to go back to her own people? Yes! Yes!

That was great luck for Sacagawea, but it was greater luck for the two captains. In the spring they broke camp, and taking Chaboneau as interpreter in case that the hostile Minnetarees were met, and little Sacagawea to spy out the land of the Snakes, and littlest Toussaint, the baby, as a peace sign to all tribes, with a picked party of thirty-one the two captains started on, up the swollen Missouri.

They made no mistake, in the Bird-woman. Of course she was used to roughing it; that was the life of an Indian woman—to do the hard work for the men, in camp and on the trail. But Sacagawea early showed great good sense.

Her husband Chaboneau almost capsized their canoe, by his clumsiness. She neither shrieked nor jumped; but calmly reaching out from it, with her baby tightly held, she gathered in the floating articles. She saved stuff of much value, and the captains praised her.

"She's a better man than her husband," asserted the admiring soldiers.

After hard travel, fighting the swift current, the strong winds, storms of rain and sleet, and monster grizzly bears, the expedition arrived at the Great Falls, as the Bird-woman had promised.

She had ridden and waded and trudged, like the rest. She had carried her baby on her back, and had built the fires for her husband, and cooked his meals, and kept right along with the men, and had not complained nor lagged.

At the Great Falls she was not so certain of the best route. This was a strange country to her, although she had known that the Falls were here. The Shining Mountains were in sight; the land of the Shoshonis lay yonder, to the southwest. All right.

The captains chose what seemed to be the best route by water, and headed on, to the southwest. Sacagawea gazed anxiously, right, left, and before. Her heart was troubled. She not only much desired to find her people, for herself, but she desired to help the great captains. "The fate of the whole party" depended upon her—and she was just a slight little Indian woman!

The Snakes did not come down, by this way. It was too far north; it was the haunts of their enemies the Blackfeet and the Minnetarees, of whom they were deathly afraid. They were a timid mountain folk, poorly armed to fight the Sioux, who had obtained guns from traders down the Missouri.

After a time the river narrowed still more, and between rough banks poured out from a canyon of high cliffs, black at their base and creamy yellow above.

"The Gate of the Mountains, ain't it?" passed the hopeful word. Sacagawea agreed. She had heard of this very "gate," where the river burst into the first plains.

"When we come to the place where the river splits into three parts, that is Shoshoni country—my people will be there."

On forged the boats, poled and hauled and rowed, while the men's soggy moccasins rotted into pieces, and the mosquitoes bit fiercely. The two captains explored by land. Hunting was forbidden, lest the reports of the guns alarm the Snakes.

Abandoned Indian camp-sites were found, but the big-horn sheep peered curiously down from the tops of the cliffs along the river, and that was not a good sign. The game was too tame.

Captain Clark the Red Head took the advance, by land, to look for the Indians. Captain Lewis, the young Long Knife Chief, commanded the boats. Small United States flags were erected in the bows of each, as a peace signal.

The boats reached an open place, where the river did indeed split into several branches.

"The Three Forks," nodded Sacagawea, brightly. "These are the Three Forks. We are on the right trail to the land of my people. Now I know."

The party proceeded at top speed. The southwest fork seemed to be the best, for boating. The stream shallowed. At the next camp Sacagawea was more excited.

"She say here in dis spot is where de Snake camp was surprise' by de Minnetaree, five years ago, an' chase' into de timber," announced Drouillard the hunter. "De Minnetaree keel four warrior an' capture four boy an' all de women. She was capture' here, herself."

Hurrah! the trail was getting warm. The canoes had to be hauled by tow-lines, with Sacagawea proudly riding in one of them and helping to fend off with a pole. She had not been here since she was a girl of eleven or twelve, but she caught more landmarks.

"Dat is w'at ze Snake call ze Beaver's Head," proclaimed Chaboneau, whose feet had given out. "Ze Snake spen' deir summer 'cross ze mountains jes' ze odder side. She t'ink we sure to meet some on dis side, to hunt ze boof'lo. Mebbe furder up one leetle way."

Captain Lewis took three men and struck out, to find an Indian trail and follow it into the mountains.

"I'll not come back until I've met with the Snakes," he asserted.

He was gone a long time. The shallow river, full of rapids and shoals, curved and forked and steadily shrank. But although Sacagawea eagerly peered, and murmured to herself, no Indians appeared.

The water was icy cold, from the snow range. This was middle August, in extreme southwestern Montana (a high country). The nights were cold, too. Game grew scarce. Three thousand miles had been logged off, from St. Louis. Unless the company could get guides and horses from the Snakes, and travel rapidly, they would be stuck, for the winter—likely enough starve; at any rate be forced to quit.

By August 16 Captain Lewis had not returned. Captain Clark set out afoot, with Sacagawea and Chaboneau, to walk across country. The Snakes simply must be found.

The toiling boats rounded a great bend, and a shout arose.

"There's Clark! He's sighted Injuns, hasn't he?"

"So has Sacagawea! Sure she has! See?"

"Injuns on horseback, boys! Hooray!"

For Captain Clark, yonder up the curve, was holding high his hand, palm front, in the peace sign. Sacagawea had run ahead, little Toussaint bobbing in the net on her back; she danced as she ran; she ran back again to him, sucking her fingers.

"Dat mean she see her own peoples!" panted Cruzatte the chief boatman, who was a trapper and trader, too, and knew Indians. "Dere dey come, on de hoss. Hooray!"

"Hooray!"

What a relief! The Indians were prancing and singing. They made the captain mount one of the horses, and all hustled on, for an Indian camp.

By the time that the hurrying canoes arrived, Sacagawea and another woman had rushed into each other's arms. Presently they and the captain and Chaboneau had entered a large lodge, built of willow branches. The Captain Lewis squad was here, too. The men had come down out of the mountains, by a pass, with the Snakes. The Snakes had been afraid of them—the first white men ever seen by the band. Old Drouillard the hunter had argued with them in the sign language and with a few Shoshoni words that he knew.

It had looked like war—it had looked like peace—and it had looked like war, and death, again. Finally, before he could persuade them, the captain had delivered over his guns, and had promised them to be their prisoner if they did not find, down below, one of their own women acting as the white men's guide.

But now all was well. The token of Sacagawea saved the day. The other woman, whom she hugged, had been captured by the Minnetarees, at the same time with herself, and had escaped.

And the chief of the band was Sacagawea's brother. He had mourned her as dead, but now he and she wept together under a blanket. Truly, he had reason to be grateful to these white strangers who had treated her so well.

Much relieved by this good fortune at last, the captains bought horses and hired guides. The Snakes were very friendly; even engaged not to disturb the canoes, which were sunk with rocks in the river to await the return trip.

There was little delay. The mountains should be crossed at once, before winter closed the trails. To the surprise and delight of all the company, Sacagawea announced that she was going with them, to see the Great Salt Water. Somehow, she preferred the white men to her own people. She had been weeping constantly. Most of her relatives and old friends had died or had been killed, during her absence. Her new friends she loved. They were a wonderful set, these white men—and the Red Head, Captain Clark, was the finest of all.

Six horses had been bought. Five were packed with the supplies; Sacagawea and little Toussaint were mounted upon the sixth, and the whole company, escorted by the Snakes, marched over the pass to Chief Ca-me-ah-wait's principal camp.

From there, with twenty-seven horses and one mule, with the happy Bird-woman and the beady-eyed Toussaint, the two captains and their men took the trail for the Great Salt Water, one thousand miles toward the setting sun. Ah, but a tough trail that proved, across the Bitter Root Mountains; all up and down, with scarcely a level spot to sleep on; with the snow to the horses' bellies and the men's thighs; with the game failing, until even a horse's head was treasured as a tidbit.

And the Bird-woman, riding in the exhausted file, never complained, but kept her eyes fixed to the low country and the big river and the Great Salt Water.

Once, in the midst of starvation, from her dress she fished out a small piece of bread that she had carried clear from the Mandan towns. She gave it to Captain Clark, that he might eat it. A brave and faithful heart had Sacagawea.

Struggling down out of the mountains, at the end of September, they changed to canoes. The Pierced Noses, or Nez Percés Indians, were friendly; and now, on to the Columbia and thence on to the sea, Sacagawea was the sure charm. For when the tribes saw the strange white warriors, they said, "This cannot be a war party. They have a squaw and a papoose. We will meet with them."

That winter was spent a few miles back from the Pacific, near the mouth of the Columbia River in present Washington.

Only once did the Bird-woman complain. The ocean was out of sight from the camp. Chaboneau, her husband, seemed to think that she was made for only work, work, work, cooking and mending and tending baby.

"You stay by ze lodge fire. Dat is place for womans," he rebuked. Whereupon Sacagawea took the bit in her teeth (a very unusual thing for a squaw to do) and went straight to Captain Clark, her friend.

"What is the matter, Sacagawea?"

She had been crying again.

"I come a long way, capitin. I carry my baby, I cold, hungry, wet, seeck, I come an' I no care. I show you trail; I say 'Snake peoples here,' an' you find Snakes. You get hosses, food, guide. When Indians see me an' my Toussaint, dey say 'Dis no war party,' an' dey kind to you. When you get hungry for bread, I gif you one leetle piece dat I carry all de way from Mandan town. I try to be good woman. I work hard, same as mens. Now I been here all dis time, near de salt water dat I trabble many days to see—an' I not see it yet. Dere is a beeg fish, too. Odders go see—I stay. Nobody ask Sacagawea. My man he say 'You tend baby!' I—I feel bad, capitin." And she hid her face in her blanket.

"By gracious, go you shall, Sacagawea, and see the salt water and the big fish," declared Captain Clark. "Chaboneau can stay home and tend baby!"

However, the Bird-woman took little Toussaint, of course; and they two viewed in wonderment the rolling, surging, thundering ocean; and the immense whale, one hundred and five feet long, that had been cast ashore. It is safe to assert that to the end of her days Sacagawea never forgot these awesome sights.

In the spring of 1806 the homeward journey was begun. On the Missouri side of the mountains the Bird-woman was detailed to help Captain Clark find a separate trail, to the Yellowstone River.

And this she did, in splendid fashion; for when the party knew not which way was the best way, out of the surrounding hills, to the plains, she picked the landmarks; and though she had not been here in many years, she showed the gap that led over and down and brought them straight to the sunken canoes.

On August 14 the whole company was at the Mandan towns once more. After her absence of a year and a half, and her journey of six thousand miles, bearing little Toussaint (another great traveler) Sacagawea might gaily hustle ashore, to entertain the other women with her bursting budget of stories.

The captains offered to take Chaboneau and Sacagawea and Toussaint on down to St. Louis. The Bird-woman would gladly have gone. She wanted to learn more of the white people's ways. She wanted to be white, herself.

But Chaboneau respectfully declined. He said that it would be a strange country, and that he could not make a living there; later, he might send his boy, to be educated by the captains. That was all.

So he was paid wages amounting to five hundred dollars and thirty-three cents. Sacagawea was paid nothing. The captains left her to her Indian life, and she followed them only with her heart.

Nevertheless, she did see her great Red Head Chief again. Captain Clark was appointed by the President as Indian agent with headquarters in St. Louis. He was a generous, whole-souled man, was this russet-haired William Clark, and known to all the Indians of the plains as their stanch friend.

So it is probable that he did not forget Sacagawea, his loyal Bird-woman. In 1810 she, the boy Toussaint, and Chaboneau, visited in St. Louis. In 1811 they were on their way up-river, for the Indian country.

Life among the white people had proved too much for the gentle Sacagawea. She had tried hard to live their way, but their way did not agree with her. She had sickened, and she longed for the lodges of the Shoshonis. Chaboneau, too, had become weary of a civilized life.

Sacagawea at last returned to her "home folks" the Snakes. No doubt Chaboneau went with her. But there is record that he was United States interpreter, in 1837, on the upper Missouri; and that he died of small-pox among the Mandans, soon afterward.

The Bird-woman out-lived him. She and her boy removed with the Snakes to the Wind River reservation, Wyoming; and there, near Fort Washakie, the agency, she died on April 9, 1884, aged ninety-six years, and maybe more.

A brass tablet marks her grave. A mountain peak in Montana has been named Sacagawea Peak. A bronze statue of her has been erected in the City Park of Portland, Oregon. Another statue has been erected in the state capitol at Bismarck, North Dakota.

So, although all the wages went to her husband, she knows that the white people of the great United States remember the loving services of the brave little Bird-woman, who without the promise of pay, helped carry the Flag to the Pacific.

CHAPTER XVII

THE LANCE OF MAHTOTOHPA (1822–1837)

HERO TALES BY FOUR BEARS THE MANDAN

WHILE the United States was getting acquainted with the Western Indians, there lived among the Mandans in the north a most noted hero—the chief Mah-to-toh-pa, or Four Bears.

Young Captain Lewis the Long Knife Chief, and stout Captain Clark the Red Head, who with their exploring party wintered among the Mandans in 1804–1805, and enlisted the Snake Bird-woman as guide, were the first white men to write a clear account of the curious Mandans; but they did not tell the half.

For a curious people indeed were these Mandans, dwelling in two villages on the Missouri River above present Washburn in central North Dakota.

They were polite, hospitable, and brave. Their towns were defended by ditches and loose timber palisades, not tight like those of the Iroquois and Hurons. Their houses were circular; of an earthern floor sunk two feet, and heavy six-foot logs set on end inside the edge of it, with a roof of timbers, woven willow, and thick mud-plaster; with a sunken fire-place under a hole in the center of the roof, and with bunks, screened by elk-hides or buffalo-robes, along the walls.

These houses were large enough to shelter twenty to

forty persons; the roofs were favorite loafing spots, for men, women, and dogs.

The Mandans formed a happy, talkative people, of strange appearance, but exceedingly clean, fond of bathing, either in the river or in wicker tubs. Their hair was heavy, sometimes reached to the ground, and was black, brown, and frequently gray or pure white even on the young. Their eyes were likely to be hazel, blue or gray, instead of black; their skin almost white. They made glassy clay vases and bowls, and remarkable blue glass beads. In fact, they seemed to have white manners, white arts, and white blood. Rumor asserted that they were partly Welsh, descended from the lost colony of the Welsh prince, Madoc.

Now this Madoc, a prince of the early Welsh people, set sail about the year 1180, with ten ships, to found a colony in a new Western continent that he claimed to have discovered.

He never was heard from. He and his ten shiploads vanished. But if he reached North America, and traveled inland, to be swallowed up amidst the red blood, the strange Mandans may have been the proof of his arrival.

Their round boats, of bowl-like wicker-work covered with hide, and their way of dipping the paddle from the front instead of from the rear, were exactly the Welsh method of canoe travel.

In the days of Mah-to-toh-pa the Mandans numbered two thousand, in two towns allied with the towns of the Minnetarees. They were beset by the tough, winter-traveling Assiniboins to the north, and by the treacherous Arikarees and the bold Sioux to the south. Therefore when in 1833 the wandering artist George Catlin of Pennsylvania, who spent eight years painting Indians in their homes all the way from Florida to the Rocky Mountains, made a long stay among the Mandans, they rejoiced him by their brave tales as well as with their curious habits.

According to all the reports, the "bravest of the braves" in the Mandan towns was Mahtotohpa; second chief by rank, but first of all by deeds. "Free, generous, elegant, and gentlemanly in his deportment—handsome, brave and valiant," says Artist Catlin. Such words speak well for Four Bears, but not a bit too well.

Before he arrived at the Artist Catlin lodge to have his portrait painted, the warning ran ahead of him: "Mahtotohpa is coming in full dress!" He was escorted by a great throng of admiring women and children. Now it was twelve o'clock noon, and he had been since early morning getting ready, so as to appear as befitted a noble chief.

His dress was complete: shirt, leggins, moccasins, head-dress, necklace, belt, robe, medicine-bag, tobacco sack, pipe, quiver, bow, knife, lance, shield, tomahawk and war-club. And as he proudly stood erect, waiting, he made a splendid sight.

His shirt was mountain-sheep skins, one before, one behind, sewed together at their edges. They were embroidered with porcupine quills brightly dyed, and fringed with the black scalp-locks of the enemies whom he had slain in combat, and tasseled with ermine tails.

They were pictured with his deeds, painted in sign language.

The leggins were of finely dressed deer-skin, worked with the porcupine quills, fringed with the scalp-locks, and fitting tightly from moccasins to thighs.

The moccasins were of buck-skin, armored with the dyed quills.

The head-dress was a crest of two polished buffalo horns set in a thick mat of ermine, from which fell clear to his heels a ridgy tail of countless eagle plumes also set in the ermine fur.

The necklace was of fifty grizzly-bear claws, strung from otter skin.

The belt was of tanned buck-skin, supporting tomahawk and broad-bladed scalping knife with elk-horn haft.

The robe slung from his shoulders like a Roman toga was the softened hide of a young buffalo bull worn fur side in; and on the white skin side all the battles of his life had been painted.

The medicine-bag was a beaver skin, ornamented with hawk-bills and ermine. He held it in his right hand.

His tobacco sack was of otter skin decorated with porcupine quills. In it were dried red-willow bark, flint and steel, and tinder.

His pipe was of curiously carved red pipe-stone from the peace quarries in present Minnesota. The stem was ash, three feet long, wound with porcupine quills to form pictures of men and animals; decorated with wood-peckers' skins and heads, and the hair of the white buffalo's tail. It was half painted red, and notched for the years of his life.

His quiver was of panther skin and filled with arrows, flint pointed and steel pointed, and some bloody.

His bow was of strips of elk-horn polished white, cemented with glue of buffalo hoof, and backed with deer sinews to give it spring. Three months had been required to make it. There was none better.

His lance had a deadly two-edge steel blade, stained with the dried blood of Sioux and Arikaree and Cheyenne and Assiniboin. The six-foot ashen shaft was strung with eagle feathers.

His shield was the hide from a buffalo's neck, hardened with hoof glue. Its center was a pole-cat skin; its edges were fringed with eagle feathers and antelope hoofs that rattled.

His battle-axe was of hammered iron blade and skull-pecker, with ash handle four feet long and deer-sinew grip. Eagle feathers and fur tufts decorated it.

His war-club was a round stone wrapped in raw-hide at the end of a cow-tail, like a policeman's billy.

After his portrait was painted, Mahtotohpa spread out his wonderful robe, and told the stories of the twelve battles and the fourteen scalps pictured on it by his own hand; and these stories included that of his Arikaree lance, and Cheyenne knife.

The lance story came about in this way. In the shaft of the lance, near the blade, there had been set an antelope prong; and when Mahtotohpa posed for his portrait, with the butt of the lance proudly planted on the ground, he carefully balanced an eagle feather across this prong.

"Do not omit to paint that feather exactly as it is," he said, "and the spot of blood upon it. It is great medicine, and belongs to the Great Spirit, not to me. I pulled it from the wound of an enemy."

"Why do you not tie it to the lance, then?"

"Hush!" rebuked Mahtotohpa. "If the Great Spirit had wished it to be tied on, it would never have come off."

Whereupon, presently, he told the story of the mighty lance. This had been the lance of a famous Arikaree warrior, Won-ga-tap. Some years back, maybe seven or eight, the Mandans and the Arikarees had met on horses near the Mandan towns, and had fought. The Mandans chased the Arikarees, but after the chase the brother of Mahtotohpa did not come in.

Several days passed; and when Mahtotohpa himself found his brother, it was only the body, scalped and cut and pierced with an arrow, and fastened through the heart to the prairie by the lance of Won-ga-tap.

Many in the village recognized that as the lance of Won-ga-tap. Mahtotohpa did not clean it of its blood, but held it aloft before all the village and swore that he would clean it only with the blood of Wongatap the Arikaree.

He sent a challenge to the Arikarees; and for four years he waited, keeping the lance and hoping to use it as he had promised. Finally his heart had grown so sore that he was bursting; and again holding the lance up before the village, he made a speech.

"Mahtotohpa is going. Let nobody speak his name, or ask where he is, or try to seek him. He will return with fresh blood on this lance, or he will not return at all."

He set out alone, on foot, like Piskaret, the Adirondack, had set out in his great adventure against the Iroquois. By night journeys he traveled two hundred miles, living on the parched corn in his pouch, until he was seven days hungry when at last he came to the Arikaree town where the lodge of Wongatap was located.

He knew the village well, for there had been brief periods when the Mandans and the Arikarees were at peace; besides, it was a warrior's business to know an enemy's lodges.

The Arikaree towns were much the same as the Mandan towns. Now Mahtotohpa lay outside and watched, until at dusk he might slip through between the pickets, and seek the lodge of Wongatap. He was enveloped in a buffalo robe, covering his head, so that he would be taken for an Arikaree.

He peeped through a crack in the Wongatap lodge and saw that his enemy was getting ready for bed. There he was, Wongatap himself, sitting with his wife in the fire-light, and smoking his last pipe. Pretty soon, as the fire flickered out, he rapped the ashes from his pipe, his wife raked the coals of the fire together, until morning; and now they two crawled into their bunk.

Hotly grasping his lance, and surrounded by the enemy, Mahtotohpa delayed a little space; then he arose and boldly stalked into the lodge and sat by the fire.

Over the coals was hanging a pot of cooked meat; beside the fire were the pipe and the pouch of red-willow smoking tobacco, just as left by Wongatap.

Amidst the dusk Mahtotohpa ate well of the cooked meat; and filling the pipe, smoked calmly, half lying down, on one elbow.

"Who is that man, who enters our lodge and eats of our food and smokes of our tobacco?" he heard Wongatap's wife ask.

"It is no matter," Wongatap replied. "If he is hungry, let him eat."

That was right. By Indian law a person in need may enter any lodge, and eat, and no questions shall be asked until he has finished.

Mahtotohpa's heart almost failed him. Had that not been the killer of his brother, he would only have left a challenge, and gone away. But he thought of his brother, and his vows, and his heart closed again.

When his pipe was smoked out, he laid it aside, and gently stirred the fire with the toe of his moccasin, for more light. He dared to wait no longer. On a sudden he grasped his lance with both hands, sprang up and drove it through the body of Wongatap, in the bunk.

With his knife he instantly snatched off the scalp. Then he uttered the Mandan scalp-halloo, and dived for the door. There he paused, for just a second, to look back, that the squaw might see his face—and in the glimmer of fire-light he noted a feather from the lance sticking in the hole in Wongatap's side.

So back he darted, plucked the feather, and carrying it in his left hand, that the Great Spirit might help him, he ran hard. Wongatap's wife was shrieking; all the village heard and answered, and the warriors streamed out of the lodges.

The whole night Mahtotohpa ran, while the Arikarees vainly searched for his trail. This day he hid, in the brush along the Missouri River. The next night he ran again; and on the sixth morning he panted into the Mandan town, with the dried blood of Wongatap on his lance's blade and the stiffened scalp of Wongatap hanging to its handle.

So that was why he cherished the lance, and that was why he considered the loose eagle's feather to be a strong medicine from the Great Spirit.

But this was only Number Six, in the twelve recorded deeds of Four Bears.

His next-biggest deed was as follows, and it is bigger, according to white man's way of thinking. By that deed he won his knife.

Early one morning one hundred and fifty Cheyenne warriors attacked the Mandan town. They took a scalp and many horses before they rode away. The Mandans had been surprised; but Mahtotohpa rallied fifty warriors and pursued.

The fifty warriors led by Mahtotohpa pursued for a day and half a day. At noon they sighted the Cheyennes driving the stolen horses; but the Cheyennes were so numerous that the Mandan warriors lost their hearts and wished to turn back.

Not so, Mahtotohpa! He galloped forward alone; he

planted his lance in the earth, to the full length of the blade; and making a circle around it with his horse he tore from his clothing a strip of red cloth and hung that to the lance shaft, for a banner.

"If you are cowards, you may go back to the women," he called to his men. "I stay here, where my lance is firm in the ground."

His men were ashamed, and hesitated. Now the Cheyennes had turned and were coming for battle. Their chief saw the planted lance of Mahtotohpa, and Mahtotohpa waiting beside it, and he galloped forward, alone, on his white horse.

"Who is it that has stuck down his lance, and defies the Cheyennes?" he shouted.

"I am Mahtotohpa."

"That is good. Mahtotohpa is a chief. Does he dare to fight?"

"Is this a chief who speaks to Mahtotohpa?"

"I wear scalps at my horse's bit, and the eagle's feathers."

"You have said enough," replied Mahtotohpa. "Come. Let us meet."

Forward hammered the Cheyenne chief, riding splendidly in circles, until he dashed in and planted his lance, also, at the side of Mahtotohpa's lance. That was his answer.

They each drew off a little way, while the Mandan warriors and the Cheyenne warriors gazed expectant. Then they charged like knights in a tournament, and shot at the same moment with their guns. After they had passed each other, and had wheeled, Mahtotohpa held up his powder-horn. The Cheyenne's bullet had smashed it, so that the powder had flowed out.

Having shown, Mahtotohpa flung away his horn, threw his gun to the ground, and setting his buffalo-hide shield upon his left arm, deliberately strung his bow and placed an arrow upon the string.

The Cheyenne chief was a mighty warrior. He likewise cast aside his powder-horn and gun, adjusted his painted shield, prepared bow and arrow. Again they charged. They circled swiftly about each other, performing many clever feats of horsemanship, while their stout bows twanged so fast that the arrows crisscrossed like darting bees.

Some thudded into the thick shields, and the shields bristled with the feathered ends. Some found legs and arms—but that mattered little. Now Mahtotohpa's horse reeled and fell, an arrow in his heart. Mahtotohpa sprang nimbly off. And off from his own horse sprang the Cheyenne chief, that he might not have the advantage.

They plied their bows, on foot. Soon the brave Cheyenne stripped his quiver from his left shoulder and flourished it. It was empty. He tossed it away, and tossed away bow and shield. Then he drew his knife.

"Ai!" responded Mahtotohpa, gladly; and ridding himself of shield and quiver he rushed forward, feeling for his knife, too.

But his knife was not in his belt. He had lost it, or left it at home! Hah! He could not stop—they had come together—the Cheyenne was upon him. So he fought with his bow. He struck aside the Cheyenne's thrust, and hit him over the head and knocked him down. They grappled. It was a terrible fight.

Mahtotohpa clutched for the knife, and the sharp blade was wrenched through his hand, cutting to the bone. The Cheyenne stabbed him many times, and many times Mahtotohpa clutched the knife blade again, before he could tear the haft from the Cheyenne's fingers.

But suddenly he succeeded, and the Cheyenne died. The warriors of both parties had formed a circle close about, watching. Mahtotohpa staggered up, with the Cheyenne's scalp and knife, and gave the kill whoop—and thus victory rested with the Mandans.

That was Mahtotohpa's most famous battle. In another battle he got his name, Four Bears. The Assiniboins had put all his warriors to flight; but he stood his ground, and shot his gun and killed an Assiniboin, and charged with lance and shield, and made them run off. He took sixty horses, besides the scalp. After this he was called Four Bears, because the Assiniboins said that he charged "like four bears in one."

His worst wound he received from the Sioux. They shot an arrow clear through his body, so that the arrow continued on, dropping blood. But he lashed his horse forward, against them, and won another victory.

Such honorable scars he kept covered with red paint, that all who saw might read.

These stories, and others, as pictured by the robe, Mahtotohpa told to Artist Catlin, while Indian trader James Kipp translated the words, and Four Bears acted out the scenes; and they three sat upon the robe itself.

The Cheyenne chief's knife he gave to Artist Catlin. He also made a copy of the pictures, on another robe, and the knife and the second robe were sent to the Catlin Indian gallery, at Washington, where they doubtless may be seen at this day.

Mahtotohpa's end came to him as follows:

In the summer of 1837, a great death attacked the Mandan towns. It was the small pox. The Sioux hedged the towns so closely that there was no escape into the prairie. The Mandan men, women and children, thus herded together, died by hundreds.

Mahtotohpa was among the last left. He witnessed all his family and friends stretched cold and lifeless, and he decided to try a sacrifice to the anger of the Great Spirit.

So he dragged his wives and children together and covered them decently with buffalo robes. Then he went out to a little hill, and laid himself down, with a vow not to eat or drink, if the Great Spirit would stay the plague.

On the sixth day he was very weak; but he crept back to his lodge, and again laid himself down, in a robe, beside his family. And on the ninth day, he, too, died.

However, the plague was not stayed for many days. Of the sixteen hundred Mandans in the two towns, only thirty-one remained alive; of all the Mandan nation there were scarce above one hundred; and today they number about one hundred and fifty.

CHAPTER XVIII

A SEARCH FOR THE BOOK OF HEAVEN (1832)

THE LONG TRAIL OF THE PIERCED NOSES

THE Nez Percés or "Pierced Noses" really were not Pierced Noses any more than any other Indians; for the North American red men, the country over, wore ornaments in their noses when they chose to.

But as the Pierced Noses this nation in the far Northwest was known. They were members of the Sha-hap-ti-an family of North Americans—a family not so large as the Algonquian, Siouan, Shoshonean and several other families, yet important.

Their home was the valley and river country of western Idaho, and the near sections of Oregon and Washington. The two captains, Lewis and Clark, were well treated by them along the great Snake River, above the entrance to the greater Columbia.

They were a small Indian; a horse Indian who lived on buffalo as well as fish, and scorned to eat dog like the Sioux; a brave fighting Indian; and withal a very honest, wise-minded Indian, whose boast, up to 1877, was that they had never shed the white man's blood.

They used canoes, but they used horses more. Horses were their wealth. They raised horses by the thousand, and the finest of horses these were. A fat colt was good meat, but without horses they could not hunt the buffalo and the buffalo supplied stronger meat.

Once a year, when the grass had greened in the spring, they traveled eastward, across the Rocky Mountains by the Pierced Nose Trail-to-the-buffalo, and hunted upon the Missouri River plains, in the country of their enemies the Blackfeet.

The Blackfeet, in turn, sought them out, west of the mountains, to steal their horses. With the Blackfeet and the Sioux, and sometimes with the Snakes, they fought many a battle; and when they had anything of a show, they won out. It took numbers to whip a Pierced Nose warrior. Like most peace-lovers, he made the hardest kind of a fighter.

The early whites in the Northwest had nothing but praise for the Pierced Nose Indians. The trapper who married a Pierced Nose woman thought that he was lucky. She would be a good wife for him—gentle, neat and always busy. Besides, as a rule the Nez Percés women were better looking than the general run of Indian women.

The early fur-hunters and explorers found that the Pierced Noses were very religious, in a way akin to the Christian way. They did not eat, drink nor sleep without first giving thanks to God. They had one day each week, like Sunday, when they did not hunt or fish or work, but listened to talks by their priests or medicine-men.

It was said that they had been taught first by a Christian Iroquois Indian, who in 1816 came in from Canada and told them the things that he had been told by the

French priests. At any rate, when the Roman Catholic priests themselves arrived to live among them, these Pierced Noses already had learned a great deal. They were anxious to learn more.

However, before the missionaries of any church visited them, the Pierced Noses tried to learn more, by themselves. In particular, they wanted a copy of the Book of Heaven. And what started them on the trail of the Book of Heaven, was this:

Among the leaders of white fur-hunters in beaver-trapping days in the west, there was Trapper-Captain Jedediah S. Smith—the Knight in Buckskin. This Captain Jedediah Smith was fearless and upright. Hunting beaver, he traveled far and wide, from the Missouri River to California, and from New Mexico to the Columbia, protected only by his rifle and his Bible.

Wherever he carried his rifle, he carried his Bible; used them both, and no man but that respected him. The Comanches of the Southwest finally killed him, in 1831, when fighting alone against great odds he died a real hero's death.

He had spent the winter of 1824–1825 in the Pierced Noses' country. Of course he told them much about the white man's religion. They saw him frequently reading in his little, black-leather book, which, they said, must be the White Man's Book of Heaven. He would not sell them the book, for any amount of horses or beaver skins. When he had left, they took counsel together and decided that they should get such a book.

Twice they sent into the East for it; and no word came back. But the Pierced Noses did not give up.

A SEARCH FOR THE BOOK OF HEAVEN

They were still without the wonderful Book of Heaven which, had said Captain Jedediah Smith the trapper, guided the white men on the straight trail to the Great Spirit above.

In the early part of 1832 they called a council of the nation, and chose four men, to set out, again, for the big, unknown village where dwelt the Red Head Chief, and where, they hoped, a copy of the Book of Heaven might be found.

The snows had scarcely melted when the four men started. Two of them were old and wise; their names are not written. Two of them were young and strong; their names were Rabbit-skin Leggins and No-horns-on-his-head.

A long, long, dangerous road lay before them: three thousand miles, across the mountains into the Blackfeet country, and across the plains guarded by the Blackfeet and the Sioux and other hungry people as bad.

But they got through all right, for they were clever and in earnest. They arrived at St. Louis in the summer.

St. Louis was then nothing like the St. Louis of today; but to the four strangers from the Columbia River basin it was amazingly large. Never had they dreamed of seeing so many white people. No one spoke their tongue; still there were trappers and Missouri River boatmen who understood signs, and by the sign language they inquired for the Red Head Chief.

The kind-hearted Governor William Clark was glad

to greet them. Their fathers, almost thirty years before, had helped him and Captain Lewis the Long Knife; he remembered the two old men when they were young. The Indians of the West might always depend upon their friend the Red Head.

So he took charge of the four Pierced Noses, and entertained them. He showed them the sights of the white man's big village beside the big rivers. They were entertained by banquets and balls and the theatre. They went to services in the Roman Catholic church, where the white people worshipped—for Governor Clark was a Catholic.

And they saw copies of the Book of Heaven—the Roman Catholic testament, and the Bible: but the books did not speak their language!

In all the white man's village there was no one who might read from the Book, in their own language.

After a few months they began to despair. The food of the white man and the close air of the lodges made them ill. The two old men died. Rabbit-skin Leggins and No-horns-on-his-head were homesick for their country beyond the mountains. In the winter they prepared to go.

A farewell banquet was given to them, but they were tired of banquets. They wanted a Book of Heaven that could talk to them. No-horns-on-his-head delivered a speech, as best he might, in sign language and broken English, through an interpreter.

> I have come to you over the trail of many moons from the setting sun. You were the friends of my fathers, who have all gone the long way.

I came with an eye partly open for my people, who sit in darkness; I go back with both eyes closed. How can I go back blind, to my blind people? I made my way to you with strong arms through many enemies and strange lands that I might carry back much to them. I go back with both arms broken and empty.

Two fathers came with us; they were the braves of many winters and wars. We leave them asleep here by your great waters and wigwams. They were tired in many moons and their moccasins wore out.

My people sent me to get the "White Man's Book of Heaven." You took me to where you allow your women to dance as we do not ours, and the book was not there. You took me to where they worship the Great Spirit with candles, and the book was not there. You showed me images of the good spirits and the picture of the good land beyond, but the book was not among them to tell us the way.

I am going back the long and sad trail to my people in the dark land. You make my feet heavy with gifts and my moccasins will grow old carrying them, yet the book is not among them. When I tell my poor blind people, after one more snow, in the big council, that I did not bring the book, no word will be spoken by our old men or by our young braves. One by one they will rise and go out in silence.

My people will die in darkness, and they will go a long path to other hunting grounds. No white man will go with them, and no White Man's Book make the way plain. I have no more words.

They left. Rabbit-skin Leggins reached his people; No-horns-on-his-head fell upon the trail and died.

But his words lived. As translated into English, they were printed in Eastern papers, and aroused great desire among the churches to give them the right answer. Should these Indians beyond the mountains remain in darkness? No!

Missionaries were called for, to carry the Book and the Word to the Columbia River. In the spring of 1834 the first party, of four Methodists, set out; others followed, the next year; soon the Roman Catholic church sent its Black Robes; and the Pierced Noses and their kin the Flatheads were made glad.

Not in vain had their warriors died, while seeking the road to the white man's heaven.

CHAPTER XIX

A TRAVELER TO WASHINGTON (1831-1835)

WIJUNJON, THE "BIG LIAR" OF THE ASSINIBOINS

THE Assiniboins are of the great Sioux family. Today there are in the United States about one thousand of them. But when they were a free and powerful people they numbered as high as ten thousand, and ranged far—from the Missouri River in northern North Dakota and northern Montana clear into Canada, above.

This cold, high country of vast plains made them hardy and roaming. In their proud bearing and good size they resembled the Dakota Sioux, but with the Sioux they had little to do, except in war. They were at war with the Mandans also, and other nations to the south. In the north they mingled with the Ojibwas or Chippewa people who had journeyed westward into Canada. The Ojibwas had given them their name, As-si-i-bo-in, meaning "They-cook-with-stones."

The Assiniboins were horse Indians and buffalo hunters. They had two peculiar customs. They did cook their meat with stones, just as the Chippewas said. Instead of using kettles, they used holes. They dug a hole about the size of a large kettle; then they pressed a square of raw buffalo-hide into it, for a lining. This they filled with water; they put their meat in, and heating stones, dropped them in, too, until the water was boiling.

Their other peculiarity lay in their style of hair. The longer the hair, the better. They divided it into strands, and plastered the strands with a paste of red earth and hoof glue, in sections of an inch or two.

When the hair did not grow long enough to suit, they spliced it by gluing on other hair, sometimes horse-hair, until it reached the ground.

In the year 1831 Wi-jun-jon, or Pigeon's-egg Head, was a leading young warrior among the long-haired Assiniboins. It was a custom of those days to have chiefs and warriors from the various Indian tribes sent to Washington, to talk with their White Father and see how the Americans lived.

This was supposed to teach the Indians the value of white man's ways, and to show them how useless was war with the white race.

The Assiniboins were still a wild people. They were located so far from St. Louis that they knew nothing about white man ways, except such as they noticed at the fur-trading posts—and here the ways were mixed with Indian ways.

So in the fall of this year Major J. F. A. Sanborn, the Indian agent at the American Fur Company's trading-post of Fort Union, where on the border between North Dakota and Montana the Yellowstone River empties into the Missouri River, decided to take a party of Indians to Washington.

The Assiniboins, the Cheyennes, the Blackfeet, the

Crows—they all came to Fort Union, to trade their furs for powder, lead, sugar and blankets.

Major Sanborn asked the Assiniboins for a warrior. They appointed Wijunjon and another.

Now, this was to be a long journey, among strangers. To be sure, from the Mandans, down-river, old Sha-ha-ka, or White Head, had made the trip, in 1806, when the Red Head Chief and the Long Knife Chief were bound home from the salty water; and he had returned unharmed. Others had gone since, from the upper Missouri, and others had died; Sha-ha-ka himself had almost been killed by the Sioux.

Nobody had gone yet, from as far away as the Assiniboin country; therefore young Wijunjon feared, but was brave. He bade his wife, Chin-cha-pee, or Fire-bug-that-creeps, and his little children goodby, and with the other Assiniboin and chiefs from the Blackfeet and Crows, set out on a fur company flat-boat under protection of Major Sanborn. The Assiniboin women on the shore wept and wailed. His people scarcely expected to see him again.

It was one thousand miles by river through the enemies of his nation, thence on to the great village of St. Louis; but he passed in safety. And when he began to see the first smaller villages of the Americans in Missouri, Wijunjon started in to count the houses, so that he might tell his people.

He had promised to report everything.

He commenced to count by making notches in his pipe stem—one notch for every lodge. The cabins became thicker, along the river banks, and his comrade needs must call off the lodges while he made the notches. Soon there was no more space on the pipe stem, and Wijunjon changed to his war club. Speedily he had filled this also.

Luckily, the barge tied up at the shore, while dinner was cooked. This gave him chance to cut a long willow stick, which surely would be enough.

In fact, so certain he was that the end of the white man's lodges must be close before them, that he worked hard to recut the pipe stem notches and the war club notches, in his willow stick, to have all together. But this very day he had filled the willow stick, and the lodges before them seemed more numerous than those behind!

Ere they arrived in sight of St. Louis itself, he and his comrade had an arm-load of willow sticks—all filled with notches. And here was St. Louis! How many people? Fifteen thousand! How many lodges? Thousands of lodges!

Pigeon's-egg Head pitched the bundle of willow sticks over-board. His knife was worn out, and his hand and brain were tired.

At St. Louis he stood for his portrait, painted by the same Artist Catlin who the next year, in the Mandan towns, listened to the hero tales of Mah-to-toh-pa. He was a great man at painting Indians, this Artist Catlin.

Wijunjon was somewhat confused by so many sounds and sights, but he made a fine figure of a chief—in his mountain-goat skin leggins and shirt, decorated with porcupine quills, and with scalp locks from his enemies; his long plaited hair, which reached to the ground; his war bonnet of eagles' plumes; his buffalo-hide robe, painted with the battles of his career; his beautiful moccasins; and his quiver and bow and bull-neck shield.

Having had his portrait painted, he continued on the long trail, of two thousand more miles by water and by stage, to Washington. And as every mile of it was amidst still more lodges of the white man, he soon saw that all the willow sticks of the Missouri River could not have counted their numbers.

This winter Wijunjon and his companions had a wonderful time among the white men. The Pigeon's-egg Head was the foremost. He was the first to shake the hand of the Great White Father. He declined nothing. The sights of Washington, Baltimore, Philadelphia, New York—he inspected them all. He scarcely rested, night or day. He learned so much that when, in the spring of 1832, he turned homeward, he was filled to bursting.

At St. Louis the first "through" steamboat, the *Yellowstone,* was waiting to ascend to Fort Union and the Assiniboin country. Artist Catlin was aboard. This was to be his first trip, also.

The steamboat *Yellowstone* made a huge sensation, as it ploughed the thick muddy current of the Missouri, frightening the Indians and buffalo along the shores. It moved without sweeps—it nosed for the deepest channels—and the Indians called it "Big-medicine-canoe-with-eyes." It spoke with its guns, and belched much smoke—and they called it "Big Thunder-canoe."

But Wijunjon feared not at all. He was used to

thunder-canoes, now; and he had seen many great sights, back there in the villages of the white men. In fact, he was a sight, himself, for on the way up he had changed his clothes, that his people might know him for a wide traveler.

Gone were his fringed and quilled goat-skin leggins and shirt; gone his war bonnet and painted robe and handsome moccasins, his bow and quiver and shield.

Instead, he wore a badly fitting colonel's uniform, of the United States Army, given to him by the Great White Father: wrinkled trousers and coat of bright blue, with gilt epaulets upon the shoulders, and a stiff collar that reached above his ears. Atop his long painted hair there was settled, to the coat collar, a stove-pipe hat, with a silver-braid band and a red wool plume two feet high. His feet were squeezed into high-heeled military boots, of shiny leather. Around his neck was a tight black stock, or collar. Around his waist was a red sash. Upon his hands were loose white cotton gloves. Upon his chest, and the ruffles of a white shirt, dangled a silver medal, on a blue ribbon. Hung by a belt across one shoulder, at his leg dangled a huge broad-sword. In one hand he carried a blue umbrella, in the other a fan, and in his arms a keg of rum.

Thus Wijunjon, the big brave, proudly strode the deck of the steamer *Yellowstone,* and impatiently looked forward to the moment when he might step off, among his people.

The moment came. Two thousand Indians had gathered on the prairie at Fort Union, to greet the thunder-canoe and the returning travelers. Wijunjon led the procession down the gang-plank.

It was not Indian etiquet to make an ado over the return. Wijunjon was roundly eyed, but nobody spoke to him. His wife, the Fire-bug-that-creeps, was here; so were his children, who scarcely knew him; so were his old parents. He felt that he was admired and that his family and friends were glad to see him; but they let him alone and he only stalked about in his glory, whistling the American war-cry of "Yankee Doodle."

After due time, of course they all loosened up. This night in his lodge in the Assiniboin village he commenced to tell his stories. But he could not tell one tenth—and yet, with the very first, several of the old men and chiefs arose and went out.

They said that this Wijunjon was a liar, and that they would not listen to him. The white people were known to be great liars, and he had learned from them!

In vain, the next day, and the next day, the Pigeon's-egg Head tried to make himself popular.

First, he let his wife cut off the tails of his frock coat, to fashion herself a pair of nice blue leggins. His silver-lace hat-band she took for garters. The rest of his coat he gave to his brother; and now he wore his white shirt with the tails outside.

He gave away his boots—which hurt his feet. He gave away the tails of his shirt, also his brass studs and sleeve-buttons. And with his keg of rum, and his broad-sword dragging and tripping him, he paid visits from lodge to lodge, and whistled "Yankee Doodle."

Pretty soon he had nothing left but his blue umbrella. That was the only thing he kept. Even his hat was gone; his sword was used by his wife, as a meat chopper. And still he was not popular.

Each night men and women gathered from near and far, to hear him talk, in his lodge. They sat silent and critical, while he told them the honest truth.

He worked very hard. He labored to describe the long journey, and the marvelous number of white man's lodges, and villages, and the stage coaches, and the railroads; the forts, and the ships-of-many-big-guns, and the tremendous "council-house" at Washington; and the patent office (great-medicine-place, filled with curious machines); and the war parade of American soldiers, and the balloon—a huge ball which carried a man to the Great Spirit in the sky; and the beautiful white squaws with red cheeks.

The people listened; and when they went out they said among themselves: "Those things are not true. The Pigeon's-egg Head is the greatest liar in the world. The other nations will laugh at the Assiniboins."

Wijunjon did not despair. He was so full of words that he simply must talk, or burst. He wished that he might bring forward the other Assiniboin who had been with him and who knew that all these stories were true; but the other Assiniboin had died on the way home. That was too bad.

However, he stuck to his stories, for he knew that he was right. His people had sent him to see, and he had seen, and he spoke only true words.

After a while, the Assiniboins took a different view

of Wijunjon. Any person who had such stories in his brain was certainly great medicine. No common liar could invent these stories about impossible wonders.

Yes, Wijunjon was doubtless taught by a spirit. He had dreamed.

Now the Assiniboin people looked upon Wijunjon with awe and fear. A person equipped with such power might be very dangerous. They decided that he ought to be killed.

Meanwhile Wijunjon went right on telling his stories. He still had hopes—and besides, it was pleasant to be the center of a gaping circle, and to walk around with folks gazing so at him.

There was a young man who agreed to rid the Assiniboins of this wizard. Beyond question, Wijunjon was too great medicine to be killed by an ordinary bullet; another way should be found.

This young man, also, was a dreamer. And in his dreams he was told, he said, how to kill Wijunjon. The wizard must be shot with an iron pot handle! Nothing else would do the work.

Accordingly, the young man appointed to kill Wijunjon for being bad medicine, found an iron pot handle, and spent a whole day filing it down to fit into the muzzle of his gun. Then from behind he shot the terrible Pigeon's-egg Head and scattered his lying brains about, and the wizard fell dead.

CHAPTER XX

THE BLACKFEET DEFY THE CROWS (1834)

"COME AND TAKE US"

SOUTHWEST from the Mandans there lived the Crow nation. They roved through the Yellowstone River country of southern Montana to the Rocky Mountains; and southward through the mountains into the Wind River and Big Horn country of western Wyoming.

West from the Mandans there lived the Blackfeet nation. They roved through the Missouri country of northern Montana, and north into Canada.

The land of the Crows and of the Blackfeet overlapped. The two peoples were at war, on the plains and in the mountains.

By reason of their wars, the Crow nation had shrunk until they were down to seven thousand people, with many more women than men. But their warriors were tall and stately, their women industrious, their garb elegant. Their buffalo-hide lodges and their buffalo-robe clothing were the whitest, finest in the West. They had countless horses. And the long hair of their men set them high in dignity.

Oiled every morning with bear's grease, the hair of a proud Crow warrior swept the ground behind him. The hair of Chief Long-hair measured ten feet, seven inches, and rolled into a bunch it weighed several pounds. When it had turned white, he worshipped it as his medicine.

The Crows' name for themselves was Ab-sa-ro-ke—Sparrow Hawk People. They were of the Siouan family and cousins of the Minnetarees, the Bird-woman's captors. They had no villages, except where they camped. They were dark, as high and mighty in their bearing as the Mohawks or Senecas, were wonderful riders and looked upon the white men not as worthy enemies but as persons who should be plundered of horses and goods.

In the white men's camps they were polite—and took away with them whatever they could. However, many white traders spoke well of the Crows.

The name of the Blackfeet was Sik-sik-a, which means the same. It referred to their black moccasins. They were Algonquins, and in power ranked with the Iroquois of the East. The Blackfeet, the Bloods and the Piegans formed the league of the Siksika nation. They warred right and left, with the Crees, the Assiniboins, the Sioux, the Crows, the Pierced Noses, and with practically all tribes; they were hostile to the white Americans who hunted in their country; but their wars had not cut them down, for they numbered close to forty thousand people.

Like the Crows their enemy-neighbors they were rovers, never staying long in one spot. They were unlike the Crows in appearance, being shorter, broad-shouldered and deep-chested. No warriors were more feared.

In November of 1834, amidst the Wind River Mountains of western Wyoming five hundred Crows were ahorse, at early morning, to chase the buffalo. And a gallant sight they made as they rode gaily out; in their white robes, their long plaited hair flying, their best horses prancing under them and decorated with red streamers.

Chief Grizzly Bear led. Chief Long-hair, now almost eighty years of age, was with another band.

In this Chief Grizzly Bear band there rode a party of white beaver-hunters who were to spend the winter with the Crows. They now were to be shown how the Crows killed buffalo.

Pretty soon, while the Crows cantered on, they sighted a group of moving figures at the base of the hills two or three miles distant across the valley. Everybody stopped short to peer. Buffalo? No! Indians, on foot and in a hurry—Blackfeet!

How, from so far away, the Crows could tell that these were Blackfeet, the white men did not know. But with a yell of joy and rage, every Crow lashed his horse and forward they all dashed, racing to catch the hated Blackfeet.

The white hunters followed hard. It was to be an Indian battle, instead of an Indian buffalo-chase.

The Blackfeet numbered less than one hundred. They were a war party. Were they hunting buffalo, they would have been on horseback; but even among the horse Indians the war parties were likely to travel on foot, so as to be able to hide more easily. They counted upon stealing horses, for the homeward trail.

These Blackfeet had been very rash, but that was Blackfoot nature. They had sighted the Crows as soon as the Crows had sighted them, and were hustling at best speed to get back into the hills.

The Crows, whooping gladly and expecting to make short work of their enemies, first made short work of the distance. Their robes were dropped, their guns loaded, their bows were strung, they spread out wider—the Blackfeet were cut off and desperately scrambling up a rocky slope—could never make it—never, never—they had halted—what were they doing?

Aha! From the hill slope there arose answering whoops; a few guns cracked; and at the base and half-way up, the Crows stopped and gazed and yelled.

The plucky Blackfeet had "forted." They were in a natural fort of rock wall. On either side of them a rock out-crop in a ridge four feet high extended up hill, to meet, near the top, a cross-ridge ten feet high.

While half the warriors defended with guns and bows, the other half were busily piling up brush and boulders, to close the down-hill opening.

Now whoop answered whoop and threat answered threat, while the Crows rode around and around, at safe distance, seeking a weak place. Chief Grizzly Bear held council with the sub-chiefs. Away sped an express, to get reinforcements from the camp.

At the first charge upon the fort, three Crows had been killed, and only one Blackfoot. That would never do: three scalps in trade for one was a poor count, to the Crows.

They were five hundred, the Blackfeet were only

ninety; but the Crows held off, waiting their reinforcements, while from their fort the Blackfeet yelled taunt after taunt.

"Bring up your squaws! Let them lead you. But our scalps will never dry in a Crow lodge!"

Here, at last, came the people from the camp: the old men, women, boys—everybody who could mount a horse and who could find a weapon; all shrieking madly until the whole valley rang with savage cries.

Matters looked bad for the Blackfeet. At least two thousand Crows were surrounding them, hooting at them, shaking guns and bows and spears at them. And the Blackfeet, secure in their fort, jeered back. They were brave warriors.

Chief Grizzly Bear called another council. In spite of all the gesturing and whooping and firing of guns, the Blackfeet were unharmed. The Crows had little heart for charging in, upon the muzzles of those deadly pieces with the fierce Blackfeet behind.

The white beaver-hunters, not wishing to anger the Blackfeet, and curious to see what was about to happen, withdrew to a clump of cedar trees, about two hundred yards from the fort. The white men had decided to be spectators, in a grand-stand.

Presently Chief Grizzly Bear and his chiefs seemed to have agreed upon a plan of battle. Had they been white men, themselves, they would have stormed the fort at once, and carried the fight to close quarters; but that was not Indian way.

To lose a warrior was a serious matter. Warriors were not made in a day. And without warriors, a tribe would soon perish. "He who fights and runs away, may live to fight another day," was the Indians' motto. They preferred to play safe.

Now the Crows formed in line, two or three hundred abreast, and charged as if they were intending to run right over the fort. It was a great sight. But it did not frighten the Blackfeet.

Up the hill slope galloped the Crow warriors and boys, shooting and yelling. The stout Blackfeet, crouched behind their barricade, volleyed back; and long before the Crows drove their charge home, it broke.

Soon several more Crow warriors were lying on the field. The wails of the squaws sounded loudly. No Blackfeet had been hurt.

The Crows changed their tactics. They avoided the fort, until they had gained the top of the hill. Then in a long single file, they tore past that end of the fort, letting fly with bullet and arrow as they sped by.

Each warrior threw himself to the opposite side of his horse, and hanging there with only one arm and one leg exposed to the fort, shot under his horse's neck.

It was an endless chain of riders, shuttling past the fort, and shooting—but that did not work.

The Blackfeet arrows and bullets caught the horses, and once in a while a rider; and soon there were ten Crows down.

The Crows quit, to rest their horses, and to talk. Their women were wailing still more loudly. War was hard on the women, too. For every relative killed, they had to cut off a finger joint, besides gashing their faces and hands with knives.

In their little fort, the Blackfeet were as boldly defiant as ever.

"Come and take us!" they gibed. "Where are the Crow men? We thought we saw Crow men among you. Come and take us, but you will never take us alive!"

"What will be done now?" the white men queried of a black man who had joined them, in the clump of cedars.

He was not all black. He was half white, one quarter negro and one quarter Cherokee. He had lived over twenty years in the Indian country of the upper Missouri River; mainly with the Crows. Edward Rose had been his name, when young; but now he was a wrinkled, stout old man, called Cut-nose, and looked like a crinkly-headed Indian.

"The Crows are losing too many warriors. They have no stomach for that kind of work," answered the old squaw-man.

The Crow chiefs and braves were seated in a circle, near the cedars, and listening to the speakers who stood up, one after another.

"Our marrow-bones are broken," some asserted. "The enemy is in a fort; we are outside. We will lose more men than he. Let us draw off; and when he is in the open, we can then attack as we please."

"He is few; we are many. Our slain warriors and their women cry for vengeance," asserted others. "We will be called cowards if we retreat. If we charge all together we may lose a few braves, but there will be no Blackfeet left to laugh at us."

These seemed to be the voices that carried. The pipe was passed around the circle, every man puffed at it, and the council broke up in a tremendous yelling.

Now the end of the Blackfeet loomed large. Ahorse and afoot the Crows massed, to charge from below and on either flank. Their chiefs hastened hither and thither, urging them. The women and children shrieked encouragement.

In their little fort the Blackfeet also listened to their chiefs. They showed not the slightest sign of fear. Their fierce faces glared over the ramparts. Their weapons were held firmly.

The Crows had aroused themselves to such a pitch that they acted half insane. Forward they charged in howling masses—but the bullets and arrows pelted them thickly, more warriors fell—they scattered and ran away. The Blackfeet hooted them.

This made old Cut-nose mad. He hastened out to where the Crows were collected in doubt what next to do, and climbed upon a rock, that they all might see him.

"Listen!" he shouted. "You act as if you expected to kill the enemy with your noise. Your voices are big and your hearts are small. These white men see that the Crows cannot protect their hunting grounds; they will not trade with a nation of cowards and women; they will trade with the Blackfeet, who own the country. The Blackfeet will go home and tell the people that three thousand Crows could not take ninety warriors. After this no nation will have anything to do with the Crows. I am ashamed to be found among the Crows. I told the white men that you could fight. Now I will show you how black men and white men can fight.''

And he leaped from his rock, and without glancing behind him he ran for the fort. The Crows did not delay an instant. Pellmell they rushed after him, caught up with him, swarmed against the brush and rock walls—the Blackfeet met them stanchly, and gave way not an inch—and the fighting was terrible.

But over the barricade poured the Crows. In a moment the whole interior was a dense mass of Indians, engaged hand to hand, and every one yelling until, as said the white men, ''The noise fairly lifted the caps from our heads.''

Guns and hatchets and clubs and knives rose and fell. The Crow women were pressing to the outskirts, to kill the wounded enemy. Gradually the weight of the Crows forced the Blackfeet back. The Blackfeet began to emerge over the upper end of the fort—their faces still to the foe.

Presently all who might escape, were outside—but their enemies surrounded them at once. The Blackfeet remaining were not many. They never faltered nor signed surrender. They only sang their death chants; and forming in close order they moved along the ridge like one man, cutting a way with their knives.

By the half dozen they dropped; even those who dropped, fought until they were dead. Soon the platoon was merely a squad; the squad melted to a spot;

there was a swirl, covering the spot; and the spot had been washed out.

Not a Blackfoot was left, able to stand. The wounded who had lost their weapons hurled taunts, as they lay helpless, until the Crows finished them also. Truly had the Blackfeet yelled: "Come and take us! But you will never take us alive!"

This night there was much mourning in the Crow camp. Thirty chiefs and braves had been killed, twice that number wounded, and many horses disabled. No prisoner had been brought in, to pay by torture. The Blackfeet nation would look upon the fight as their victory.

So the Crow dead were buried; and into each grave of chief or brave were placed his weapons and the shaved off mane and tail of his best horse—for every hair would become a horse for him, in the spirit world.

CHAPTER XXI

THE STRONG MEDICINE OF KONATE (1839)

THE STORY OF THE KIOWA MAGIC STAFF

THE Kiowas are of the great Athapascan family of Indians. In their war days they ranged from the Platte River of western Nebraska down into New Mexico and Texas. But their favorite hunting grounds lay south of the Arkansas River of western Kansas and southeastern Colorado.

It was a desert country, of whity-yellow sand and sharp bare hills, with the Rocky Mountains distant in the west, and the only green that of the trees and brush along the water-courses. Nevertheless it was a very good kind of country.

It had plenty of buffalo. The timber and the streams supplied winter shelter. The wagon-road of the white merchants, between the Missouri River and Santa Fe of New Mexico, ran through the middle of it and furnished much plunder. In the south, where lay Comanche land and Apache land, there were Mexican settlements that furnished horses.

With the Comanches and Apaches, and with the Cheyennes and Arapahos north, the Kiowas were friends. To the Pawnees they were enemies, and their name carried dread through many years of fighting.

Now in the summer of 1839, twenty Kiowa warriors

left their village near the Arkansas River in present southern Kansas, to go down across Comanche country and get horses and mules from the Pasunke, or the Mexicans of El Paso, which is on the Rio Grande River border between northwestern Texas and Mexico. However, in those days all that region was Mexico.

The head chief of the party was old Do-has-an, or Bluff. But he did not command. Gua-da-lon-te, or Painted-red, was the war chief. Dohasan would take command only in case Gua-da-lon-te was killed. Among the warriors there were Dagoi, and Kon-a-te, whose name means "Black-tripe."

After several days' travel horseback clear across New Mexico they came to El Paso town, where many goods were stored on the way between New Mexico and Old Mexico, and where the people got rich by trading and by making wine from grapes. But they could see soldiers guarding El Paso; so they did not dare to charge in and gather horses and mules from the frightened Pasunke.

Dohasan, who was wise as well as brave, advised against it.

"Another time," he said. "We are too few, and we are a long way from home. Let us go, and come again. Maybe on the way up we will meet with luck among the other villages."

They rested only the one night, and turned back, thinking that they had not been discovered. At the end of a day's journey through a bad, waterless land, they halted and camped by a spring, of which they knew.

It was a big rock-sink or round, deep basin, with a pool of water at the bottom, and a cave that extended under a shelf.

The Mexican soldiers must have struck their trail, or perhaps had followed them from El Paso; for early in the morning there was a sudden shooting from all around, and much yelling. Bullets whined and spatted, and horses screamed and fell over.

"Into the cave!" shouted Painted-red. "Quick!"

Hustled by old Bluff and Painted-red, into the cave they bolted. Nobody had been hurt, and the soldiers were afraid to venture in after them, but right speedily they found themselves badly off.

The soldiers camped along the edge of the well, above, so as to kill them by thirst and hunger. Only in the darkness might the Kiowas, two or three at a time, crawl out of the cave, gulp a few swallows from the pool, maybe slash a strip of horse-meat, and scuttle in again.

While doing this, Dagoi was shot in the leg, so that he could not walk. In a couple of days the dead horses began to decay, for the sun was very hot. The smell grew sickening. The flesh was sickening. One or two of the dead horses lay in the pool, and the water got sickening. The Mexican soldiers stayed close and watchful, and yelled insults in Spanish.

But they had with them several Apache scouts; and one of the Apaches called in Comanche, so that the soldiers would not understand.

"Be of good cheer, brothers," he called. "Be strong and hold out, until these dogs of Mexicans tire."

YOUNG KIOWA GIRL

Courtesy of The Field Museum.

The Kiowas had no thought of surrendering. They would rather die where they were, because if they surrendered, they would be killed anyway. Old Dohasan and others among them belonged to the society of Ka-itse-nko or Real Dogs—whose members were under a vow never to surrender.

Part of them guarded the cave's mouth, and the rest explored back inside. At the very end there was a hole which let in daylight. Konate was boosted up; but when he stuck his head through, a soldier saw it and he had to duck down. Thereupon the soldiers stopped the hole with a large rock.

When ten days and nine nights had passed, they all decided that they would either escape or be killed. The horse meat could not be touched; neither could the water. It was better to die in the open, like men, than to die in a hole, like gophers.

The soldiers guarded the only trail that led up the side of the cliff wall, out of the well; but at another side there was a cedar which had rooted in a crack and almost reached the rim. By hard climbing a man might manage to scramble up and gain the open.

But what to do with Dagoi, who had only one leg and was weak from pain?

"You will not leave me, my brothers?" implored Dagoi. "It is true I am wounded, but if you leave me, I shall surely die. Perhaps you can carry me on your backs. Or wait a day or two, and the soldiers will grow tired."

"No," said old Dohasan. "That is impossible. We must move fast, and to get you up the tree would make noise. If we wait, or if we stay, we will all die, and it is better that one should die than that all should die. Have a strong heart, my son. You are a warrior, and you must die like a warrior."

Dagoi bowed his head.

"Those are good words," he answered. "I hear them and they make me strong. I am a man, and I am not afraid. When you get home, tell my friends to come and avenge me."

In the darkness Dagoi dragged himself to the pool, and sat beside it, waiting for daylight and the bullets of the soldiers.

Old Dohasan sang the death-chant of the Real Dogs. Then he stepped silently out, leading the file of warriors to the wall under the tree, that he might be the first to climb and meet the soldiers in case they were on watch.

Up he went, into the cedar, and on; up went all, one after another, as fast as they could. The camp-fires of the Mexican soldiers were glowing, right and left and behind and before, along the rim; but without a sound the nineteen gaunt Kiowas, bending low, stole swiftly forward, at the heels of Dohasan.

They succeeded. But in finding horses, somebody made a little noise, and the Mexicans fired wildly into the darkness. However, answering not, and leading the horses out a short way, step by step, they were ready to vault on.

"Anybody hurt?"

"A bullet has gone through my body," said Konate. "But I will try to ride."

"We must hurry," spoke Painted-red. The camp was all aroused. "Someone help Konate."

Away they dashed, several riding double, and Konate supported in his seat by a comrade. Behind, in the well, Dagoi sat beside the pool and kept his heart strong for the end that would come by daylight.

All that night and all the next day they rode, making northeast toward the desolate desert region of the Staked Plain, on the homeward way across western Texas. No Mexican soldiers would follow into the Staked Plain.

When after hard riding they arrived at Sun-mountain Spring, on the top of a high, bare-rock hill near the Staked Plain, Konate's wound had spoiled in him and he could not sit upright on his horse. He was very ill.

"I am about to die, friends," he gasped. "Do not try to carry me farther. But go, yourselves; and some day come back for my bones."

He spoke sense. Any one might see that he had only a few hours to live, and that soon his comrades would be carrying only a body across the Staked Plain, where the sun beat hotly and water was far apart.

It was better that they leave him here, at the spring where they might find his bones. So on the water's edge they built a shade for Konate, with a few crooked cedar branches, and bidding him goodby they rode on, into the great Staked Plain.

They expected that they would never seen him again.

What happened now to Konate, he often told, and he told it always the same; therefore it must be true.

For the rest of the long day he lay there, with the sun beating down around him, and his mind and body very sick from his wound. He was unable to sleep. The sun set, and the air changed to cool, the twilight deepened to dusk; alone on his hilltop he closed his eyes, and waited for the spirit of the tai-me, or Sun-dance medicine, to bear him to his fathers.

In the star-light he heard a wolf howl, far off. He listened, and the howl sounded again, nearer, from another direction. Then he knew that the wolf had scented him and was ranging to find his spot. That would be bad—to be eaten by a wolf and have one's bones scattered!

Konate groaned. His heart had been strong, until this moment. He had hoped that his bones would be cared for.

Soon he heard the wolf, at hand; there was the soft patter of its pads, and the sniffing of its inquiring nose, seeking him out. And now he saw the wolf, with shining eyes peering into the bough shelter where he lay helpless, unable even to speak.

That was an agonizing moment, for Konate. But lo, instead of jumping upon him, the wolf trotted forward, and gently licked his wounds, and then lay quietly down beside him.

Konate was amazed and thankful. While the wolf lay there, next he heard another sound, in the distance: the shrill eagle-bone-whistle music of the great Sun-dance of the Kiowa nation. The music drew nearer, and he heard the Sun-dance song; and while he listened, strong of heart again, he saw the medicine spirit of the Sun-dance standing before him, at the entrance to the shelter.

"I pity you and shall not let you die," said the medicine spirit. "You shall see your home and friends."

Then the medicine spirit brought down a rain, to wash Konate's wounds and cool his fever. The medicine spirit sat with Konate most of the night, and told him many things: told him how to make a new kind of Sun-dance shield, and also an a-po-te, or sacred forked staff, that should be a medicine staff and have magic powers.

Toward morning the medicine spirit left, saying:

"Help is near."

Every bit of this Konate firmly insisted was true, although white men claimed that he dreamed. For, listen:

Meanwhile the Painted-red party were riding on, and in the Staked Plain they met six Comanches, bound to Mexico after plunder. They spoke to the Comanches regarding Konate, and asked them to cover his body so that the wolves should not get it.

This the Comanches promised to do, and continued to the Sun-mountain Spring where Konate had been left to die.

But when they reached the spring, they found Konate alive and stronger than when his comrades had bid him goodby! That astonished them. They then knew that he was "medicine." Therefore they washed him, and gave him food, and putting him on an extra horse they turned back and took him home.

The village, and all the tribe, also, were astonished

to see him again. As proof that he had been visited by the medicine spirit, he made the medicine shield, of a new design, and the apote, or sacred forked stick.

He took the name Pa-ta-dal, or Lean Bull. After that the keepers of the medicine stick bore the same name.

Konate carried the medicine stick in the Sun-dance, for several years, and then handed it on to his nephew K'a-ya-nti, or Falls-over-a-bank, who became Lean Bull the second—but the white people called him Poor Buffalo.

This apote was a two-pronged stick about four feet long, decorated with wild sage. It was smooth and had no bark, and was brought out only once a year, for the Sun-dance. The keeper of it used it for beating time, in the dance. At the close of the dance it was stuck, forks up, in the ground in the center of the medicine lodge, and left until the next year.

When the stick was eighteen years old Konate's nephew planted it as before, at the close of the Sun-dance, in the center of the medicine lodge on the plain; and when the Kiowas returned, the next summer, for another Sun-dance, they discovered that the apote had been planted the other end up, and was putting forth green leaves!

For a stick eighteen years old, without bark, to do this, was certainly great medicine. No one now might doubt the story of Konate, to whom the taime spirit had talked, under the bough shelter by the Sun-mountain Spring.

None of the Kiowas dared to touch the apote, this

time—or to stay near the medicine lodge. The dance was held at another place.

When, ten years later, or in October, 1867, the Kiowas met in a treaty council with the United States, near the present town of Medicine Lodge on Medicine Lodge Creek, southern Kansas, they were enabled to show that the apote had grown to be a large tree.

Such had been the strong medicine of Konate, to whom, about to die from his wounds, in his shelter by the Sun-mountain Spring beyond the Staked Plain, the taime spirit had talked.

Konate was dead; but K'a-ya-nti, his nephew, the other keeper of the stick, was still alive; and he knew.

CHAPTER XXII

RED CLOUD STANDS IN THE WAY (1865–1909)

THE SIOUX WHO CLOSED THE ROAD OF THE WHITES

THE name Sioux comes down from a longer Chippewa word meaning "adder" or "enemy." The Indians who bore this name were the powerful Dakotas —the true Sioux of history.

The wide Nation of the Lakota, as these Sioux called themselves, was a league of seven council fires.

The four divisions of the Santees lived in Minnesota; the two divisions of the Yanktons lived between them and the Missouri River; the one large division of the Tetons lived in their Dakota country, west of the Missouri River.

The Santees, the Yanktons and the Tetons spoke their own dialects. They differed in appearance from one another. They were separated into tribes and bands.

Even as late as 1904 they numbered twenty-five thousand people in the United States. By mind, muscle and morals they have been rated as leaders of the Western red men. They roamed hither-thither, and depended upon the buffalo for food. They waged stout war.

The Tetons were the strongest, and formed half of the Dakota nation. It was chiefly they who fought the

RED CLOUD

Courtesy of The American Bureau of Ethnology.

United States soldiers for so long. The war opened in 1855, over the killing of a crippled cow by a Min-i-con-jou, at Fort Laramie of Wyoming, on the Oregon Trail of the emigrants.

The Brulés, or Burnt Thighs; the Og-la-las, or Scatter-one's-own; the Hunk-pa-pas, or Those-who-camp-by-themselves; the Min-i-con-jous, or Those-who-plant-beside-the-stream; the Si-ha-sa-pas, or Black-moccasins: these were the Teton Sioux who battled the hardest to save their buffalo and their lands from the white man.

Red Cloud at first was chief of the Bad Faces band of Oglala Sioux. They were a small fighting band, but he was a noted brave. His count showed more coups, or strike-the-enemy feats, than the count of any other warrior of the Oglalas. Before he retired from war, his coups numbered eighty.

He was born in 1822. His Sioux name was Makh-pia-sha, meaning Red Cloud. In the beginning it probably referred to a cloud at sunrise or sunset; later it referred to his army of warriors whose red blankets covered the hills.

When he was forty years old, there was much excitement among the white men to the west of the Sioux range. From the mines of Idaho the gold-seekers had crossed to the eastern base of the Rocky Mountains in western Montana. Mining camps such as Helena, Bozeman and Virginia City sprang up.

The Oregon Trail of the emigrants already passed through the Sioux country, and the Sioux had agreed to let it alone. Now the United States asked permission to make a new road, which from Fort Laramie of southern Wyoming would leave the Oregon Trail, and branch off northwest, through the Powder River and the Big Horn country of Wyoming, and on west across Montana, as a short-cut to the gold-fields.

This part of Wyoming really was Crow Indian country; but the Sioux had driven the Crows out, and with the Northern Cheyennes were using the region for a hunting ground. The white man's trails to the south had frightened the buffalo and reduced the herds; the Powder River valleys were the only ranges left to the Sioux, where they might hunt and always find plenty of meat.

Some of the Sioux chiefs did sign a treaty for the new road. The only Oglalas who signed were subchiefs. Red Cloud did not sign. The United States went ahead, anyway. Troops were sent forward, to begin the work of building the road. Red Cloud, with his Oglalas and some Cheyennes, surrounded them and captured them; held them prisoners for two weeks, until his young men threatened to kill them. Then he released them, with a warning.

"I shall stand in the trail," he said. Those were the words of Pontiac, to Major Rogers, one hundred years before.

United States officials were ordered to Fort Laramie, to talk with the angry Red Cloud. He declined to meet them.

But already a number of white gold-seekers had entered by this Bozeman Trail, as it was known. In June, of the next year, 1866, the United States tried again to get Red Cloud's name on the paper. A council was called at Fort Laramie.

During the last year, another fort had been located. It was Fort Reno—the first out-post of the new trail, at the Powder River, one hundred and sixty-seven miles along from Laramie.

Red Cloud, and his lieutenant, They-fear-even-his-horses, came in to talk with the United States, at Fort Laramie. A great throng of Indians was present, for Fort Laramie was a busy post.

Nothing could be done with the Red Cloud band. The United States was willing to promise that nobody should be allowed to leave the new road, or to disturb any game. Red Cloud only shook his head. He well knew that the white travelers would not obey the law. They would hunt and camp, as they chose.

"Wah-nee-chee!" he said. "No good! Why do you come here and ask for what you have already taken? A fort has been built, and the road is being used. I say again, we will not sell our hunting grounds for a road."

But the United States had decided. The Government had been assured by the treaty makers that all the Sioux would finally yield. There was last fall's treaty, as a starter. The Sioux from every band had signed. Besides, the Government could not give up the right to open roads. A railroad had the power to take right-of-way through towns and lands; and a Government wagon road should have the same license.

So certain was the Government that the road would be opened, that even while the council with the Red

Cloud Oglalas was in session, there arrived at Fort Laramie Colonel Henry B. Carrington of the Eighteenth Infantry, with seven hundred soldiers.

Red Cloud saw the camp.

"Where are those soldiers going?"

"They are sent to open the new road and build forts."

"The Americans seek to steal our land whether we say yes or no!" angrily uttered Red Cloud. "They will have to fight."

He and They-fear-even-his-horses (whom the white men called "Young-man-afraid-of-his-horses") seized their rifles, and rode away, and three hundred of their warriors followed them.

"Red Cloud means war," warned the Indians who remained. "The Great Father makes us presents, to buy the road; but the white soldiers come to steal it first. In two moons the white war chief will not have a hoof left."

An express sent after Red Cloud, to ask him to return, was whipped with bows and ordered to get out and tell the white chiefs that Red Cloud would not talk about the road.

Colonel Carrington marched on, into the forbidden land. The officers' wives were with them. Traders along the line insisted that the Indians were determined to fight; but some of the emigrant outfits bound over the trail to the mines were scornful of danger. One emigrant captain laughed, when the women were timid.

"You'll never see an Injun unless he comes in to beg

for sugar and tobacco," he said. "I've been on the plains too long to be scared by such trash."

This was at Fort Reno. That very morning, in broad daylight Red Cloud's band ran off all the post sutler's horses and mules while the soldiers looked on. Eighty men pursued, and captured only one Indian pony loaded with goods obtained at Fort Laramie.

Colonel Carrington left a detachment here at the Powder River, to build a better Fort Reno. He marched on.

Meanwhile Red Cloud had been growing stronger. Sioux warriors were hastening to join him. Spotted Tail of the Brulés had declined to accept the treaty for opening the road—he waited for Red Cloud; but he was wisely staying at home. However, his Brulé young men were riding away in large numbers, and he told the white people at Fort Laramie that if they "went far on the trail they had better go prepared to look out for their hair."

Red Cloud was watching the march of the soldiers. He did not attack; but when he saw them pushing on, and finally making camp to locate another fort, fifty miles northwest of Reno, on Piney Fork of Lodge-pole Creek, in the Big Horn Mountains of northern Wyoming, he again sent a message, by a party of soldiers whom he met and turned back.

"The white chief must take his soldiers out of this country. Let him decide for peace or war. If he wants peace, he can go back to Powder River. The fort there can stay. But no forts shall be built farther on the road, and no soldiers shall march over the road which has never been given to the white people."

Red Cloud wanted an answer at once. He also asked that the white chief come to him with an interpreter, and settle matters in a council. But the messenger was held at the fort for a short time, and Red Cloud moved his warriors to a new place.

Colonel Carrington invited the Sioux to come to the camp; and went ahead building his fort. Some bands of Northern Cheyennes appeared for a talk. They said that Red Cloud had urged them to join the Sioux in keeping the white men out of the hunting grounds, and that he knew what the soldiers had been doing every hour since they left Fort Laramie.

The Cheyennes seemed a little fearful of the Sioux; but said that if they were given provisions, they would stay away from the white trail.

When the Cheyennes returned to the Sioux, Red Cloud asked them what the white chief had said.

"Is he going back to the Powder River?"

"No," answered Black Horse, of the Cheyennes. "The white chief will not go back, and his soldiers will go on."

"What presents did he give you?"

"All we wanted to eat. He wishes the Sioux and the Cheyennes and all the other Indians to go to Fort Laramie, and sign the treaty, and get more presents. I think that we had better take the white man's hand and presents, rather than fight him and lose everything."

"No!" replied Red Cloud. "The white man lies and steals. My lodges were many; now they are few. The white man wants all. He must fight, and the Indian will die where his fathers died."

With that, the Sioux unstrung their bows and whipped the Cheyennes on the face and back, crying, "Coup!" as if they were striking the enemy.

So Black Horse sent word that the Sioux intended war.

The fort was named Fort Phil Kearney. It was built of timber cut in the pine woods seven miles distant, and was surrounded by a palisade or high fence of thick pickets set upright.

Saw mills were placed in the woods, and the wood-camps were protected by block-houses. Almost one hundred wagons were used, to haul the logs and boards.

One hundred miles onward, another fort was started: Fort C. F. Smith.

The Crows informed Colonel Carrington that Red Cloud had tried to enlist even them—that all the Sioux were uniting to drive out the white men from this region, and that in the fall there would be a "big fight" at the two forts.

White Mouth and Rotten Tail said that they were half a day in riding through the Sioux village; there were fifteen hundred lodges. In truth, Chief Red Cloud had over two thousand warriors, with whom to stand in the path.

And there he stood. Nobody might doubt that. His raiders watched every mile of the trail back to Powder River, and not an emigrant train got through. He himself, with two thousand warriors, guarded Fort Kearney, where the white chief lived.

Nobody might venture from it to hunt game. The wood wagons might move only when many together and well armed. Not a load of hay could be brought in without strong escort. After a time no mail could be sent on to Fort Smith.

Colonel Carrington had five companies of infantry and one company of the Second Cavalry. The infantry was mostly recruits. Their guns were old style muzzle loaders; but the band had the new Spencer breech-loaders.

He asked for better guns and more ammunition. The Government was not certain that the Sioux could do much against soldiers of a country which had just been trained by a four years' war, and Carrington was left to prove it.

Chief Red Cloud had his first chance to prove the opposite on December 6. He had been amusing his warriors by letting them gallop past the fort and shout challenges to the soldiers to come out and fight; then when the cannon shot at them, they dodged the shells—but did not always succeed.

The big guns that shot twice surprised them.

On the morning of December 6 Red Cloud struck in earnest, and had planned to strike hard. He had a line of signal flags seven miles long, by which to direct his army. Then he sent a company to attack a wood train.

The attack on the wood train brought the troops out of the fort. One detachment of thirty-five cavalry and a few mounted infantry was commanded by Captain William J. Fetterman. He was very anxious to fight

Indians; in fact, the officers all had set their hearts upon "taking Red Cloud's scalp."

Captain Fetterman rescued the wagon train, by chasing the Sioux away; but in about five miles Red Cloud faced his men about and closed. It was an ambuscade. The troopers of the cavalry were stampeded, and the captain found himself, with two other officers and a dozen men, surrounded by yelling warriors.

Colonel Carrington arrived just in time to save him; but young Lieutenant H. S. Bingham of the Second Cavalry was killed, and so was Sergeant Bowers.

When Captain Fetterman had returned to the fort he had changed his mind regarding the prowess of the Sioux, whom he had thought to be only robbers.

"I have learned a lesson," he remarked. "This Indian war has become a hand-to-hand fight, and requires great caution. I'll take no more risks like that of today!"

Red Cloud was not satisfied. His warriors had not done exactly as he had told them to do. He bided his time.

On the morning of December 21 he was again ready. His men were stationed, waiting for a wood train to appear. It appeared, starting out to chop timber in the pine woods, and haul the logs to the fort.

It was an unusually strong train—a number of heavy wagons, and ninety armed men.

Red Cloud let it get about four miles along, and ordered it attacked. He had spies upon a ridge of hills, to watch the fort.

When the attack was heard at the fort, soldiers

dashed out. The Red Cloud warriors allowed the wagon train to think that it had whipped them. He withdrew, across the ridge.

The leader of the soldiers was Captain Fetterman, again. He had asked for the command. With him was Captain Fred H. Brown, who expected to go back to Fort Laramie, and wished, first, to get a scalp. He and Captain Fetterman were rivals for scalps and had almost forgotten the affair of December 6. They were gallant soldiers, but reckless.

Altogether the detachment numbered seventy-nine officers and men, and two scouts named Wheatley and Fisher.

Captain Fetterman was distinctly ordered by Colonel Carrington to do nothing but rescue the wagon train. He must not cross the ridge in pursuit of the Sioux.

Captain Fetterman did not move directly for the place of the wagon train. He made a circuit, to cut off the attacking Sioux, at their rear, or between the wagon train and the ridge to the north of it.

He had taken no surgeon, so Dr. Hines was hurried after him. The doctor came back in another hurry. He reported that the wagon train was on its way to the timber, without the captain; and that the captain had disappeared, over the ridge! Many Indians were in sight, and the doctor had been obliged to stop short.

Now, on a sudden, there was a burst of distant gunfire. In twelve minutes a second detachment of soldiers was on the run, from the fort for the battle; wagons and ambulances and more men followed; and soon only one hundred and nineteen men remained.

The firing was very heavy, in volleys—then in fire-at-will; then it died down—quit. Not a sound could be heard, as the women and men in Fort Kearney strained their ears and eyes.

Presently a courier from the second detachment galloped headlong in. He said that the valley beyond the ridge was swarming with Sioux; they yelled and dared the soldiers to come down to the road there. But of the Captain Fetterman command, no trace could be sighted.

The soldiers and the reinforcements stayed out all the afternoon. They returned at dark; but of the eighty-one others, none came back. All of them, the entire eighty-one, had fallen to the army of Red Cloud.

Nobody was alive to tell the story of the fight. The signs on the field were plain, though; and of course the Red Cloud warriors knew well what had occurred.

Captain Fetterman had crossed the ridge, to chase the Sioux. Two thousand Red Cloud men were waiting for him. They permitted him to advance to the forbidden road. The white soldiers fought until their ammunition was almost spent. Then the Red Cloud men rushed. Only six of the white soldiers were shot; the rest were killed by hand.

The plan of Red Cloud and his chiefs had been laid to get all the troops out of the fort, together; kill them and seize the fort.

But the warriors had not waited long enough. Their victory was too quick, and they lost too many men, themselves, in the one fight: seventy, of killed and wounded, they said; sixty-five of killed, alone, said the red blotches on the field.

Still, Red Cloud had closed the road with the bodies of the soldiers. He had made his word good.

The garrison in Fort Kearney gave up all thought of glory by capturing Red Cloud; and this winter there was no more fighting. How many warriors Red Cloud had, to "cover the hills with their scarlet blankets," nobody knew; but the count ran from three thousand to five thousand.

The spring came, and the summer came, and the road had not been opened. In more than a year, not a single wagon had passed upon it, through the hunting grounds of the Sioux.

Another white chief had been sent to take command of Fort Phil Kearney. He was Brigadier General H. W. Wessels. All this summer the soldiers were having to fight for wood and water. The contractor in charge of the teams hauling lumber complained that he must have more protection or he would be unable to do the work.

Captain James Powell of the Twenty-seventh Infantry was ordered out to protect the lumber camps. He took Lieutenant John C. Jenness and fifty-one men.

The wood choppers had two camps, about a mile apart. The captain detailed twenty-five of his men to guard the one camp, and escort the wagon trains to the fort; with the twenty-six others he made a fort of wagon boxes, at the second camp.

He arranged fourteen of the wagon boxes on the ground, in a circle. Some of the boxes had been lined with boiler iron. Two wagons were left on wheels, so that the rifles might be aimed from underneath. The boxes were pierced low down with a row of loop-holes. The spaces between the ends of the boxes were filled with ox-chains, slabs and brush. He had plenty of ammunition and plenty of new breech-loading rifles.

The little fort was located in an open basin, surrounded by gentle hills. He directed the men of the other camp to come in at the first sign of trouble.

The Sioux were at hand. Red Cloud had been merely waiting for the soldiers to march out and make it worth his while to descend. He was resolved to destroy Fort Kearney this year, before the snows.

It seemed to him that again he had the soldiers where he wanted them. Word of the flimsy little corral spread a laugh among his two thousand warriors. The squaws and old men were summoned from the allied Sioux and out-law Cheyenne village, to come and see and be ready with their knives.

On the morning of August 2 he so suddenly attacked the unfortified wood camp that he cut it off completely. Two hundred of his men captured the mule herd; five hundred of them attacked the wagon train there, burned the wagons and drove the soldiers and teamsters and choppers who were outside the corral, in flight to Fort Kearney. Scalps were taken.

Now it was the turn of the puny corral, and the rest of the soldiers.

He could see only the low circle of wagon-boxes. They were covered with blankets; underneath the blankets there were soldiers—few and frightened.

The hill slopes around were thronged with his people, gathered to watch and to plunder. He felt like a great chief indeed. And at wave of his hand eight hundred of his cavalry dashed in a thundering, crackling surge of death straight at the silent circle.

On they sped, and on, and on, and were just about to dash against the circle and sweep over, when suddenly such a roar, and sheet of flame, struck them in the face that they staggered and melted. Now—while the guns were empty! But the guns were not yet empty—they belched without pause. Veering right and left around a bloody lane the warriors, crouching low, tore for safety from the frightful blast.

Red Cloud could not understand. His own men were well armed, with rifles and with muskets captured from the soldiers during the past year or supplied at the trading post. It seemed to him that there were more soldiers under those blankets than he had reckoned. But he knew that his men were brave; his people were watching from the hills; he had no mind for defeat.

In the corral Captain Powell had told his twenty-six soldiers and four civilians to fight for their lives. The poor shots were ordered to load guns and pass them as fast as possible to the crack shots.

Red Cloud rallied his whole force, of more than two thousand. He dismounted eight hundred and sent them forward to crawl along the ground, as sharpshooters; they ringed the corral with bullets and arrows.

He himself led twelve hundred, afoot, for a charge.

His young nephew was his chief aide—to win the right to be head chief after Red Cloud's death.

But although they tried, in charge after charge, for three hours, they could not enter the little fort. Sometimes they got within ten yards—the soldiers threw augers at them, and they threw the augers back—and back they reeled, themselves. The guns of the little fort never quit!

Red Cloud still could not understand. He called a council. In the opinion of his chiefs and braves, the white soldiers were armed with guns that shot of themselves and did not need reloading.

The squaws on the hills were wailing; his men were discouraged; many had fallen. So finally he ordered that the bodies be saved, and the fight ended. His braves again crawled forward, behind shields, with ropes; tied the ropes to the bodies, in spite of the bullets, and running, snaked the bodies away behind them.

"Some bad god fought against us," complained the Red Cloud people. "The white soldiers had a great medicine. We were burned by fire."

And all the Indians of the plains, hearing about the mystery, when the breech-loading rifles mowed down the Sioux and the Cheyennes, spoke of the bad god fight that defeated Chief Red Cloud.

The Sioux reported that they had lost eleven hundred and thirty-five warriors. Red Cloud's nephew was sorely wounded in the charge. Captain Fetterman's loss was Lieutenant Jenness and two men killed, two men wounded. He said that when the reinforcements, with the cannon, arrived from Fort Kearney, while the

Sioux were removing their dead, he was in despair. Another charge or two and he would have been wiped out.

But the road remained closed. Red Cloud remained in the path. This fall the Government decided that, after all, it had no right to open the road. In April of the next year, 1868, another treaty was signed with the Sioux and the Cheyennes, by which the United States gave up any claim to the Powder River and Big Horn country, and the Indians promised to let the Union Pacific Railroad alone.

Red Cloud did not sign. "The white men are liars," he insisted; and he waited until the three forts, Smith and Kearney and Reno, were abandoned. Then, in November, after his warriors had burned them, and all the soldiers were gone out of the country, he put his name to the treaty.

Thus he won out. He had said that he would close the road, and he had done it.

Through the following years he remained quiet. He had had his fill of fighting. His name was great. He was head chief of the Red Cloud agency, later called Pine Ridge. Spotted Tail of the Brulés controlled the other agency, later called Rosebud.

Red Cloud always closely watched the whites. He was at peace, but suspicious. When the Black Hills were finally demanded by the United States, he sent out men to count the buffalo. The number in sight was too small. Some day, soon, the Indians would have no meat on their hunting grounds. Therefore Red Cloud decided that the red men must begin to live by aid of the white man; and he favored the reservations —even the sale of the Black Hills so that his people would be made rich enough to settle down.

He was looked up to as a warrior and a councillor, but the United States did not trust him; and after a time, put Spotted Tail over him, in charge of the two agencies. This made bad feeling, and Red Cloud and Spotted Tail did not speak to each other. However, his own people, who rose under Sitting Bull, urged him to join with them, in vain.

Red Cloud lived to be a very old man. He became almost blind, and partly paralyzed. He stuck to his one wife. They were together for many years.

He died in December, 1909, in a two-story house built for him by the Government on the Pine Ridge agency in South Dakota. He was aged eighty-seven. Five years before he had given his chief-ship over to his son, young Red Cloud, who carried the name. It is a name that will never be forgotten.

CHAPTER XXIII

STANDING BEAR SEEKS A HOME (1877-1880)

THE INDIAN WHO WON THE WHITE MAN'S VERDICT

THE Ponca Indians were members of the large Siouan family. They had not always been a separate tribe. In the old days they and the Omahas and the Kansas and the Osages had lived together as Omahas, near the mouth of the Osage River in eastern Nebraska.

Soon they divided, and held their clan names of Poncas, Omahas, Kansas and Osages.

The Poncas and Omahas clung as allies. Finally the Poncas remained by themselves, low down on the Niobrara River in northern Nebraska.

When the captains, Lewis and Clark, met some of them, the tribe had been cut by the small-pox to only some two hundred people. They never have been a big people. Their number today, about eight hundred and fifty, is as large as ever in their history.

They and the Omahas warred with the Sioux, but they never warred with the white men. They have always been friendly to the white men, except once; and that once brings up the story of Standing Bear.

Back in 1817 the Poncas made a treaty of friendship with the United States; and in 1825 they made another treaty, allowing white traders to live among them, and

Standing Bear

Courtesy of The American Bureau of Ethnology.

agreeing to let their own bad men (if any) be punished by the United States; and in 1859 they made another treaty, selling their hunting grounds to the United States, and keeping a tract on the Niobrara River for their own homes.

None of these treaties did they break. They were at peace with even the Sioux. They had good farms, and were prospering.

But in 1868 the United States laid out a new reservation for the Sioux. By a mistake this took in the Ponca reservation in Nebraska, and the Poncas were not told. The way they found out, was this: The Sioux began to come in and claim the land.

"That is not right," said the Poncas. "You do not belong here. All this country is ours. Go back. We do not want you."

So there was fighting, every little while, and the Poncas lost many warriors. This continued for nine years, until, by the raids of the Sioux, one fourth of the Poncas had been killed or captured.

Still they had not been told by the United States that these lands were theirs no longer; but, suddenly, in 1877, they were told that they must get out.

At this time they had three villages, on the lower Niobrara River, and eight bands, each under a chief. The chiefs were Standing Bear, White Eagle, Big Soldier, Traveling Buffalo, Black Crow, Over-the-land, Woodpecker, and Big-Hoofed Buffalo.

The United States informed the eight chiefs that they must remove their people to the Indian Territory, but did not say why.

Standing Bear had been born in 1829, so he was forty-eight years old. He stood high among the Poncas, because of his clan, the Wa-zha-zhe—a clan that could cure rattle-snake bites and work other wonders.

He strongly opposed giving up the Ponca home-land, upon which the tribe had lived for almost one hundred years, and which the United States had agreed, on paper, to give them in exchange for their hunting grounds. The other chiefs thought the same. They could not understand why they all should be thrown off, when they had done nothing wrong.

But the white men paid no attention. One of them, who was the United States Indian Inspector, only answered:

"The President says that you must sell this land. He will buy it and pay you money, and give you new land in the Indian Territory."

"We do not know your authority," argued Standing Bear. "You have no right to move us until we have held a council with the President."

"If you like the new land, then you can see the President and tell him so," offered the inspector. "If you don't like it, then you can see him and tell him so."

So Standing Bear and nine other chiefs went; but they were dubious.

The inspector showed the three pieces of land, and told them to choose. All the pieces were bad pieces. It was a hot country and a bare country, and not suited to the Poncas, who had good corn-fields and houses in their own country of the Niobrara.

Besides, now the white man said that they were to have no pay for their Niobrara land. He told the chiefs, according to Standing Bear:

"If you do not accept what land is offered you here, I will leave you here alone. You are one thousand miles from home. You have no money. You cannot speak the language."

Then he slammed the door.

"But we do not like this land," explained Standing Bear. "We could not make a living. The water is bad. Now send us to the President, as you promised."

The man would not send them. He would not take them home. He would not give them any of the Indian money, for buying food. He would not give them a paper, to show to the people along the way. He would not give them the interpreter, to talk for them. He would not take them to a railroad.

"He left us right here," said Standing Bear. "It was winter. We started for home on foot. At night we slept in hay-stacks. We barely lived till morning, it was so cold. We had nothing but our blankets. We took the ears of corn that had dried in the fields; we ate it raw. The soles of our moccasins wore out. We were barefoot in the snow. We were nearly dead when we reached the Oto reservation. It had been fifty days."

Their feet made bloody marks on the Oto reservation. The Otos and the Oto agent treated them kindly. They stayed ten days, to rest; then the Otos gave them each a pony, and in two more weeks they were home.

It had been a cold, hungry journey, of five hundred

miles, and their relatives and friends were glad to see them again.

But the United States inspector was waiting for them. He was angry. He said that the Great Father had ordered the Poncas to change homes. It did not seem to matter whether or not they liked the new home. And he called for soldiers, and all the Poncas were bundled out of their villages and taken to the hot country of the south. On the way women and children died. Standing Bear's daughter died.

Just as Standing Bear and the other chiefs had tried to explain, the new country was not a good country for the Poncas. It was humid and hot; their Niobrara country had been dry and bracing. Within one year a third of them were dead from sickness; the rest were weak and miserable. They pined for the villages that they had built and loved, and that they had lost without any known reason.

After a year and a half Standing Bear's boy died, as so many others had died; and the heart of Standing Bear was heavy. He did not sleep, by thinking that his son's bones must lie here in this unfriendly country. His medicine demanded that the boy should rest with their ancestors, in the Ponca ground along the dear Niobrara.

Therefore, in January, 1879, he placed the bones in a sack, and tied the sack to his neck, and taking his people who could travel, he set out to walk to Ponca land.

That was hard work. They made their way as best they could, but had been over three months on it when, in May, they arrived at the reservation of their friends the Omahas, near the Missouri River in northeastern Nebraska.

Chief Standing Bear asked the Omahas if they might rest, and plant a few acres of ground, so as to get food. The Omahas gave them seed and ground. Standing Bear still had the bones of his son, in the bag. When he had started a crop, he was going on with the bones, and bury them at the Niobrara, where the Poncas of happier years had been buried.

Before the crop was in, soldiers appeared, and arrested him and all his party, to take them back to the hot country.

This much alarmed the Omahas. They had heard how the Poncas had been moved off without warning and without reason. Standing Bear was not being allowed to stay; he had lost his country forever. The same thing might happen to the Omahas.

They had a similar treaty with the United States. They thought that they owned their lands. They had been improving them and living on them for years. They had spent much money of the tribe, for tools and buildings, and were becoming like white men. The Government had issued papers to them, showing which land each man possessed.

Now they were liable to lose their lands, as the Poncas had lost.

The Omahas hastened to ask white lawyers about it. They were told that the papers did not show that they owned the land; the papers only showed which lands each man had a right to farm.

The Omahas were Indians, and not white citizens, and could not own lands, man by man. When a man died, his land might be given to somebody else.

Now dread fastened upon the Omaha tribe. They hastened to draw up a petition to Congress, asking that the lands which their men owned or thought they owned be put down on paper forever. They wanted titles such as the white men had, so the lands could be recorded.

Miss Alice Fletcher, from Washington, had been sent to study the Omaha people; and they appealed to her. She helped them. The petition went to Washington, but the months passed without an answer.

Meanwhile Standing Bear and his bag of bones and his party were being taken south, by the soldiers from Fort Crook, Omaha, to the sickly hot country. When they camped on their way, near Omaha, a newspaper man talked with them. His name was Mr. T. H. Tibbles.

The story was printed in the Omaha papers, and at once Standing Bear had many white allies.

The Omaha City people invited him to come in and talk to them; and so he did, in a church that was crowded with listeners. Two lawyers, Mr. Poppleton and Mr. Webster, adopted him as a client; and before the soldiers had started on with him, the lawyers asked the court for a writ of habeas corpus—a challenge to the United States to surrender him, as a person who had been unlawfully arrested.

The United States argued that Standing Bear was an Indian, and that an Indian was not a "person," under the laws of the United States; he did not have any rights, in court.

Standing Bear had left his tribe, and was nobody, until he returned; and even then, he would be only an Indian.

Standing Bear's lawyers brought witnesses into court, to state that the Standing Bear party had traveled peacefully, like good citizens; had not even begged along the way.

Standing Bear was told to arise and repeat his story. Part of it is contained in this chapter. It was a remarkable speech. The people in the court-room believed it. Standing Bear's heart warmed. He was no Indian; he was a man.

The judge decided. He said that an Indian was a person, and had a right to the courts, and to liberty when he had not done wrong. The Poncas had been unjustly removed by force from their lands, and Standing Bear's party had been unjustly arrested. Therefore they should be released.

When this word was carried to Standing Bear by his lawyers, he was so pleased that he almost wept.

"Before this," he said, "when we have been wronged we went to war to get back our rights and avenge our wrongs. We took the tomahawk. We had no law to punish those who did us wrong, and we went out to kill. If they had guns and could kill us first, it was the fate of war. But you have found us a better way. You have gone into court for us, and I find that our wrongs can be righted there. Now I have no more use for the tomahawk. I want to lay it down forever." So he put it on the floor. "I lay it down. I have found a better way. I can now seek the ways of peace."

He gave the tomahawk to Attorney Webster, "to keep in remembrance of the great victory."

And a great victory it was, not only for the Poncas, but for all the Indians. Standing Bear's trip with the bones had gained him many new friends.

Now he traveled straight to the Niobrara, and nobody dared to stop him.

The next winter he made a tour of the East, with interpreters, and with Mr. Tibbles the newspaper ally. He spoke from many platforms, telling of the wrongs of the Indians. The newspapers everywhere spread his talk wider. Soon letters from white people and their societies began to pour into Washington, for the President and for the Congressmen.

As a result, in the spring of 1880 the Senate of the United States sent a commission into the West, to find out if Standing Bear's stories were really true.

They were true. Therefore the Poncas were told that they might go back to the Niobrara, if they wished. Some did so. They were called the Cold Country Band. Those who were willing to stay in the Indian Territory were granted better lands, and they were paid for the lands that they had lost in the north. They were called the Hot Country Band.

Each band was given titles to the lands held by it. The Omahas, too, won out, and were given titles. They and the Poncas secured the rights of citizens of the United States.

As for Standing Bear, he died, well satisfied and

much honored, in 1908, aged seventy-nine, and was buried there near the Niobrara, in ancient Ponca country, where his ancestors slept. He had saved his tribe.

CHAPTER XXIV

SITTING BULL THE WAR MAKER (1876-1881)

AN UNCONQUERED LEADER

THE treaty that Chief Red Cloud at last signed in the fall of 1868 was half white and half red. The white part made the Sioux agree to a reservation which covered all of present South Dakota west of the Missouri River. Here they were to live and be fed. The red part, put in by Red Cloud, said that the whole country west of the reservation to the Big Horn Mountains of northern Wyoming, and north of the North Platte River, should be Indian country. Here the Sioux and their Indian friends were to hunt as they pleased.

This closed the road, and gave the Powder River region to the Sioux. They might chase the buffalo, from central Wyoming up across Montana clear to Canada, and no white man could interfere. It was their own game reserve—and the best game reserve in the United States.

The Sioux numbered thirty thousand. Many of them preferred living in their hunting grounds instead of upon the reservation. That was their natural life—to hunt and to war. Besides, they found out that the United States was not doing as had been promised. There were to be cows, seeds, farm tools, teachers, and so forth, for the reservation Indians—and scarcely a third of these things was supplied.

The Indians upon the reservation did not live nearly so comfortably as those who did as they pleased, in the hunting grounds.

So the treaty did not work out well. The hunting-ground Indians were perfectly free. They had guests from other tribes; and in the passing back and forth, white men were attacked. The Crows of western Montana complained that the Sioux invaded them, and that they might as well go to war, themselves, as try to stay at home.

The Government had intended that the Sioux should settle upon the big reservation, and from there take their hunting trips. Speedily, or in 1869, General Sherman, head of the army, declared that the Indians found outside of the reservation might be treated as hostiles, and brought back.

Nevertheless, by the terms of the Red Cloud treaty, the Sioux had a right to be in this country, which was all theirs, if they behaved themselves.

Among the leaders of the hunting-ground Sioux, Sitting Bull ranked with the foremost. He was a Hunkpapa Sioux, of the Teton division—in which Spotted Tail was leader of the Brulés and Red Cloud of the Oglalas.

But Sitting Bull was no chief. By his own count he laid claim to being a great warrior; by the Sioux count he had powerful medicine—he could tell of events to come. And this was his strong hold upon the Sioux. They feared him.

He had been born in 1834, in present South Dakota. The name given him as a boy was Jumping Badger. His father's name was Four Horns, and also Ta-tan-ka Yo-tan-ka or Sitting Buffalo-bull. When Jumping Badger was only fourteen years old he went with his father on the war trail against the Crows. A Crow was killed, and little Jumping Badger touched the body first, and counted a coup, or stroke.

To be the first to count coup on a fallen enemy was high honor. Frequently a wounded warrior only pretended to be dead, and when his foe approached him close, he shot.

Upon their return home, old Sitting Bull gave a feast, and distributed many horses, and transferred his own name to Jumping Badger.

After this, although young Sitting Bull counted many coups, he practiced making medicine until he gained much reputation as a future-teller. He openly hated the whites. His hate was as deep as that of O-pe-chan-can-ough, the Pamunkey.

He grew to be a burly, stout man, with light brown hair and complexion, a grim heavy face pitted by small-pox, and two shrewd, blood-shot eyes. He limped, from a wound.

His band was small; but his camp was the favorite gathering place for the reservation Indians, on hunting trips. They took presents to him, that he might bring the buffalo.

Thus matters went on, broken with complaints. It was hard to tell which were reservation Indians and which were wild Indians. When the Sitting Bull peo-

SITTING BULL

Courtesy of The American Bureau of Ethnology.

ple and other bands came in to the reservation, and drew rations of flour, they emptied the flour on the prairie and used the sacks as clothing. This helped to make the reservation Indians ill content. The wild Indians evidently were living very well indeed.

Along in 1871 the Northern Pacific Railroad wished to build westward. The route would take them through the country given to the Sioux, and the Sioux said no. Their treaty protected them against the white man's roads. They attacked a surveying party escorted by soldiers, and killed two. This was in 1872.

It was a brutal killing. Rain-in-the-face was arrested for this, on the reservation; but he escaped and vowed vengeance. He went to Sitting Bull, and was safe.

In 1874 the United States began to ask for the Pahsap-pa, or Black Hills, in South Dakota. To the Sioux and the Cheyennes, Pah-sap-pa was medicine ground. Spirits dwelt there; it was the home of the Thunder Bird and other magic creatures; it contained much game, and quantities of tent poles, for lodges.

Spotted Tail of the Brulés went in. He hung around the white men's mining camps, and found out that the white men were crazy for the gold.

The United States had been accustomed to buying Indian land cheap, and getting rich out of it. Now it offered to buy the Black Hills for six millions of dollars, or to rent them for four hundred thousand dollars a year.

Coached by Spotted Tail and by Red Cloud, the Sioux laughed, and asked sixty millions of dollars.

So the deal did not go through, this time. However, the Sioux lost Pah-sap-pa, just the same.

The United States Government was unable to keep the gold-seekers out. They dodged through the troops. There were fights with the Sioux, and the Sioux became angered in earnest.

They saw their Black Hills invaded by a thousand white men. Other white men, guarded by soldiers, were planning to run a railroad right through the Powder River country. On the Great Sioux reservation Spotted Tail and Red Cloud were the head chiefs; but out on the hunting grounds the Sitting Bull people stayed and prepared to make war and hold the Sioux lands.

The Sioux on the reservations began to leave, and join Sitting Bull. They felt that Red Cloud's heart was with them. He had notified the United States that it must keep the white men out of Sioux country.

The United States also was alarmed. The Sioux seemed to be using the reservation as a sort of supply depot; they got provisions and clothing there, and took them to the hunting grounds.

General Alfred H. Terry, who commanded the Military Department of Dakota, sent scouts to inform Sitting Bull that unless he came in, with all his people, out of the Big Horn Valley and the Powder River country, before a certain time, troops would bring him out. There would be war.

Sitting Bull answered:

"When you come for me you need bring no guides.

You will easily find me. I shall be right here. I shall not run away."

In February, this 1876, the United States started to go after him, but the cold weather delayed the plans. Then, in May, matters were all arranged. There were to be three columns, to surround the unruly Sitting Bull.

General George Crook, the famous Indian fighter, was to march into the Big Horn country from the south with thirteen hundred men; Colonel John Gibbon was to march in from the west with four hundred men; General Terry's infantry, and General George A. Custer's Seventh Cavalry, one thousand men, were to march in from the east.

They were to meet at the Powder River, and capture Sitting Bull.

A great many Indians had rallied to Sitting Bull and his comrade chief Crazy Horse—an Oglala who commanded the Cheyennes. Sitting Bull was making medicine. He told the warriors that in a short time there would be a big fight with the soldiers on the Big Horn, and that the soldiers would be defeated.

Crazy Horse struck the enemy first. He met General Crook's column and stopped it. Then he joined Sitting Bull again.

Now in June the Sitting Bull camp upon the Little Big Horn River in the Big Horn Valley of southern Montana was three miles long and contained ten thousand people. It had twenty-five hundred good fighters. It was not afraid, but its people were here to hunt and dance and have a good time. Although they listened to the prophecy of Sitting Bull, they really did not expect that the soldiers would find them.

Chief Gall, a fine man, of the Hunkpapas, was head war chief; his aide was Crow King. Crazy Horse commanded the Northern Cheyennes. The head of the Miniconjou Sioux was Lame Deer. Big Road commanded the Oglalas. There were other Sioux also—some Brulés, and some Without Bows; and a few Blackfeet and Arapahos.

General Custer, whose regular rank was lieutenant-colonel, found the village with his Seventh Cavalry. He had left General Terry, in order to scout across country; and when his scouts told him that the Sioux camp was before him, he rode on to the attack.

About noon of June 25th he divided his troops into three columns, to attack from different directions. The largest column, of five companies, he led, himself.

Not until that morning did the Sitting Bull people know that the soldiers were near. There was much excitement. The ponies were saddled, and the women began to pack their household stuff; but the warriors did not intend to run away.

Sitting Bull was certain that the white men would be defeated. The night before, his medicine had been very strong. An eagle had promised a great victory. Now he said that during the fight he would stay in the village and make more medicine. So Chief Gall it was who commanded.

But Sitting Bull did not stay in the village. When the bullets of the soldiers pelted into the lodges he lost faith in his own prophecy. Taking his two wives and whatever else he might gather, he bolted for a safer place. He missed one of his twin boys, but he did not stop to look for him.

He was ten miles out, when he received news of the victory. And a terrible victory that had been: of the five companies of General Custer, the Long Hair, only one man had escaped—although the Sioux did not know of that escape. He was Curly, a Crow scout. At any rate, the Long Hair's warriors, to the number of two hundred and twelve, had been killed in an hour.

The other soldiers were penned up, and could be killed, too.

So Sitting Bull rode back again, with his family. He said that he had not intended to run away. He had been out in the hills, making his medicine; and the bodies of the soldiers would prove it.

That certainly seemed true. The Indians had lost only twenty, and had killed more than two hundred.

Sitting Bull was greater than ever. Never before had such a victory been won at such little cost. This night the village danced and sang, and Sitting Bull kept by himself, and accepted the presents given to him.

Chief Gall had thought to starve out the soldiers who were penned up, and were being watched by warriors. These were the two other columns, of the Seventh Cavalry. But the next day, General Terry and Colonel Gibbon approached, in order (they had planned) to meet the Custer detachment. When Chief Gall heard that the "walking soldiers" were nearing, he decided that there had been fighting enough.

So he ordered the village to be broken, and the warriors to come in; they all left before dark, depending upon the medicine of Sitting Bull to lead them to new hunting grounds.

Soon Crazy Horse took his band and branched off for himself. He was a nephew of Chief Spotted Tail, but fierce against the whites. The rest followed Chief Sitting Bull and Chief Gall.

For a while they saw no more soldiers. Now and then other Indians from the reservation joined them, bringing supplies; and now and then parties left, to scout by themselves. Sitting Bull and Gall and all knew this country very well; it was Sioux country. They knew it far better than the soldiers did. There were many hiding places.

When the weather began to grow cold, in the fall, the Sitting Bull people commenced to think of winter. They received word that the soldiers were stopping everybody from leaving the reservation. This cut down the supplies.

The Gray Fox, who was General Crook, struck several bands in the midst of the hunting grounds. He had wiped out American Horse and had pressed Crazy Horse very hard. More soldiers were pouring in.

The Sitting Bull band numbered three thousand. They used lots of meat. The buffalo were being frightened by so much travel of soldiers, and for the band to stay long in one spot was dangerous. Some of the women and men got faint-hearted, and deserted. They carried word to the soldiers, and asked to be sent to the reservation. Sitting Bull's medicine did not prevent them from running away.

He and Gall planned to march farther northward, across the Yellowstone River, to a better buffalo country, and make camp for a big hunt. A store of meat ought to be laid in, before winter.

A new fort was being located on the Yellowstone at the mouth of the Tongue River, southeastern Montana. They marched to cross the Yellowstone below this fort; and while near the Yellowstone they drove back a soldiers' wagon-train that was trying to reach the fort.

The wagons tried again, five days later, and there was another fight. Sitting Bull sent a note to the white chief.

Yellowstone.

I want to know what you are doing traveling by this road. You scare all the buffalo away. I want to hunt in this place. I want you to turn back from here. If you don't, I will fight you again. I want you to leave what you have got here and turn back from here.

I am your friend.

SITTING BULL.

I mean all the rations you have got and some powder. Wish you would write as soon as you can.

This was a "feeler," to see what kind of a man the white chief was. The white chief, whose name was Lieutenant-Colonel E. S. Otis, of the Twenty-second Infantry, answered at once.

To Sitting Bull:

I intend to take this train through to Tongue River, and will be pleased to accommodate you with a fight at any time.

Sitting Bull and his chiefs held council. If they might make a peace, they could stay out all winter with their families, and when the grass greened in the spring they could travel as they pleased. The white soldiers had the advantage, in the winter.

So two Indians were sent forward with a flag of truce, to say that the Sitting Bull people were hungry and tired, and to propose a peace talk. The white chief said that there was a higher chief at the mouth of the Tongue River, with whom they must talk, but he sent them some bread and bacon.

Sitting Bull and Chief Gall, Low Neck, Pretty Bull and the others did not go to find the white commanding chief; they continued on, and in a few days the American commander caught up with them, himself, north of the Yellowstone.

He agreed to meet Sitting Bull between the lines, for a talk. They each took six men. The white chief was Colonel Nelson A. Miles. He had only about four hundred soldiers, and one cannon. Sitting Bull had one thousand warriors, and was not afraid.

"What are all these soldiers doing in this country?" he demanded. "Why don't they stay in their forts, where they belong? It is time they went there, for the winter."

"The soldiers are in this country to bring you and your men out and put them on the reservation," replied Colonel Miles. "We do not wish war. But if you insist on war, then you will be shut up. You cannot roam about over the country, and cause trouble."

"This country belongs to the Indian and not to the white man," retorted Sitting Bull. "We want nothing to do with the white man. We want the white man to go away, and leave us alone. No white man ever lived who loved an Indian, and no true Indian ever lived that did not hate the white man. God Almighty made me an Indian. He did not make me an agency Indian, and I'll fight and die fighting before any white man can make me an agency Indian. How did you know where I was to be found?"

"I not only knew where you were, but I know where you came from and where you're going," asserted Colonel Miles.

"Where am I going?"

"You intend to remain here three days, and then move to the Big Dry and hunt buffalo."

This showed Sitting Bull that he had been betrayed by spies. He flared into a rage, and his words were hot. He hated the whites; he had a thousand warriors at his back, and his power was great.

He would make peace, but only if all the white men got out of the country. There must be no forts or roads or towns. He wanted no presents of food or clothing from the United States. If the United States would leave a few trading posts, he would trade for powder and flour, but he would live free, to do as he chose.

So this talk and other talks amounted to nothing new. The white chief told him to prepare for war, and there was a battle. At one moment, the Sitting Bull warriors had the soldiers surrounded; but the cannon shells were too much to face, the walking soldiers stood stanch, and finally the Sioux had to retreat with their families.

The white chief, Miles, proved to be a stubborn

fighter. He pursued and captured almost all the camp supplies. This broke the hearts of the Sitting Bull band. His medicine had grown weak. Five chiefs, with two thousand of the warriors and women and children, surrendered, so as to be kept warm and to be sure of food. But Sitting Bull and Gall went on, leading four hundred northward.

The weather got very cold and snowy. They stayed for a time near the Missouri River in northern Montana. Sitting Bull's medicine failed entirely. The soldiers marched upon them right through the blizzards, and no place seemed safe.

The other bands were being captured. The walking soldiers and the big-guns-that-shot-twice were everywhere, to south, east and west. The Crazy Horse Cheyennes and Oglalas were taken. They agreed to go upon the reservation.

When Sitting Bull heard of this, he resolved to get out of reach of the Americans altogether. He and Gall headed north again, and crossed into Canada.

This was Sioux country, too. The Sioux never had had any dispute with the Great White Mother; she seemed better than the Great White Father. Accordingly Sitting Bull plumped himself and his band down upon Canada ground, and defied the United States to meddle with him.

Other runaways joined him. It was now spring. Some of the runaways were from the reservation. They reported that they had almost starved, there, during the winter.

So when the United States sent up after Sitting Bull,

he laughed. General Terry, his old enemy, was in the American party, and did the talking.

The President invited the Sioux to come back into the United States, and give up their arms and their horses, in exchange for cows. Sitting Bull replied scornfully.

"For sixty-four years you have kept me and my people, and treated us bad. What have we done that you should wish us to stop? We have done nothing. It is all the people on your side who have started us to do as we did. We could not go anywhere else, so we came here. I would like to know why you come here? I did not give you that country; but you followed me about, so I had to leave and come over to this country. You have got ears, and eyes to see with, and you see how I live with these people. You see me. Here I am. If you think I am a fool, you are a bigger fool than I am. You come here to tell us lies, but we don't want to hear them. I don't wish any such language used to me. This country is mine, and I intend to stay here and raise this country full of grown people. That is enough, so no more. The part of the country you gave me, you ran me out of. I don't want to hear two more words. I wish you to go back, and to take it easy going back. Tell them in Washington if they have one man who speaks the truth to send him to me and I will listen. I don't believe in a Government that has made fifty-two treaties with the Sioux and has kept none of them."

Back went the commission, to report that they could do nothing at all with Sitting Bull.

Other parties from the American side of the line crossed over to talk with Sitting Bull. He laid down the law to them.

"If the Great Father gives me a reservation I don't want to be held on any part of it. I will keep on the reservation, but I want to go where I please. I don't want a white man over me. I don't want an agent. I want to have a white man with me, but not to be my chief. I can't trust any one else to trade with my people or talk to them. I want interpreters, but I want it to be seen and known that I have my rights. I don't want to give up game as long as there is any game. I will be half white until the game is gone. Then I will be all white."

"Did you lead in the Custer fight?"

"There was a Great Spirit who guided and controlled that battle. I could do nothing. I was supported by the Great Mysterious One. I am not afraid to talk about that. It all happened—it is past and gone. I do not lie. Low Dog says I can't fight until some one lends me a heart. Gall says my heart is no bigger than a finger-nail. We have all fought hard. We did not know Custer. When we saw him we threw up our hands, and I cried, 'Follow me and do as I do.' We whipped each other's horses, and it was all over."

By this it is seen that Sitting Bull was a poser, and had lost the respect of the Sioux. Chief Gall despised him. The camp was getting unhappy. The life in Canada was not an easy life. The Great White Mother let the red children stay, because it was Indian country, but she refused to feed them, or help them against the United States.

There were no buffalo near. When the Sioux raided into the United States, the soldiers and the Crow scouts were waiting. Their old hunting grounds were closed tight.

Rain-in-the-face and other chiefs surrendered, to go to the reservation. Chief Gall defied Sitting Bull, and took two thirds of the remaining Indians and surrendered, also.

Sitting Bull now had only forty-five men and one hundred and forty women and children. They all were starving. A white scout visited them, with promise of pardon by the United States. So in July, of 1881, after he had stayed away four years, he surrendered, at Fort Buford at the mouth of the Yellowstone River.

He came in sullen and sour and unconquered, but not as a conqueror. They all were dirty and shabby and hungry. With Sitting Bull there rode on ponies his old father, Four Horns, and his elder children. In a wagon piled high with camp goods rode his two wives, one of whom was named Pretty Plume, and his small children.

A long train of other wagons and carts followed. There was no glory in this return.

At the Standing Rock Sioux agency he found that Chief Gall was the real ruler. The people there now thought little of Sitting Bull. His medicine had proved weak. He tried to make it strong, and he was laughed at.

Soon the Government deemed best to remove him

and his main band, and shut them up for a while. Sitting Bull was kept a prisoner of war for two years. After that he took a trip through the East, but he was hissed. He rode in the Buffalo Bill Wild West show for a short time. But the white people never forgot the Custer battle, and looked upon Sitting Bull as a thoroughly bad Indian.

He assumed to settle down, at peace, upon the Standing Rock reservation, in a cabin not far from the place where he had been born. But as he had said, he was not "an agency Indian," and did not want to be an agency Indian.

There is another chapter to be written about Sitting Bull.

CHAPTER XXV

CHIEF JOSEPH GOES TO WAR (1877)

AND OUT-GENERALS THE UNITED STATES ARMY

AFTER Colonel Nelson A. Miles of the Fifth Infantry had driven Sitting Bull and Chief Gall of the Sioux into Canada and his troops were trying to stop their raids back, at present Fort Keogh near Miles City on the Yellowstone River in southeastern Montana he received word of another Indian war.

The friendly Pierced Noses of Oregon had broken the peace chain. They had crossed the mountains and were on their way north, for Canada.

That the Pierced Noses had taken the war trail was astonishing news. For one hundred years they had held the hand of the white man. Their proudest boast said: "The Nez Percés have never shed white blood."

They spoke truly. During the seventy years since the two captains Lewis and Clark had met them in 1805, only one white man had been killed by a Pierced Nose. That was not in war, but in a private quarrel between the two.

Hunters, traders and missionaries had always been helped by the Pierced Noses. The white man's religion had been favored. The Good Book had been prized.

Young Chief Joseph was now the leader of the

Pierced Noses upon the war trail. His Indian name was Hin-ma-ton Ya-lat-kit—Thunder-rising-from-the-water-over-the-land. But his father had been christened Joseph by the missionaries; so the son was called Young Chief Joseph.

A tall, commanding, splendid-looking Indian he had grown to be, at forty years of age. He was every inch a chief, and had a noble face.

His people were the Lower Nez Percés, who lived in the beautiful Wallowa Valley—their Valley of the Winding Waters, in northeastern Oregon. Here they raised many horses, and hunted, but put in few crops. Old Chief Joseph had believed that the earth should not be disturbed; the people should eat only what it produced of itself. The earth was their mother.

He believed also that nobody owned any part of the earth. The earth had been given to all, by the Great Creator. Everybody had a right to use what was needed.

Twenty years ago, or in 1855, Old Chief Joseph had signed a paper, by which the United States agreed to let the Pierced Noses alone on their wide lands of western Idaho, and eastern Oregon and Washington.

But it was seen that the Pierced Noses did not cultivate the better portion of this country; the white men wanted to plough the Valley of Winding Waters; and eight years later another treaty was made, which cut out the Winding Waters. It narrowed the Nez Percés to the Lapwai reservation in Idaho.

Old Chief Joseph did not sign this treaty. Other chiefs signed, for the Nez Percés. The United States thought that this was enough, as it considered the Pierced Noses to be one nation. The Valley of the Winding Waters was said to be open to white settlers.

The Old Chief Joseph Pierced Noses continued to live there, just the same. They asserted that they had never given it up, and that the Upper Pierced Noses had no right to speak for the Lower Pierced Noses.

As Young Chief Joseph afterwards explained:

"Suppose a white man comes to me and says: 'Joseph, I like your horses and I want to buy them.' I say to him: 'No; my horses suit me; I will not sell them.' Then he goes to my neighbor, and says to him: 'Joseph has some good horses. I want them, but he refuses to sell.' My neighbor answers: 'Pay me the money and I will sell you Joseph's horses.' The white man returns to me and says: 'Joseph, I have bought your horses and you must let me have them.' That is the way our lands were bought."

When Old Joseph died, Young Joseph held his hand and listened to his words:

> My son, my body is returning to my mother earth, and my spirit is going very soon to see the Great Spirit Chief. When I am gone, think of your country. You are the chief of these people. They look to you to guide them. Always remember that your father never sold his country. You must stop your ears whenever you are asked to sign a treaty selling your home. A few years more, and white men will be all around you. They have their eyes on this land. My son, never forget my dying words. This country holds your father's body. Never sell the bones of your father and your mother.

Young Joseph promised.

"A man who would not love his father's grave is worse than a wild animal," he said.

After that he was careful never to accept any presents from the United States.

Even before the treaty of 1863 which was supposed to cover the Winding Waters valley, the white men had invaded the Pierced Nose country. Gold had been discovered in Idaho. In 1861 the white man's town of Lewiston had been laid out, among the Nez Percés—and there it was, without permission.

The Black Hills were being taken from the Sioux, in the same way.

Now trouble occurred between the Indians and the whites in the Valley of the Winding Waters, also. The Government started in to buy the settlers' claims, so that the Pierced Noses might remain undisturbed, but Congress did not appropriate the money.

In order to force the Indians off, the settlers stole their horses, and their cattle; Indians were whipped, and killed. Chief Joseph's brother was killed. The murderer was not brought to trial, because Joseph would not allow his people to appear in court.

"I have decided to let him escape and enjoy life," said Joseph. "I will not take his life for the one he took. I do not want anything in payment for what he did. I pronounce the sentence that he shall live."

All that the Nez Percés asked, was that the white men get out.

Among the Indians of this Columbia River region there had sprung up a prophet, as in the days of Tecumseh. His name was Smo-hal-la. He preached the doctrine that the land belonged to the Indians, and that the red man was the real child of the Great Spirit.

A day was nearing, when the Great Spirit would re-people the earth with Indians, and the white race would be driven out. In the meantime the red men must live in their own way, and have nothing to do with the white men. They must not dig into the body of their "mother," the earth.

The followers of Smohalla were called Dreamers. Chief Joseph was a member of the Dreamers; so were many of his band.

As the Chief Joseph people would not come in upon the Lapwai reservation, and the missionaries and Indian agent and soldiers could not persuade them, General Oliver O. Howard, who commanded the Military Department of the Columbia, met in council with them, at Fort Lapwai, in April and May, 1876.

General Howard was a brave soldier who had lost his right arm in the battle of Fair Oaks, during the Civil War. He was a kind, just man, one whom the Apaches and other tribes greatly trusted; but he could do little with the stubborn Pierced Noses.

They usually dressed like white people. When they came to the council they were painted, and wore buckskins and blankets, according to the custom of the Dreamers.

Chief Joseph finally appeared. His younger brother, Ollicut, whom he dearly loved, was here. So were Hush-hush-cute, chief of the Palouse tribe who mingled with the Pierced Noses in friendship; and Sub-Chiefs Looking Glass and White Bird; and old Too-hul-hul-so-te, a Too-at, or Drummer Dreamer chief.

In the principal councils Too-hul-hul-so-te was the

most out-spoken, for the Pierced Noses. Chief Joseph and Ollicut his brother were more quiet. But General Howard and Toohulhulsote had several tilts.

The white chiefs stated that the Nez Percés were to go upon the Lapwai reservation; then they would be given the privilege of hunting and fishing in the Winding Waters country.

"The earth is our mother. When the earth was made, there were no marks or lines placed upon it," grunted the surly, broad-shouldered Toohulhulsote. "The earth yields enough, of itself. It is not to be disturbed by ploughs. It is not to be bought or sold. It carries its own chieftain-ship. Nobody can sell possession of it. We never have made any trade. Part of the Indians gave up their land. We never did. The Great Spirit made the earth as it is, and as he wanted it, and he made a part of it for us to live upon. I don't see where you get the right to say we shall not live where he placed us."

"You have said twenty times that the earth is your mother," replied General Howard, growing angry. "Let us hear no more about it, but come to business."

"Who are you, that you ask us to talk and then tell me I sha'n't talk?" retorted the saucy old Toohulhulsote. "Are you the Great Spirit? Did you make the world? Did you make the sun? Did you make the rivers to run for us to drink? Did you make the grass to grow? Did you make all these things, that you talk to us as though we were boys? If you did, then you have the right to talk as you do."

"But," argued General Howard, "you know very

well that the Government has fixed a reservation and that the Indian must go upon it."

"What person pretends to divide the land and put me on it?" growled old Toohulhulsote.

"I am the man," General Howard answered. "I stand here for the President."

"The Indians may do as they like, but I am not going on the reservation," announced Toohulhulsote.

His words were causing much excitement and bad feeling, and General Howard ordered him arrested. The young men murmured among themselves, and would have begun war at once by rescuing him; but Chief Joseph spoke to them and quieted them.

Toohulhulsote was kept locked up for five days. Meanwhile Chief Joseph had resolved to permit no war.

"I said in my heart," related Joseph, "that rather than have war I would give up my country. I would rather give up my father's grave. I would give up everything, rather than have the blood of white men on the hands of my people."

Thirty days was named as the time within which he must gather his people and goods and remove to the reservation. He counseled everybody to obey. When Toohulhulsote came home he urged the Nez Percés men to fight, and not be driven like dogs from the land where they were born; but Joseph stood with a strong heart.

The time seemed too short for moving so many families, their horses and cattle. Still, he worked hard, and all was going smoothly, when without warning some bad white men raided the gathered cattle, and killed one of the herders.

This aroused the young men, again. A grand council of the Pierced Noses met, and talked war and peace both. Chief Joseph talked peace. He was very anxious to get his people into the reservation before more killings took place. The thirty days were almost up.

Then, on the very last day, or June 13, his young men broke away from him. There was one, whose father had been killed by the settlers. There were the young man's father's relatives. There were two Indians who had been whipped.

The young man rode away from the council, vowing war. He and his friends went out; they killed the white murderer, and others; they came back and shouted to the council:

"Why do you sit here like women? The war has already begun."

So it had. Joseph and Ollicut were not here, but Chief White Bird hastened about, crying:

"All must join now. There is blood. You will be punished if you stay back."

More went out. The man who had whipped the two Indians was killed. A dozen of the settlers were killed. Chief Joseph found that war had been declared; plenty of ammunition had been collected without his knowing it; there was no use in any peace talk now.

He tried to make his people agree not to injure more settlers. Then he moved the camp to White Bird Canyon, at the Salmon River in Idaho just across from the northeast corner of Oregon.

They did not have long to wait. General Howard at once sent two troops of the First Cavalry against him. Troop F was commanded by Captain David Perry, and First Lieutenant Edward Russell Theller of the Twenty-first Infantry; Troop H was commanded by Captain J. G. Trimble and First Lieutenant William R. Parnell. The two troops numbered ninety men. Ten settlers joined them, so that the whole number was one hundred.

Chief Joseph and Chief White Bird his assistant had sixty warriors. At dawn of June 17 Ollicut, through a spy-glass, saw the soldiers entering the narrow canyon.

Ollicut and White Bird wished to cross over the Salmon River with the women and children, and fight from the other side.

"No, we will fight them here," said Joseph.

He had never fought a battle. The soldiers and settlers did not expect him to do much; he himself did not know what he could do; but he was a born general, he had watched the white soldiers drill, and, as he explained: "The Great Spirit puts it into the heart and head of man to know how to defend himself."

Now he stowed the women and children in a safe place, and posted his warriors. White Bird commanded the right flank; he, the left. He cleverly seized upon the high ground on the broken sides of the canyon.

The soldiers rode in, by column of twos, until at the wide spot they changed to column of fours. Chief Joseph's men suddenly fired. Captain Perry used all his military skill, but in short order he was thoroughly defeated.

Joseph missed not a point. No white man could have done better. He threatened the right flank—Captain Perry hastened men to strengthen it and then White Bird turned the left flank. The volunteers ran away, Chief Joseph grabbed the best position; now he had the soldiers under his thumb, and they retreated helter-skelter.

He cut off the rear guard, and every one in it was killed fighting. Captain Perry had worked hard to rally his men. No use. The Chief Joseph men pressed furiously.

The actual battle had occupied only a few minutes. The soldiers lost Lieutenant Theller and thirty-two men shot dead, out of the ninety; seven were wounded. The volunteers lost four men. The Pierced Noses did not try to take any scalps.

Chief Joseph's warriors pursued for twelve miles, and quit. During the battle his wife was presented by the Great Spirit with a little daughter. So now he had a baby to look out for.

Captain Perry was much mortified by the easy victory over him. The Pierced Noses of Joseph and White Bird rejoiced. They had done better than they had expected. The soldiers had proved to be not very great.

Joseph had planned to take his people only beyond the Bitter Root Mountains of northeastern Idaho, by the Pierced Noses' Road-to-the-buffalo, and stay in the Powder River country of Montana until he might come to terms with the United States. He was willing to risk the Sioux.

But General Howard did not sleep. He summoned troops from all his wide department of the Columbia. The telegraph carried the word into California, and down into Arizona.

When he had two hundred soldiers he led them, himself. Chief Joseph ferried his women and children over the roaring Salmon River on skin rafts towed by swimming ponies, and put the river between him and General Howard.

General Howard viewed the position, and was puzzled. His rival general was a genius in defense. He crossed the river, to the attack. Chief Joseph dodged him, crossed the river farther north, and circling southward cut his trail and his communications with Fort Lapwai; fell upon Captain S. G. Whipple's First Cavalry, which was in his path—surrounded it, wiped out Lieutenant Sevier Rains and ten cavalrymen, scattered the reinforcements, and passed on, for the Road-to-the-buffalo.

General Howard heard that he had been side-stepped, and that the Nez Percés were beyond his lines. With almost six hundred men, two field-pieces and a Gatling gun he followed at best speed. The "treaty" or friendly Pierced Noses aided him; so did the Bannock Indians.

Chief Joseph had been joined by his friend Chief Looking Glass. Now he had two hundred and fifty warriors—also four hundred and fifty women and children, two thousand horses, as many cattle, and much lodge baggage. In all the history of wars, no general carried a greater burden.

On July 11 he turned at the banks of the south Clearwater, in northern Idaho, to give battle again. He had thrown up dirt entrenchments, and was waiting for General Howard's infantry, cavalry, artillery and scouts.

General Howard formed line. He had graduated with honors at West Point in 1854, and had won high rank in the Civil War. But Joseph wellnigh defeated him—nearly captured his supply train, did capture a spring and keep him from the drinking water; and had it not been for reinforcements coming in and creating two attacks at once on the Pierced Noses' position, he would have made General Howard retire.

The battle lasted two days. It was really a victory for Chief Joseph.

"I do not think that I had to exercise more thorough generalship during the Civil War," General Howard confessed.

Chief Joseph withdrew his people in good order. General Howard in desperation sent the cavalry, under Chief-of-Staff E. C. Mason, to find the Pierced Noses and hold them. Colonel Mason did not find them—they found *him*, and he was very glad to return in haste to General Howard.

The Joseph people were now safely in the Lo-lo Trail, or the Road-to-the-buffalo, that wound up the Bitter Root Range, and down on the other side. On this trail the two captains Lewis and Clark had almost perished. What with the great forest trees fallen crisscross, the dense brush and the sharp tumbled rocks, no trail could be rougher.

Over and under and through the trees and rocks Chief Joseph forced his women and children, his ponies and cattle and baggage. Behind him he left blood and disabled horses and cows. One hundred and fifty miles behind him he left the toiling, panting soldiers, whose forty axe-men were constantly at work clearing a passage for the artillery and the packs.

Even at that, the soldiers marched sixteen miles a day; but the Pierced Noses marched faster.

The telegraph was swifter still. Fort Missoula, at the east end of the trail, had been notified. Captain C. C. Rawn of the Seventh Infantry hastily fortified the pass down, with fifty regulars and one hundred volunteers. Chief Joseph side-stepped him also, left him waiting, and by new trails turned south down the Bitter Root Valley on the east side of the mountains!

The Bitter Root Valley was well settled. The Pierced Noses molested no ranches or towns. They traded, as they went, for supplies.

Colonel John Gibbon, who had campaigned against Sitting Bull, now took up the chase. Chief Joseph did not know about Colonel Gibbon's troops, and made camp on the Big Hole River, near the border in southwestern Montana. He was preparing lodge-poles, to take to the buffalo country.

Here, at dawn of August 9, Colonel Gibbon with two hundred regulars and volunteers surprised him completely. A storm of bullets swept his lodges, before his people were astir. Everybody dived for safety.

Some of the warriors left their guns. The white soldiers charged into the camp. All was confusion; all was death—but the warriors rallied.

In twenty minutes the white soldiers were destroying the camp with fire. In an hour they were fighting for their lives. The Pierced Noses had not fled, as Indians usually fled in a surprise; they had stayed, had surrounded the camp place, and were riddling the soldiers' lines.

The squaws and boys helped. On the other side, Colonel Gibbon himself used a rifle. He ordered his troops into the timber. The Chief Joseph people rushed into their camp, packed up under hot fire, and bundled the women and children and loose horses to safety. The warriors remained.

The soldiers threw up entrenchments. Colonel Gibbon was wounded. The Indians captured his fieldpiece, and a pack mule loaded with two thousand rounds of rifle ammunition. They disabled the cannon and drove off the mule. They fired the grass, and only a change of wind saved the soldiers from being driven into the open.

All that day and the next day the battle lasted. At dusk of August 9 Colonel Gibbon had sent out couriers, with call for reinforcements. "Hope you will hurry to our relief," he appealed, to General Howard. Couriers rode to the Montana forts, also. The whole country was being stirred. Even Arizona was getting troops ready.

This night of August 10 Chief Joseph learned from one of his scouts who had been posted on the back trail, that General Howard was hurrying to the rescue. So he withdrew his people again, to make another march.

He had lost heavily. Eighty men, women and children were dead. Out of one hundred and ninety men in the battle of the Big Hole, Colonel Gibbon had lost sixty-nine in killed and wounded, including six officers.

But the white men could easily get more soldiers; Chief Joseph could get no more warriors. He decided to join with Sitting Bull's Sioux, in Canada.

Canada was a long way; maybe a thousand miles. General Howard and Colonel Gibbon pursued. Joseph crossed the mountains again, into the southward. He veered east for the Yellowstone National Park. On the road he found two hundred and fifty fresh ponies. General Howard sent Lieutenant G. R. Bacon with cavalry to cut in front of him and defend a pass; and camped, himself, for a short rest, on the Camas Meadows, one day's march behind the enemy.

Chief Joseph turned on him, deceived his sentries with a column of fours that looked like Lieutenant Bacon's men coming back, and ran off all of General Howard's pack mules.

"I got tired of General Howard, and wanted to put him afoot," said Chief Joseph.

And he almost did it; for had not the cavalry horses been picketed close in, they would have been stampeded, too.

General Howard had to wait for mules from Virginia City. Lieutenant Bacon wearied of watching the pass; left it—and Chief Joseph marched through, into the Yellowstone Park.

Now Colonel Miles, at Fort Keogh, far in the east, had been notified. He sent out Colonel S. D. Sturgis and six companies of the fighting Seventh Cavalry, with Crow scouts, to head Joseph off.

Colonel Sturgis made fast time to the southwest. But Chief Joseph fooled him; pretended to go in one direction and took another, leaving the Seventh Cavalry forty miles at one side.

Colonel Sturgis obtained fresh horses from General Howard, and started in chase. On September 17 he came up with Chief Joseph's rear guard, captured several hundred ponies and sent back word to General Howard that there was to be a decisive battle.

General Howard hurried. He marched all night. When he got to the battle-field he found only the Seventh Cavalry there, with three killed and eleven wounded, and everybody exhausted. Chief Joseph was marching on, north, in a great half circle. Somebody else must head him off.

General Howard sent a dispatch to Colonel Miles.

"The Nez Percés have left us hopelessly in the rear. Will you take action to intercept them?"

From Fort Keogh on the Yellowstone, one hundred and fifty miles eastward, Colonel Miles sallied out. It was a relay race by the white chiefs. He took four mounted companies of the Fifth Infantry, three companies of the Seventh Cavalry, three companies of the Second Cavalry, thirty Cheyenne and Sioux scouts and some white scouts, a Hotchkiss machine gun, a twelve-pounder Napoleon field-piece, a long wagon train guarded by infantry, and a pack train of mules.

A steamboat was ordered to ascend the Missouri, and meet the troops with more supplies. Telegraph, steamboats, trained soldiers, supplies—all the military power of the United States was fighting Chief Joseph.

Joseph reached the Missouri River first, at Cow Island. There was a fort here, guarding a supply depot. He seized the depot, burned it, and leaving the fort with three of its thirteen men killed, he crossed the river.

Canada was close at hand. Pretty soon he thought that he had crossed the line, and in the Bear Paw Mountains he sat down, to rest. He had many wounded to care for; his women and children were worn out. He had marched about two thousand miles and had fought four big battles.

"I sat down," said Joseph, "in a fat and beautiful country. I had won my freedom and the freedom of my people. There were many empty places in the lodges and in the council, but we were in a land where we would not be forced to live in a place we did not want. I believed that if I could remain safe at a distance and talk straight to the men sent by the Great Father, I could get back to the Wallowa Valley and return in peace. That is why I did not allow my young men to kill and destroy the white settlers after I began to fight. I wanted to leave a clean trail, and if there were dead soldiers on it I could not be blamed. I had sent out runners to find Sitting Bull, to tell him that another band of red men had been forced to run from the soldiers, and to propose that we join for defense if attacked. My people were recovering. I was ready to move on to a permanent camp when, one morning, Bear Coat and his soldiers came in sight, and stampeded our horses. Then I knew that I had made a mistake by not crossing into the country of the Red Coats; also in not keeping the country scouted in my rear."

For he was not in Canada. The Canada border lay a day's march of thirty-five miles northward yet. And he had not known anything about Colonel Miles, the Bear Coat.

Colonel Miles brought three hundred and seventy-five soldiers, and the cannon. Chief Joseph had already lost almost one hundred of his men and women. But his brother Ollicut, Chief White Bird, and the Drummer Dreamer, old Too-hul-hul-so-te, were still with him; and one hundred and seventy-five warriors.

The first charge of the Bear Coat cavalry, early in this morning of September 30, 1877, scattered the camp and cut off the pony herd. Chief Joseph was separated from his wife and children. He dashed for them, through the soldiers. His horse was wounded, his clothes pierced, but he got to his lodge.

His wife handed him his gun.

"Take it. Fight!"

And fight he did; his people fought. They dug rifle-pits, the same as white soldiers would. There was fighting for four days. The Bear Coat lost one fifth of his officers and men. He settled to a close siege, shooting with his cannon and trying to starve the Pierced Noses. He was much afraid that Sitting Bull was coming down, and bringing the Sioux. He sent messages to notify General Terry, in the east, and General Howard, in the south.

Chief Joseph's heart ached. His brother Ollicut was dead. Old Toohulhulsote was dead. Looking Glass was dead. Twenty-four others had been killed, and forty-six were wounded. He had over three hundred women and children. Of his own family, only his wife and baby were left to him. Sitting Bull did not come.

"My people were divided about surrendering," he said. "We could have escaped from the Bear Paw Mountains if we had left our wounded, old women and children behind. We were unwilling to do this. We had never heard of a wounded Indian recovering while in the hands of white men. I could not bear to see my wounded men and women suffer any longer."

So he rode out, on the morning of October 5, and surrendered. General Howard had arrived, at the end of his long thirteen-hundred-mile chase, but the surrender was made to Colonel Miles.

Chief Joseph handed over his gun.

> "I am tired of fighting. Our chiefs are killed. Looking Glass is dead. Toohulhulsote is dead. The old men are all dead. It is the young men who say yes or no. He who led the young men is dead. [That was Ollicut.] It is cold and we have no blankets. The little children are freezing to death. My people, some of them, have run away to the hills, and have no blankets, no food. No one knows where they are—perhaps freezing to death. I want to have time to look for my children and see how many of them I can find. Maybe I shall find them among the dead."

He raised his hand high, toward the sun.

"Hear me, my chiefs. I am tired. My heart is sick and sad. From where the sun now stands I will fight no more forever."

White Bird had taken a company and escaped to Canada. Colonel Miles promised Chief Joseph that he would ask to have the surrendered people sent back to the Nez Percés' country. Those were the terms. The surrendered people numbered eighty-seven men, three hundred and thirty-one women and children.

"Thus," reported General Sheridan, the head of the army, "has terminated one of the most extraordinary Indian wars of which there is any record. The Indians throughout displayed a courage and skill that elicited universal praise; they abstained from scalping, let captive women go free, did not commit indiscriminate murder of peaceful families, which is usual, and fought with almost scientific skill, using advance and rear guards, skirmish lines and field fortifications."

The Government did not send the Chief Joseph Pierced Noses to their own country. It was claimed that White Bird had broken the terms, by his escape. At any rate, the Joseph people were kept a long, long time in Indian Territory. Many of them sickened and died. They were mountain Indians. They missed their cold streams and their pure air. They fell away from over four hundred to two hundred and eighty.

Chief Joseph's heart broke utterly. He issued an appeal—his own story—which was published in the *North American Review* magazine, in 1879.

"If I cannot go to my own home, let me have a home in some country where my people will not die so fast. . . . Let me be a free man—free to travel, free to stop, free to work, free to trade, where I choose; free to choose my own teachers, free to follow the religion of my fathers, free to think and talk and act for myself —and I will obey every law or submit to the penalty."

Not until 1884 was he permitted to return to the mountains of the Northwest. The majority of his people were located again in Idaho, among their kindred. He himself was placed upon another reservation, near Spokane, Washington.

He pleaded for the Wallowa Valley—his Valley of the Winding Waters; but that had been settled by the white men. All that he found was his father's grave. A white man had enclosed it with a picket fence. Chief Joseph wept.

He lived to a good age. In 1903 he visited the East; he talked with President Roosevelt and General Miles. He met General Howard. The next year he exhibited himself in an Indian show at the St. Louis fair. That hurt his pride. He was ashamed to sell his face for money.

When he went home, he was sick. This September he died, on the Washington reservation. The doctor asserted that he died from a broken heart.

He was the last of the great chiefs of the American Indians. The Historical Society of the State of Washington has erected over his grave a noble monument. Under it he lies, while people read his name, translated: "Thunder-rolling-in-the-mountains."

CHAPTER XXVI

THE GHOST DANCERS AND THE RED SOLDIERS (1889–1890)

AND SITTING BULL'S LAST MEDICINE

IN 1889 the Sioux, upon their reservations in South Dakota, were much dissatisfied. Their cattle were dying, their crops had failed, there were no buffalo, and the Government supplies were not being issued according to promise.

The Sioux no longer occupied the Great Sioux reservation of western South Dakota. By several treaties they had sold the greater portion of that land. The last treaty, signed only this year, had left them five tracts, as reservations.

On the Missouri River at the middle north line of South Dakota there was the Standing Rock reservation, where lived Sitting Bull and many of the Hunkpapas and Oglalas whom he had led.

Next to it, on the south was the Cheyenne River reservation, for the Miniconjous, Without Bows, Two Kettles, and others.

Then there was a wide strip of land which had been sold, with the small Lower Brulé reservation in the east end of it.

Then, side by side against the Nebraska line, south, there were the Rosebud reservation, for the other

Brulés; and Chief Red Cloud's Pine Ridge reservation, for his Oglalas, and various bands.

The Sioux numbered twenty-five thousand. The lands left to them were the poorest of the lands. White men had failed to make a living upon such lands. The Sioux were supposed to help themselves by farming and cattle raising, but they found themselves starving.

Sitting Bull had been placed upon the Standing Rock reservation in May, 1883. His home was a log cabin with a stable and corral, on the Grand River in the southern part of the reservation. He still kept a peace pipe, as sign that he would not go to war.

He had been among those who opposed the selling of the lands. After the last sale, this year, he was asked what the Indians thought about it.

"Indians!" he angrily blurted. "There are no Indians left now but me."

He viewed the Sioux police sullenly. These were a fine company of fifty young Sioux under First Lieutenant Bull Head and Second Lieutenant Chatka. They were drilled as United States soldiers, wore the army uniform of blue, and were well armed. Their duty was that of keeping order for the Indian agent. They were proud of their trust, and faithful to it.

Now in the fall of 1889 the restless Sioux heard a voice. Their young people were being educated at the Indian schools of the East, and at the agency schools, and were learning to read and write.

The eastern school Indians exchanged letters with Indian friends whom they had met or of whom they knew; the agency school Indians in different parts of the country also wrote letters. Word came by letters from the west, to Sioux at the Pine Ridge agency, that beyond the Rocky Mountains a man who claimed to be Christ, the Son of God, had appeared upon earth.

The white people once had tried to kill him by nailing him to a cross. He was back again, to punish them for their treatment of him, and for their treatment of the Indians. The Indians were to be his people, and possess the land. This sounded reasonable.

It aroused curiosity and hope. It was only the same old story, as spread by other prophets, and here put in a little different form; but the red people of America had never yet ceased to look forward to a miracle that would restore to them their game and their liberty and their loved country.

Old Chief Red Cloud, Young-man-whose-horses-are-feared and other head men of the Pine Ridge reservation called a council, to choose delegates who should travel into the west and find out if the Arapahos and Shoshonis of Wyoming were telling the truth.

Kicking Bear from the Cheyenne River reservation and Short Bull from the Rosebud reservation, were the leaders selected. The other men were Good Thunder, Flat Iron, Yellow Breast, and Broken Arm, from Pine Ridge.

Without permission from their agents they traveled west into Wyoming, to talk with the Arapahos and Shoshonis at the Fort Washakie reservation. Some Cheyenne delegates from the Tongue River reservation in Montana were there also, seeking information.

The Arapahos and Shoshonis said that the word was

true. The Messiah had come; he did not live among them, but was living west of the mountains, among the Fish-eaters. A Bannock Indian had brought the news across to them. They had sent men to see. The men had seen the Messiah, and had talked with him. They had seen the dances that he had ordered, which would waken the dead to life and populate the earth again with Indians.

Porcupine and his Cheyennes, and Kicking Bear and Short Bull and their Sioux were much impressed. They decided to go on, and see for themselves. So they did. They got on the train at Rawlins, Wyoming, and rode all day and branched off by another train, and rode still farther, and arrived at Fort Hall of Idaho, in the Bannock country.

From here the Bannocks guided them onward, by train and by wagon, until at last they reached the country of the Fish-eaters, or Pai-Utes, at Pyramid Lake in western Nevada!

The Pyramid Lake Fish-eaters sent them south, to Walker Lake of the Pai-Utes. Here they met the Christ, listened to his talk, danced the sacred dances, and felt that everything was true.

Kicking Bear and Short Bull and their Sioux were absent from the Sioux reservations all winter. They sent back letters from Wyoming, Utah, Idaho and Nevada, telling of their progress. In April, of 1890, they returned.

They reported to the council. They had seen the Messiah. Delegates from many other tribes had been there, too. The Messiah talked to each tribe in its own language. He bore the scars of nails, on his wrists. He looked like an Indian, only lighter in color. He taught them dances called Ghost Dances, which would bring the spirit people back upon earth. He fell into a sleep, and went to heaven and saw all the spirit Indians. The earth was too old; it was to be made new and would stay green and new, and the Indians who obeyed his teachings and lived good would never be more than forty years old, themselves. This fall all the good people were to be made young; and after that they would be made young every spring. Anyone who had shaken hands with the Messiah could call him in sleep.

The Sioux delegates told their story over and over again. At the Cheyenne reservation in Montana, Porcupine talked for five days and four nights.

There was indeed a Pai-Ute prophet, named Wo-vo-ka or the Cutter. He later took the name Kwo-hit-sauq, or Big Rumbling Belly. To the white people he was known as Jack Wilson. He had worked on ranches near the Walker Lake reservation, until, when he was about thirty years old, while sick with a fever he went into a trance, during an eclipse of the sun.

On waking up, he said that he had been to heaven, had visited God and the spirits, and had received command to preach a new gospel.

The Pai-Utes were glad to believe whatever he claimed for himself. He seemed to hypnotize them. The word that Wo-vo-ka was the Messiah and could perform miracles spread through the Pai-Utes of Nevada and the Utes of Utah; it crossed the Sierra

Nevada Mountains into California on the west, and the Rocky Mountains into Wyoming on the east; and it kept going, east and north and south.

This spring Good Thunder, Short Bull, Cloud Horse and Yellow Knife journeyed to see the Messiah again.

When they came back they reported that he had appeared to them out of some smoke. He welcomed them, and showed them a land that bridged the ocean, and upon the land all the Indians of all nations were on their way home again.

They saw lodges, of buffalo hides, in which the dead were living. They talked with dead Sioux whom they had known.

The Messiah had given them red and white paint, that would ward off sickness, renew youth, and cause visions. He had told them to have the Sioux send their children to school, and to attend to farming. There was to be no fighting with the white people. But the whites were to be destroyed, by a great landslide that would cover the world with new earth. Upon the new earth would roam the buffalo and deer, as of old. The Indians who obeyed the Messiah would be lifted up, above the landslide, and gently dropped back again, there to live forever with all their friends and relatives who had come with it from spirit land.

This reunion was to occur the next spring, of 1891, when the grass was knee high.

The Good Thunder party brought what they said was a piece of buffalo meat. The Messiah had told them that if on their way home they killed any buffalo, they were to leave the hoofs and tail and head on the prairie, and the buffalo would spring up, whole, when they turned their backs.

All the buffalo would act this way, in the happy time to come.

The day of buffalo herds on the plains was past; but the party asserted that they did find a herd, and killed one buffalo—and he sprang up, from the hoofs and tail and head, just as the Messiah had promised.

The Cheyennes, the Shoshonis, the Arapahos, the Kiowas, the Utes, the Pai-Utes, were dancing the Ghost Dance. The Sioux now danced.

The Ghost Dancers danced in a circle, holding hands and chanting, until they fell over and went to spirit land. From the spirits they brought back signs, such as buffalo tails, buffalo meat, and other things of an Indian country.

The Sioux Ghost Dancers wore Ghost shirts, of white muslin. These Ghost shirts would turn a bullet; no enemy weapon could pierce a Ghost shirt! That was the word of Kicking Bear and Short Bull.

The Ghost Dance ceremonies were many, and the dance was noisy.

Away up on the Standing Rock reservation, which had not yet joined in the craze, Sitting Bull, the former great medicine leader of the Sioux, was much interested. The agent, Mr. James McLaughlin, refused to permit him to visit Kicking Bear, the prophet on the Cheyenne River reservation, south. Kicking Bear was hard at it, preaching the Messiah religion to his Miniconjous and the other Sioux there.

But Sitting Bull was anxious to learn. So he sent

six of his young men down, to ask Kicking Bear to come up for a visit at the Grand River in the Standing Rock reservation.

Kicking Bear appeared, in October, this 1890, with several of his followers, and preached to the Sitting Bull people.

"My brothers, I bring to you the promise of a day in which there will be no white man to lay his hand on the bridle of the Indian's horse; when the red men of the prairie will rule the world, and not be turned from the hunting grounds by any man. I bring you word from your fathers the ghosts, that they are now marching to join you, led by the Messiah who came once on earth with the white men, but was cast out and killed by them. I have seen the wonders of the spirit land, and have talked with the ghosts. I traveled far, and am sent back with a message to tell you to make ready for the coming of the Messiah and return of the ghosts in the spring."

This was the commencement of Kicking Bear's sermon, as reported to Agent McLaughlin by One Bull, an Indian policeman who was Sitting Bull's nephew.

Kicking Bear spoke for a long time. He told Sitting Bull everything. The new earth, that would bury the whites, was to be five times the height of a man. It would be covered with sweet grass, and with herds of buffalo and ponies. The Pacific Ocean would be filled up; the other oceans would be barricaded. The white man's powder would not burn, against the Ghost Dancers. The whites who died would all belong to the Evil Spirit. Only the Indians would enjoy life, under the

Good Spirit, with no white people to molest them.

To the unhappy, starving Sioux this was a promise full of hope. Sitting Bull at once took the lead at Standing Rock. He danced himself, reported Agent McLaughlin, "to mere skin and bone." He introduced new wrinkles of his own.

Down at Pine Ridge reservation old Red Cloud had adopted the new belief. On the Rosebud reservation Short Bull, who also "had seen the Messiah," was making the Brulés defiant. Now at Standing Rock Sitting Bull had the fever, and was tireless.

Kicking Bear proved to be a nuisance. The Sioux feared him. It was said that in the dark there was a halo around his head, and a star over him; that he had the power to strike unbelievers dead, with a look, or change them into dogs.

Agent McLaughlin sent thirteen police under Sergeant Crazy Walking, to arrest Kicking Bear and put him off the reservation.

Crazy Walking went, and found Kicking Bear and Sitting Bull in the midst of a Ghost Dancer meeting. He listened to the stories, and was afraid of the medicine. He returned to the agency, and said that Sitting Bull had promised that Kicking Bear should leave, the next day.

Agent McLaughlin called Second Lieutenant Chatka. Lieutenant Chatka had good sense. He was a soldier and did not put much faith in such "medicine." He asked for only two men, and rode straight to Sitting Bull's camp, on the Grand River, forty miles south of the Agency quarters.

The Sioux there were dancing—which made no difference to Lieutenant Chatka, although some of them were his relatives. He broke through the circle, told Kicking Bear and his Cheyenne River reservation squad that they must get out; and escorted them twenty-five miles south, to the line between the two reservations.

Thus Lieutenant Chatka proved himself to be a faithful officer.

This night Sitting Bull snapped his peace pipe in two, before his Ghost Dancers. His heart had swelled within him.

"Why did you break your pipe, Sitting Bull?"

He replied hotly:

"Because I want to fight, and I want to die, if need be, for this new religion."

He declared that the dancing must continue. The spirits had said that the Sioux must dance or they would lose their lives.

Four hundred and fifty of the Standing Rock Indians were his devoted followers. It was he who translated the messages received for them from the spirit world. It was he who anointed them, after the sweat baths, with the sacred oil. It was he who urged them to dance until they dropped at the wave of his sacred feather. He was all-powerful, again.

First Lieutenant Bull Head, of the Sioux police, lived three miles west of him, up river, and was watching him. Sitting Bull did not like to be watched. The police irritated him.

The constant dancing, day and night, on the reservations, alarmed the white officials. It was a threat, like the threat of Tecumseh and the Open Door.

Down at Pine Ridge, Short Bull, the Messiah's prophet there, announced:

"My friends and relations: I will soon start this thing in running order. I have told you that this would come to pass in two seasons, but since the whites are interfering so much, I will advance the time from what my father has told me to do, so the time will be shorter. Therefore you must not be afraid of anything. Some of my relations have no ears, so I will have them blown away."

He told them all to gather in one place and dance and make ready. Even if the soldiers surrounded them four deep, no harm would occur.

At last, on request of the agents at Pine Ridge and Rosebud the troops entered, to keep order. Short Bull, Kicking Bear and other prophets of the Messiah led their people into the Bad Lands, in the northwest corner of the Pine Ridge reservation, there to await the promised time.

They had destroyed their houses, and the houses in their path. Many of the Sioux who had not danced went with them, or joined them, because of fear of the soldiers. They feared being arrested and held as hostages. Soon there were three thousand of the Sioux in the Bad Lands.

This left Sitting Bull and his dancers alone, up at Standing Rock, with the police watching them. He felt that he ought to go to the Ghost Dance big camp, in the Bad Lands. And he decided that he would.

Agent McLaughlin had asked him to come to the agency for a talk; but Sitting Bull well knew that if he did go to the agency, he probably would be arrested. So he declined.

Next, Agent McLaughlin arrived, in person, and roundly scolded him for encouraging the "foolish" dancing.

Sitting Bull proposed to Agent McLaughlin that they journey together into the west; and that if they could find no Indians there who had seen the Messiah, he would tell his people that it all was a lie.

But Agent McLaughlin refused to do this, although it seemed to be a fair proposition. When he rode away, the Ghost Dancers threatened him; but Sitting Bull would permit no violence. He had been bathing, and wore only his breech-clout. He stood almost naked in the cold, and kept his people from attacking, until the agent was out of sight.

Sitting Bull prepared to join the other Ghost Dancers, who would be expecting him. His horses had been doing nothing. They were well fed and strong, and if he got a head start, he knew that he could keep it. So, to show that his heart was not all bad, he had his son-in-law, who could write a little in English, write a note to Agent McLaughlin.

Bull Ghost, who was called "One-eyed Riley" by the white people, and who was his chief assistant in medicine making, took the note to the agency. This was December 13. The note said, as far as Agent McLaughlin could read it, that Sitting Bull had decided to go to Pine Ridge, in order to know more about the prayers. He did not like to be called a fool, and to have his prayers interrupted by gun and knife.

Lieutenant Bull Head was as smart as he. The lieutenant knew exactly what was in Sitting Bull's mind; and he, too, sent a note to Agent McLaughlin, saying that if Sitting Bull got away on his fresh ponies, the police would not be able to catch him. The arrest ought to be made at once.

The troops already had been directed to arrest Sitting Bull. "Buffalo Bill" Cody, the famous scout, had arrived, to manage the arrest by help of the soldiers. But Agent McLaughlin warned that if the soldiers went down, there surely would be a fight, and many persons would be killed. He was certain that his Indian police could do the work with less trouble.

By return courier, who was Second Sergeant Red Tomahawk, this evening of December 14 he sent orders in English and in Sioux, to Lieutenant Bull Head, that Sitting Bull should be arrested the first thing in the morning, and must not be permitted to escape.

Sergeant Red Tomahawk rode the forty miles in the dark, over a rough trail, in four hours and a quarter.

Other couriers were dispatched, to take orders to the police squads stationed elsewhere. Lieutenant Bull Head was to have thirty-eight regular police and four specials, with First Sergeant Shave Head as his assistant.

Two troops of the Eighth Cavalry under Captain E. G. Fechet were to be stationed on the trail part way to Sitting Bull's camp, in readiness to support Lieutenant Bull Head, if necessary.

The Ghost Dancers had been guarding Sitting Bull's house, for several nights; but this night of December 14 they had danced until they were tired out.

When before sunrise in the morning Lieutenant Bull Head led his troops into the camp, few persons were stirring. Before the camp, which extended several miles along the Grand River, could pass the word that the police were there, Lieutenant Bull Head had rapidly thrown a line of dismounted police around the houses of Sitting Bull.

There were two log cabins, one larger than the other. The police did not know in which cabin Sitting Bull would be found. Lieutenant Bull Head ordered eight policemen to enter the smaller cabin; he and First Sergeant Shave Head and ten other policemen entered the larger cabin.

Sitting Bull was here, asleep on the floor, with his two wives and his son Crow Foot, seventeen years old.

His wives saw the police standing over them, and began to cry. Sitting Bull sat up.

"What is wanted?" he asked, but he knew very well.

Lieutenant Bull Head briefly told him.

"You are under arrest, and must go to the agency."

"Very well," answered Sitting Bull, calmly. "I will dress and go with you."

"Bring me my best clothes," he said to his wives. "And I shall want my best horse—the gray horse."

His clothes were brought. Sergeant Shave Head ordered one of the policemen to saddle the gray horse and have it at the door.

While he dressed, Sitting Bull began to complain,

and to scold the police for arresting him, who was a Sioux and an old man, when they were Sioux, themselves. But Lieutenant Bull Head said nothing. He was here to do his duty.

He placed himself upon one side of Sitting Bull; First Sergeant Shave Head took the other side, Second Sergeant Red Tomahawk closed in behind; and they all went out.

Now trouble awaited them. One hundred and fifty angry Ghost Dancers had gathered. They were armed, they were yelling threats, they were jostling the line of police and shoving them about. The stanch police were holding firm, and keeping the space before the door cleared. At the same time they argued with their friends and relatives and acquaintances in the crowd, telling them to be careful and not cause blood-shed.

Sitting Bull's gray horse was standing in the cleared space. He started for it, as if to go with the police, when young Crow Foot, his son, taunted him.

"You call yourself a brave man. You said you would never surrender to a blue-coat, and now you give up to Indians in blue clothes!"

That stung Sitting Bull. He resisted. He began to speak rapidly to his Ghost Dancers.

"These police are taking me away. You are more than they. You have guns in your hands. Are you going to let them take me away? All you have to do is to kill these men on either side of me. The rest will run. Our brothers are waiting for us in the Bad Lands, before they make the whites die. When the whites die, only the Indians will be left. But the whites mean to try to kill us all first." Suddenly he shook an arm free, and raised it. "Shoot!" he cried. "Kill the police. They are none of us!"

Two of the Ghost Dancers, Catch-the-bear and Strikes-the-kettle, sprang through the line of police, and fired.

Catch-the-bear's bullet struck Lieutenant Bull Head in the side. Strikes-the-kettle's bullet struck Sergeant Shave Head in the stomach. Private Lone Man shot and killed Catch-the-bear. With his revolver Lieutenant Bull Head instantly shot Sitting Bull through the body. Red Tomahawk shot him through the head. Then, down together, fell Sitting Bull, Bull Head and Shave Head.

Now it was a big fight, of the forty-one police against almost two hundred Ghost Dancers. Lieutenant Bull Head and First Sergeant Shave Head were mortally sick from their wounds; Second Sergeant Red Tomahawk took the command.

The fighting at first was hand to hand, with clubbed guns and knives. The squaws helped the Ghost Dance men.

"Do not hurt the women and children," shouted Red Tomahawk. And as fast as possible the women were grabbed and hustled into the small cabin.

The police were trained soldiers, and used their revolvers freely, although not trying to kill. They drove the Ghost Dancers into the timber along the river south of the Sitting Bull place.

"I will run and tell the soldiers," cried Hawk Man No. 1.

"Run!" panted Red Tomahawk, to Hawk Man No. 1. "Tell the soldiers."

And Hawk Man No. 1 did run, like a deer, through the storm of bullets. His uniform was cut, but he was unharmed. He ran eight or ten miles.

Bull Head and Shave Head were disabled. Fourth Sergeant Little Eagle, Private Afraid-of-soldiers, were lying dead; Special Policeman Hawk Man No. 2 and John Armstrong were nearly dead; Private Middle was bleeding badly.

Sitting Bull was stone dead. So was young Crow Foot; so were Ghost Dancers Catch-the-bear, Blackbird, Little Assiniboin, Chief Spotted Horn Bull; Chief Brave Thunder and Chase, another Dancer, were fatally wounded.

The fight had lasted only a few minutes. Now the Red Tomahawk men carried their dead and wounded into the Sitting Bull large cabin, to stand off the Ghost Dancers until the soldiers came.

They occupied the corral, too, and kept the Ghost Dancers from getting the ponies that had been put there in readiness for fleeing to the Bad Lands.

For two hours they held their own, against the raging mob, because they had been sworn into the service of the United States Government. But they did not shoot to kill, except in defense of their own lives. They were Sioux, and had relatives and old-time friends among those people outside.

When the cavalry galloped into sight, over the hill beyond, Red Tomahawk raised a white flag, as a signal. But the soldiers either did not see, or else thought it was a trick; for they brought a cannon and fired two shells at the cabin.

So Red Tomahawk ordered his men out of the cabin, and mounted them in line upon their horses. Then he took the white flag and rode forward alone, until the soldiers saw who he was, and that the men behind him were the loyal police.

The fighting Ghost Dancers ran away. Captain Fechet did not pursue them far. He sent word to them that they had better come back, and they would not be harmed. Sitting Bull was dead, and their religion had not protected them from bullets.

Many did come back, cured of their craze. Only a few joined the Bad Lands Ghost Dancers.

When the news of the death of Sitting Bull, by bullets, was carried into the Bad Lands, and several leaders on the reservation had surrendered, the Indians in the Bad Lands broke camp, to return to their reservations. But some clung to their Ghost shirts. Their hearts were set upon the promises of the Messiah.

When they were gathered near Wounded Knee Creek, on the Pine Ridge reservation, and the soldiers were about to disarm them, on the morning of December 29 Yellow Bear, one of the medicine prophets, suddenly called upon them to resist—now was the hour—their Ghost shirts would make the soldiers powerless.

Young Black Fox, a Ghost Dancer of the Cheyenne River reservation, threw up his gun, from under his blanket, and fired at a soldier. All the soldiers fired; the Indians fought back; the machine guns opened; and in a twinkling two hundred Sioux men, women and children, and sixty soldiers, were piled, dead or wounded, upon the snowy ground.

This was the battle of Wounded Knee, and was the last of the Ghost Dancers.

Meanwhile, after the cavalry had rescued the police, Red Tomahawk put the body of Sitting Bull into a wagon, and with two prisoners took his troop up to the Standing Rock agency, to report.

Little Eagle, Afraid-of-soldiers, John Armstrong and Hawk Man No. 2 were dead; Lieutenant Bull Head and First Sergeant Shave Head died in the hospital several days later. Bull Head had four wounds.

The four dead police were buried in the reservation cemetery on the second day, December 17. A company of the Twenty-second Infantry fired three volleys over their graves, and a great throng of the Sioux were present, to mourn. The police had been brave men.

The police troop and the majority of the other Sioux there, asked that Sitting Bull be not buried in this cemetery. His medicine had been bad. Therefore this same morning he was buried, wrapped in canvas in a neat coffin, in the military cemetery near by. His age was fifty-six.

The white head-board says simply:

SITTING BULL
Died
December 15, 1890

That was his end, on this earth; for, as far as known, he never came back from spirit land. The pretended Messiah's promises proved false. The white men remained stronger than the ghosts. The Indians seemed to have no "medicine" to equal the terrible shoot-without-loading guns of the blue-coat soldiers.

THE END